The
Battered
Body
Beneath
the Flagstones
& Other

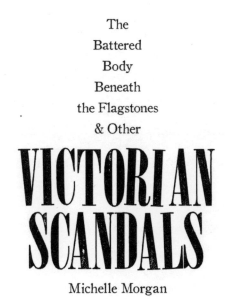

VICTORIAN
SCANDALS

Michelle Morgan

Also by Michelle Morgan:

Madonna
The Mammoth Book of Hollywood Scandals
Marilyn Monroe: Private and Undisclosed

The
Battered
Body
Beneath
the Flagstones
& Other

VICTORIAN SCANDALS

Michelle Morgan

ROBINSON

ROBINSON

First published in Great Britain in 2018 by Robinson

1 3 5 7 9 10 8 6 4 2

A CIP catalogue record for this book is available from the British Library

ISBN: 978-1-47213-947-4

Typeset in Adobe Garamond by Hewer Text UK Ltd, Edinburgh
Printed and bound in Great Britain by Clays Ltd, Plc

Papers used by Robinson are from well-managed forests and other responsible sources

Robinson
An imprint of
Little, Brown Book Group
Carmelite House
50 Victoria Embankment
London EC4Y 0DZ

An Hachette UK Company
www.hachette.co.uk

www.littlebrown.co.uk

I would like to dedicate this book to my senior school headmaster and English teacher, Mr Brian Tyler. Without his attentive teaching skills, I may never have travelled this road.

And to my junior school headmaster, John Lord, for giving me a safe and happy place to explore my creative dreams.

Contents

Acknowledgements

W RITING A BOOK is never something one can do completely alone. It takes many people behind the scenes to turn an idea into a manuscript, and then into the book you are currently holding in your hand. With that in mind, I would like to thank the following, who have all given me much support during the writing of this book:

Christina Rice. I know it sounds clichéd to say that I could not have written this book without you, but it really is true. Your support and friendship mean the world to me. Thank you!

My agent, Robert Smith; my editor, Duncan Proudfoot, the wonderful Howard Watson, and everyone at Robinson/Little, Brown. We have worked together on many projects over the years, and I very much look forward to many more!

I am very grateful to the stall holders and organisers of the Peterborough Antiques Fair. Without them, I would never have bought the Victorian postcard album that inspired me to write this book. Thank you for that and countless other little treasures!

A huge thank you must go to my readers. That people buy my books and enjoy reading them is something I will never take for granted. I thank each and every one of you for your support, encouragement and friendship.

I'd like to thank my friends, Claire and Helen. I must say, I'm glad that this book doesn't deal with 1980s scandals, because I have a feeling we'd have all ended up in it (or at least Claire would have!).

A huge and heartfelt thank you must go to my mum and dad. They always support my career and have literally travelled across the world to be with me for important events. Their love knows no bounds, and I am extremely lucky and privileged to have them. Thanks also to Mum for forcing me to take typing lessons all those years ago. Without them, this book would have taken twice as long to write!

To Paul, Wendy and Angelina – you are the best brother, sister-in-law and niece that I could ever wish for. Angelina – look, your name is in this book twice! ☺

Finally, thank you so much to my wonderful husband, Richard, and my beautiful daughter, Daisy. I could never do what I do without them, and I am thankful every day that they are in my life. Thanks especially to Richard for buying me a new keyboard when my old one stopped working twenty thousand words before the end of this book!

Introduction

I HAVE ALWAYS BEEN interested in the Victorian era; particularly the 'ordinary' folk, who lived, worked and died during that time. When I was ten years old, I was really envious when my friend bought a book that not only told the story of Victorian day-to-day life, but also popped out to become a huge, four-storey mansion, complete with paper family, servants and furniture. I searched for years for a replica of that house and I was twenty-one by the time I found one. Did I buy it? Absolutely! Then just a few months ago I spotted a Victorian street scene with stick-on people and props. I bought that too, much to the embarrassment of my teenage daughter!

The way Victorian people lived their lives is fascinating to me. From those who inhabited the foggy streets of London, to the English country farmers and then the American prairie dwellers. There is something mysterious, often dark about those years from 1837 to 1901, and stories are everywhere apparent.

When I first began this project, I was aware, of course, of the high-profile scandals of the day, such as Jack the Ripper and Dr Crippen. However, when I scratched the surface, I discovered a plethora of other stories, mysteries and tales that had not been reported for well over a hundred years. I decided very early on that I would not replay the well-known scandals, and concentrate on the ones that had received scant – or no – attention since they first made headlines. If you are a Jack the Ripper 'fan', don't worry; he still features in the book, but I concentrate on one lesser-known story, instead of those that have been investigated over and over again.

Working on this book has really given me a sense of what Victorian people went through during often exceptional times. Their lives and stories have come alive to such a degree that I often found myself thinking and worrying about the characters for many days after I had finished exploring their lives. It is my hope that the following chapters will enlighten and sometimes even entertain. If readers find tales of their own family history here too, then that will be the icing on Queen Victoria's wedding cake, as far as I'm concerned.

Oh, one more thing – while officially the Victorian era didn't begin on 1 January 1837 and end on 31 December 1901 (Victoria reigned from 20 June 1837 to 22 January 1901), I've used those dates when compiling my research. Why? Well, for one thing, there were some great stories that popped up just a month or so out of the official Victorian era and, for another, it just made it easier for a girl who is scared of numbers.

So, without further ado, I bring you the best, worse, funniest, most gruesome tales from those six decades of Victorian life. I hope you enjoy reading them as much as I have enjoyed writing them.

Michelle Morgan

A Fine Line Between Love and Hate

JUST AS IN modern times, Victorians knew how to love and hate each other in equal measure. The archives are full of stories of all kinds of atrocities, including husbands murdering their wives, suicidal lovers, and mistresses taking revenge on their love rivals. They range from the toe-curling to the utterly ridiculous, but most have one thing in common – bloodshed and lots of it.

One example of a ludicrous murder was the case of a Hungarian woman who 'mistakenly' killed off her husband. According to her, a lodger had moved into her home and gave her a packet to look after. Overcome with curiosity, she opened the envelope and found the equivalent of £1000 inside. The woman told the court that she was determined to get her hands on the money, so stabbed the man to death while he slept. It was only later that she examined the contents of the packet more closely and discovered her wedding certificate and various other documents related to her husband.

The woman had not seen her other half in many years and was curious to know how the lodger had got his hands on such things. Of course, she could no longer ask him, but as she stood over the very dead man in her spare bedroom, it suddenly dawned on her that the person she had butchered was actually none other than her long-lost spouse.

By her own admission the woman was guilty of murder, but whether she was recalling the true version of events was another matter. Newspapers were abuzz with the story for some weeks, calling it 'A Weird Story from Hungary'. One went so far as to declare it the fascinating outline for a sensational novel or play; such was the believability of the mysterious crime.

Another lethal wife came in the shape of Mrs Gossan, who took a voyage from Le Havre to New York in 1881. During the trip, the murderous woman poisoned her husband and then attempted to throw him overboard. She was caught by members of the crew before she was able to hoist the man over the side, but it was far too late to save his life. When the ship reached New York, the woman was charged with the man's murder and sentenced to death. Her last words were not related to sorrow or remorse. Instead, she took the opportunity to confess that, several years ago, she had killed her first husband too. Her accomplice? Her current husband, of course; the one she had poisoned just a few weeks before.

Then there is the case of Isadore Stasiulis and Annie Rakaszis, from Pittsburgh. The two sweethearts had been 'stepping out' for nine years when they got into a massive fight and broke up. Shortly afterwards, in 1900, Annie announced her intention to marry love-rival John Kancewicz, in a small church ceremony. Unfortunately for everyone involved, the wedding party got more than they bargained for when the rejected Rakaszis came storming into the church in an effort to stop the wedding.

When he discovered the couple had already married, the man flew into a rage, took out his revolver and aimed it straight at the bride. Luckily for her, members of the wedding party dived onto him and wrestled the gun from his hands. He then stormed off, declaring that if he couldn't have Annie, he might as well commit suicide in the Monongahela River. When it became clear that nobody actually cared what he did, he changed his mind about killing himself, and went on his merry way.

There are literally thousands of similarly mysterious and shocking scandals among Victorian family members, friends and lovers. Here, then, is a handful of the most scandalous.

The Battered Body Beneath the Flagstones

On 13 November 1849, thirty thousand people stood outside a London prison in order to witness the execution of twenty-eight-year-old former servant Maria Manning, and her thirty-year-old travelling salesman husband Frederick. The very public hanging of a married couple caused absolute chaos, as the crowd chanted, booed, shouted, sung songs and laughed. But the story did not start there, of course. Instead, it began months before, when Frederick and his wife decided to commit a crime so grizzly that few could believe it had actually taken place.

Patrick O'Connor worked on the docks, but also had interests in financial shares, which meant he was never short of money. This made him very attractive to the married Maria

Manning, who became his lover and enjoyed spending his money. Perhaps knowing that this was why the woman pursued him, O'Connor seemingly endeavoured to have a bit of fun at her expense. He encouraged her to rent a bigger house at 3 Miniver Place, which would cost her and Frederick a lot of money to maintain. In return, O'Connor promised he would move in as a lodger, but after staying there for just one night, he announced that he'd changed his mind and returned to his regular lodgings. Knowing that the couple had spent a lot of money on the bigger house, and probably feeling shunned and humiliated by her lover, Mrs Manning became absolutely enraged and vowed never to forgive him.

Over the course of the affair with O'Connor, Maria encouraged her lover to be on friendly terms with her husband. Together, the threesome was frequently seen either at their house or his lodgings. Whether or not Mr Manning was concerned about his wife carrying on with O'Connor is debatable, but certainly the knowledge that the man was particularly well off seemed to lessen the blow. However, the relationship soured after the lodging incident, and any remaining friendship was purely superficial.

Needing to pay the rent, the couple took in another lodger – William Massey – a medical student who was at the house for over two months. However, in July 1849, the Mannings suddenly announced their intention to leave the property, and requested that the young man leave. He was surprised at this turn of events, particularly because they seemed very anxious to be rid of him. There was a reason why the couple wanted him gone so quickly, and it had nothing to do with them moving house.

O'Connor had been a nice distraction for Maria, but now she had grown bored and resentful of him. She was not, however, irked by his money and, together with Frederick, had come up with a plan to get rid of the man but keep all of his cash, shares and other belongings. The only way they could do this, they decided, was to murder O'Connor and dispose of his body. A deadline of August 1849 was set, and the couple busied themselves with the grand plan.

The lodger William Massey had met O'Connor on several occasions. He had also sat in the front room and heard Mr Manning talk rather obsessively about the amount of money the man was worth. At one point, he even bragged that O'Connor had written his will, and was leaving everything to Mrs Manning. Massey did not know whether Frederick was merely trying to impress him but, for the sake of a quiet life, he just nodded and feigned interest.

Because William Massey was a medical student, this would often be the topic of conversation in the house. However, these conversations sometimes took a dark twist, especially when Mr Manning asked what part of the head was the most tender; where the brain was located; and whether or not Massey had any experience of air rifles. On one particular day, he asked the lodger if he believed murderers went to heaven. Massey replied with just one word – 'No.'

As Frederick and Massey were talking, the former mentioned how he wanted O'Connor to sign a promissory note for a considerable amount of money. It seemed to be just a passing remark, but then moments later the medical student was shocked when Manning asked him if he had any knowledge of drugs that would produce stupefaction or intoxication. When Massey disclosed that perhaps morphine would do the job, the landlord added that he was particularly looking for a drug that would entice someone to write something he may not normally have written.

Since they had only just been talking about O'Connor, it was clear to Massey that the two subjects were certainly intertwined. He explained that yes, there were drugs that could be used for negative purposes, and left it at that.

This seemed to please Mr Manning considerably, and he came up with an idea. He planned to get O'Connor to come to the house, where something would be said to convince the man he was about to fall foul to cholera, a disease that particularly frightened him. After scaring him enough, Manning would then offer him a drink of brandy, which of course would contain the drugs. He repeated the plan out loud to Massey, who sensibly chose not to reply to this bizarre statement. The lodger did note, however, that during the entire conversation, Mrs Manning was in the same room and heard every word that was being said, but stayed eerily silent. Shortly after this exchange, Massey happily moved out of the Manning's home, and the couple continued with their plans to be rid of Patrick O'Connor.

On 25 July, Mr Manning walked the short distance to a local building supplier, where he placed an order for some grey lime. Lime was well known as something that hastened the decomposition of a body, destroying the features very rapidly and effectively. It was delivered later that day, and the merchant was told to take it down to the back kitchen, and empty it into a basket. Also that day, Manning went to another merchant and ordered a crowbar measuring five inches long. It was specially made for him and, on 28 July, the porter headed to Miniver Place to deliver it. Along the way he met Frederick Manning, and handed the tool over to him. 'You should have wrapped it up,' he complained. 'I do not wish for everybody to see what I am purchasing.'

The man insisted that the porter come with him to a stationery store, where he bought some brown paper and wrapped the crowbar. Manning then told the boy to take the tool to his home, as he had further errands to do. The address was written on a piece of paper, which was later submitted into evidence in court. When the porter arrived at Miniver Place, Mrs Manning opened the door, looked at the bill and complained bitterly about the cost. However, anxious to get it inside before anyone should see, she paid the money and bid the delivery boy farewell.

On 3 August, Mrs Manning went to a stockbroker who had been recommended to her by O'Connor. Once there she asked what kind of shares would be best to buy, if she intended to sell them abroad. The man asked where she was planning to sell and after a long pause she replied, 'Paris.' He made the recommendations and she then asked if it was possible to buy without registering them. Her intention, the stockholder later revealed, was to sell them without her husband's knowledge or permission.

The man answered all of Mrs Manning's questions, and she seemed pleased with the replies. The woman said she would be back shortly to buy the shares she required, but the stockbroker never saw her again. This meeting was repeated with another seller in the area, though that too did not lead to any sales. Both men, however, knew O'Connor well and had sold numerous shares to him in the months leading up to August, so thought nothing of Maria Manning mentioning his name.

On 8 August, Mrs Manning went to an ironmonger on Tooley Street to look at their range of shovels. After talking to the shopkeeper for a few minutes, he recommended she take a regular, wood-handled spade. The woman refused to entertain this idea and said she would buy a dust shovel instead. 'I will make this one do,' she murmured aloud.

Later that evening, O'Connor arrived at 3 Miniver Place with his friend, Pierce Walsh. It was late and they were greeted by Maria, who wanted to know why her former lover had not been over for dinner that day. He denied ever receiving an invitation; then he and the Mannings began talking about money and unpaid bills. Apparently, he was chasing up some debts with a local grocer, and this seemed to interest the couple no end.

After a few minutes, the subject changed to general chitchat, and O'Connor and Frederick Manning settled down to smoke their pipes and partake in a glass of brandy. Unfortunately, the former suddenly became faint and slumped down into the sofa in a fearful manner. According to Pierce Walsh, Maria proceeded to take out some perfume and began massaging the man's temples with it, before he finally came around. O'Connor was then given some brandy and water, before he and his friend left the premises and headed home.

On 9 August, the plan to murder O'Connor was in full swing. Pretending that he was invited to dinner, the Mannings brought him to their home under false pretences. Once there, he was hit around the head with some kind of instrument, shot through the brain and then buried under the flagstones in the back kitchen. How the crime took place, who was ultimately responsible and how his body was disposed of would be discussed copiously in the months ahead, as we shall see.

No sooner had the murder taken place than Mrs Manning travelled to O'Connor's lodgings where she was seen by his unsuspecting landlady and her sister, just before 6 p.m. Brazenly, she asked if Mr O'Connor was at home, and hearing that he was not, headed towards his bedroom anyway. Maria was on a mission to find his cash box, to which – thanks to pretending she wanted to invest in railway shares several weeks before – she had been previously introduced. When she left an hour later, the money and shares went too.

Back at Miniver Place, Mr Manning was deep in thought as he sat on his garden wall, smoking a pipe. His neighbour entered into a conversation with the man, though it was noted that he was not in the mood to continue with it. Claiming he had an appointment he had forgotten about, Frederick suddenly jumped down from the wall, excused himself and went back into his house.

Mrs Manning came home shortly afterwards, and then returned to O'Connor's house again the next day, 10 August, where she was once more seen by his landlady. The home was attached to a small shop and, after picking through her former lover's possessions, she went through and bought a biscuit for herself. Here she was witnessed as being very pale, and shaking as she handed over the money. O'Connor's landlady witnessed that under her right arm, Mrs Manning carried a parcel, though she felt it wasn't her place to ask what was in it.

On 11 August, twelve-year-old Hannah Firman was sitting close to the Miniver Place house when she saw Maria Manning. 'Do you want your steps cleaned?' the girl asked. Mrs Manning replied that she did not, but then having a change of heart, asked if she was prepared to clean other items. The girl said she would for 5d and then went into the house. 'I did not know that she would keep me from half past nine in the morning until night,' she later said.

Once the woman got Hannah inside, she seemed extraordinarily anxious for her to clean some blinds. The girl said no as her hand was injured, so Mrs Manning tried to have her clean out the basket which had previously carried the lime. Once again the girl said no, so the woman had no choice but to do it herself. Hannah later recalled that she cleaned the basket for such a long time that the water in the house ran out.

Eventually Hannah was asked to clean the kitchen, even though Mrs Manning admitted that she had scrubbed it herself the day before. During this time, the girl witnessed the couple being fairly argumentative with each other. At one point, Frederick Manning insisted his wife give him an item, which the girl thought looked like a comb. When Maria refused to hand it over, he stamped his foot until she changed her mind.

While Hannah was in the house, she did not have any cause to think there was anything particularly wrong, and actually felt confident enough to rifle through their drawers while she was supposed to be working. By the time she left that night, the little thief had in her pockets an egg, a razor, a purse and a pair of stockings.

The girl wasn't the only one busy that day. Mr Manning was on a mission to sell some of O'Connor's shares for the maximum profit he could obtain. Wandering into Killick and Co. brokers, the brazen man told of his intention to sell. He was then shown into a private room, where he signed over several shares in exchange for cash. The signature he used when doing so? That of Patrick O'Connor.

William Patrick Keating was a friend and colleague of O'Connor. Through him, he was also acquainted with Maria Manning and had seen them together on many occasions, both on the street and in his friend's lodgings. He last saw O'Connor on 9 August, when he was on London Bridge, heading towards Bermondsey. They spoke for a while with David Graham, another colleague, whereupon O'Connor showed them both a dinner invitation from the Mannings. He then said goodnight and carried on with his journey. Around the same time, he was also spotted by another old friend, who swore later in court that he was about a hundred yards from the Mannings' house, headed in that direction. According to him, O'Connor had looked confused; as though he was wondering whether to go one way or the other.

On 12 August, when the man had been missing for several days, O'Connor's colleagues were becoming more and more concerned. Knowing that he was often seen at the Mannings' house, colleague William Flinn went to Bermondsey but found nobody in the house. However, colleagues Keating and Graham were luckier. They too visited Miniver Place, and this time Maria was at home. However, she denied all knowledge of O'Connor ever being at her house on the night he had disappeared. Instead, she admitted going to his lodgings on that evening, but only to enquire about his health, since he had felt so faint the night before.

She then claimed that the man had not been home that evening, or again when she returned the following day. Keating was not sure he believed her, and informed Maria that he had actually seen O'Connor heading in the direction of her home, on 9 August. The woman made no direct reply to the question, but was bolshie enough to make up a story about her husband being upset at O'Connor for not turning up to dinner.

Something wasn't right, and the two men knew it. One asked if he could speak to Mr Manning. The woman said he had gone out to church, but Keating then insisted on knowing when he would be back, so that he could question him, too. Maria ignored the request and claimed that the couple had a dinner appointment that evening and would not return until late. Keating and Graham eventually gave up and went home, which is just as well, considering that their friend was currently buried underneath the kitchen floor. Who knows what would have happened had they returned to the house later that night.

On Monday 13 August, Flinn returned to the Miniver Place property, only this time he brought with him a plainclothes policeman. Sitting in the front parlour, Mrs Manning once again denied having seen O'Connor after 8 August, but mentioned Keating's story of seeing him at the bridge on the 9th. Maria proceeded to tell the men just what a fickle person O'Connor was, but then suddenly her demeanour changed and she announced that he was the best friend she had ever had in London. 'Poor Mr O'Connor,' she exclaimed, shaking her head sadly.

Flinn was concerned by this sudden change of mood, and asked if the pale woman was okay. She insisted she had been ill six weeks previously, and had not felt herself since then. She then admitted once again to having been at O'Connor's lodgings on the 9th, and the men got up to leave. As they were at the door, Maria suddenly blurted out, 'You gentlemen are very susceptible.' Flinn thought this was a strange thing to say, but she never offered an explanation and he did not question her further.

The two men left and Mrs Manning presumed that both were undercover police officers. When her husband returned, she complained bitterly that they had been sniffing round, then dramatically fainted when the realisation that she could be found out suddenly swept over her. She was right to be worried. After visiting the house, Flinn's suspicions were heightened.

There was something about Mrs Manning that he just did not trust. To that end, he called a police officer and several colleagues, and together they went to O'Connor's digs. It was common knowledge among his friends that the man's money was kept in a cash box inside a trunk. They opened both boxes and, sure enough, apart from a few notes and IOUs, there was absolutely no money to be found. Furthermore, O'Connor's railway shares were also gone.

The idea that she was about to be found out filled Mrs Manning with absolute horror. Several days before Flinn's visit, she had told her husband that there was no way they could stay in the house, and proposed they should move to America. He agreed that a clean break was in order, and contacted a local dealer about buying their furniture. When the purchaser came, he took a good look round the house, made a deposit and promised to come back to collect the items in the very near future.

While they had hoped that O'Connor's money would bring them great happiness and satisfaction, the reality was the complete opposite. Suddenly Frederick Manning became extremely jealous that all of the cash and shares were in his wife's possession, and demanded she hand over half to him. When she refused, he threatened her with a knife, and said he would chop her head off if no money was forthcoming. She gave him a handful of railway shares and later said that cash had been the chief cause for arguments in the days after the murder. The fact that they had a body underneath their floor seemed to be the least of their problems.

Despite the frequent arguments, Mr Manning was still planning their getaway. After Flinn's visit on 13 August, he was encouraged by his wife to visit Charles Bainbridge, the dealer who had promised to buy his furniture a few days before. Mrs Manning told him not to hurry back; to stay awhile, smoke his pipe and relax. This he did, and on doing so discovered that Bainbridge wasn't just in the furniture business, but the letting one too. At that moment, an idea came to Frederick and he told the man that his plans had changed slightly. He would be staying in town longer than he originally thought, so while he did not need him to buy the furniture at the moment, he would very much like to rent an apartment instead.

There was a reason why Maria Manning had told her husband to take his time. If she had the nerve to murder her lover for money, then she certainly had the audacity to double-cross the man who wanted half of it. Maria had thought about running away to Paris even before O'Connor's murder, hence the enquiries made to several stockbrokers. Now, after days of arguments, fending off questions from strangers, and with a body still under the floor, the woman decided to take off with O'Connor's money. Taking the opportunity of her husband running errands, she packed her belongings and then, at 3.15 p.m., she was seen by neighbour, Mary Ann Schofield, coming out of the house with a cab driver.

After helping her downstairs with various boxes and packages, the driver took Mrs Manning to several places, including a stationery store to pick up cards, and then on to a railway station. There Maria told a porter to write the words, 'Mrs Smith, passenger, Paris', onto the cards, and then place them onto the boxes. She told him that the packages were to stay at the station until collected. She was then driven to another station, Euston this time, where she got out with her remaining luggage and headed for the first train to Edinburgh. After the long journey, Maria finally checked into lodgings under a new name: Mrs Smith.

Back in London, and happy that he had found a relatively safe place to stay, Mr Manning told his new landlord that he would go back to the Miniver Place house in order to collect his wife. When he got there, however, the doors were locked and nobody responded to his calls. After tapping on the door and window for some time, the man went over the road to Mrs Schofield's house and asked if she had seen his wife. 'Yes,' was the reply. 'I saw her go out in a cab.' The man enquired as to whether or not his wife had luggage with her. When the reply was affirmative, he then crossed the road to number 2 Miniver Place to ask his neighbour if she could say where Maria had gone. She could not.

Devious Frederick Manning had plotted and planned the murder of an innocent man, in the hope of receiving some money for himself. Now though, he realised that his wife had no intention of sharing it with him, and he was pretty much penniless. In order to get some money quickly, Frederick pawned his pistols and, when he returned to his new digs, he was carrying a bottle of brandy and in an antsy mood. 'I've sent my wife into the country,' he said, before announcing that he too would be moving away after all. When Mrs Bainbridge asked if he would be spending the night in his own house, Manning replied that he would not sleep there if someone paid him. He gave no explanation for this comment, and then stayed at the Bainbridges' house for several nights.

On Tuesday 14 August, the furniture dealer asked a PC Burton to go with him to the Mannings' house in order to collect the furniture he had been promised. Why he asked a policeman when Frederick was still in his house is unclear.

However, the men were let in using a neighbour's key and then had a look around. They found thirty pieces of clean linen, all neatly stacked on a shelf in the front kitchen. There were also boxes with nondescript items inside, and in the back kitchen of the property there was a shovel. Bainbridge packaged up everything he had been promised – including the shovel – and took it all back home.

In charge of unpacking the items, Mrs Bainbridge discovered the shovel, which she proceeded to use around the house. She also found a bag of dresses and noted that one had been washed but not dried properly and had developed mildew. Interestingly, there were also scorch marks, as if the wearer had tried to dry it too close to the fire. Attached to the dress was a cape, and as Mrs Bainbridge examined the material she found a rather large stain: a mark she soon decided was washed-out blood. She did not say anything to Mr Manning about her discovery, though she did think it rather strange.

The next morning Frederick Manning left, but first instructed the Bainbridges' servant that should anyone call for him, she should say he had not been seen for the last two weeks. He then climbed into a cab with what was left of his belongings, and was taken to Waterloo station. After he'd gone, Mrs Bainbridge became ever more curious about the blood on the cape, and disclosed the information to PC Burton, the man who had searched the Miniver Place house the day before.

While the officer had not found anything suspicious on his first visit to the home, Mrs Bainbridge's revelation was enough to send him back again. On 17 August, he and colleague PC Barnes headed to the house, where they got the shock of their lives. On performing a thorough examination of the back kitchen, the men found two large, damp flagstones, which looked as though they had been recently moved. With the help of a crowbar and shovel, Burton and Barnes began removing not only the stones, but also a quantity of earth and then lime underneath them. It wasn't long before they came across a human toe, and then the buttocks and back of O'Connor. Shortly afterwards, his entire naked torso was revealed, lying face down, his legs tied up and under with a washing line.

By this time, several surgeons had been called and arrived at the property. One of the doctors, Samuel Meggitt Lockwood, reached into the hole and removed the dentures from the body, as part of the investigation. The remains of Patrick O'Connor were then removed and placed in the front kitchen, where they were examined by the doctors. It was found that there was a bullet lodged in the skin above the right eye, and the back of the head was severely fractured where the man had been shot. The brain was so decomposed that it had almost turned to fluid, and the head was covered in scars and injuries from what appeared to be a sharp instrument. Sixteen individual pieces of bone were removed from the skull; such was the damage done by the bullet and the beating. There followed a full post-mortem, and then the body was left in the house until an inquest could be called.

In Edinburgh, 'Mrs Smith' was settling into her new surroundings. However, after the discovery of O'Connor's body, the newspapers had run wild with the story and circulated the Mannings' descriptions everywhere. It wasn't long before other people in the boarding house noticed that Mrs Smith looked awfully like Maria Manning, and when she began offering railway shares to local residents, the police were called. On 21 August, Superintendent Richard John Moxey arrived at the premises.

Mrs Manning let the man into her room without a fuss, and proceeded to answer his questions, albeit falsely. Yes, her name definitely was Mrs Smith. Yes, she was married, but her husband had sadly passed away. No, she hadn't been in Edinburgh long – perhaps since last Tuesday or Wednesday. When asked why she was in the city, Maria replied that she had come just for the good of her health. She remained calm and cooperative until the Superintendent asked if she knew anything about shares.

'What do you mean by that?' she boomed. Moxey leaned down and told the woman he suspected that she was really the wife of Frederick Manning. She didn't need to answer, however, as at that point a neighbour entered the room and positively identified her as being the local railway-share seller. With an arrest firmly in his sights, Moxey asked if he could look through Maria's luggage and, to his surprise, she gave her full permission.

The man looked briefly through her possessions and then hit the jackpot when he discovered a box and trunk. Inside the box was a bill addressed to Mrs Manning, and inside the trunk were hundreds of shares, Bank of England notes, seventy-three sovereigns, tickets from London to Edinburgh and many other articles. One item of particular interest was a bundle of references from affluent London people, claiming that Mrs Manning was 'kind, affectionate and piously inclined'. The police did not agree, and the woman was arrested and taken to the local police station.

Of course, once officers had Maria Manning in the station, they wanted to know where her husband was, too. Shaking her head, the woman admitted that she did not have a clue as to his whereabouts. 'I came from London suddenly,' she said, 'while he was out.' She also said that at the point of departure, she had not made up her mind whether to go to Scotland or Paris;

hence her decision to leave some of the luggage at another station. When asked if she had murdered Mr O'Connor, Maria seemed shocked to the core. According to her, the man had been the kindest friend she had ever known, and was something of a father figure to her.

The questions continued and the well-rehearsed woman told a story of Mr O'Connor coming to her house on the Wednesday night. However, instead of admitting that he had become ill after drinking the Mannings' brandy, she told police that he had been thoroughly intoxicated on his arrival, and had to return home shortly afterwards. According to her, he did not show up for dinner the next night, and she could not believe how rude that was, especially considering the way he had behaved the night before.

Maria then gave the police a sob-story about how terrible it had been to live with her husband, and how he had continually misused her. The subject of money came up, and she admitted that the man had threatened her for his share. She did not, of course, admit to coming by the money in such a foul way. Instead, the woman told the story that she had bought the shares on the advice of O'Connor, who had apparently put her in touch with a stockbroker.

Nearly six hundred miles away, Frederick Manning was making a new life for himself on the island of Jersey, a place he had visited before. As luck would have it, on the way over he was spotted by the daughter of the landlord in charge of the guesthouse where he had previously stayed. She had not heard of the murder, but did not speak to Manning regardless, since she was suffering from seasickness. However, as soon as she read about the ghastly deed in the newspapers, she tipped off a London police station.

Coincidentally, Police Sergeant Edward Langley had known Manning previously, so he volunteered to travel with several other officers to the island on 25 August. The fugitive had been staying at a local inn, where he was reported as being intoxicated for much of the time. He made absolutely no secret of who he was, and even delighted in drawing attention to himself through his over-the-top behaviour. Still, the future was on his mind and he begged an associate to let him travel to France with him. The man declined, so Manning made plans to travel on to Guernsey. However, he was so stupefied on the day he was due to sail, that he had been unable to get out of bed and missed the boat.

Despite his bravado, Frederick Manning must have been tipped off that the police were heading his way because he suddenly checked out of the inn, although he left several belongings and asked that his room should be kept for his return. He disappeared for a few nights and finally turned up at another guesthouse, where Langley and his colleague eventually found him.

It seems that his final mistake came from his ever-present love of brandy. When he kept ordering from the same shop, it wasn't long before the shopkeeper recognised his description and told police where he was. Apparently, Sergeant Langley had walked past that house on many occasions during the search for Manning, but having never seen or heard anything of him, decided that he must surely have moved on or committed suicide. He was relieved and very grateful to be told otherwise.

When the police burst into his room, one of the officers threw himself across the bed, thinking that Manning would try to escape. He need not have worried, though, as the man was too tired and drunk to run anywhere. On seeing intruders, Frederick exclaimed, 'Are you here to murder me?' before recognising the sergeant. 'Sergeant, is that you?' he asked. When the detective replied in the affirmative, Manning then told the man that he had just decided to return to London to explain himself.

As officers looked around the room, they saw an open blade lying on the table. This sighting took a gruesome twist when it was revealed that he had been asking fellow boarders if his landlord and wife had any children. When it was revealed that they did not, Manning answered, 'They must have money, then.' Detectives wondered if the man was planning another murder for financial gain, since he had travelled to Jersey with very little money of his own.

Other murder ambitions aside, the man made no secret of his current dislike for his wife, and asked Sergeant Langley if the 'wretch' had been found yet. When it was answered that she had been, Manning happily replied, 'I am glad of it. That will save my life.' Pushing further, he then asked if the money was found on her person. The policeman was in no mood for small talk, however, so instead of answering his questions, he read the man his rights and told him he was under arrest for the murder of Patrick O'Connor.

'Oh, very well,' Manning replied. 'I am perfectly innocent.' He was then handcuffed (much to his chagrin, since he assumed the policeman would not do such a thing to someone he knew), and loaded into a van heading to the St Helier police station. Undoubtedly he was nervous, but trying desperately to hold onto his wits, Manning proceeded to tell his version of events to Langley and another policeman called Captain Chevalier. They soon discovered that his idea was to throw any hint of blame firmly in his wife's direction.

According to Frederick Manning, Maria asked O'Connor to dinner, and when he came into the house, the table was laid as if she were about to serve up. The woman asked if he would go and wash his hands, and as O'Connor descended the staircase into the back kitchen, she placed one hand on his shoulder and shot him in the back of the head with the other. Langley had no wish to hear a confession in the van, and was appalled when his colleague asked what had happened to the body. Manning very carefully replied that his wife had dug a grave for the unsuspecting man, and he was placed in there.

It was decided to move Manning to Southampton quickly after cholera broke out at the St Helier jail. The worry was that he would contract it and die before his trial, so every effort was made to get him out alive. However, knowing that he was unlikely to get back to Jersey again, the prisoner asked if he could take one last walk in St Helier and enjoy a cigar in the company of officers. The request was granted, and he walked from the station to the pier where he was to make the crossing back to England.

Three hundred Jersey citizens came out to see the man being taken onto the boat; a small number, which the newspaper said was 'a proof, at any rate, of the good taste of the residents of St Helier's'. After the eleven-hour crossing, Frederick Manning and the officers eventually arrived on the mainland, where he was booed by the crowds. Reporters described him as a 'bull-headed, thick-necked man, with a half-effeminate expression, arising from a very fair complexion, and light hair . . . He behaves with vulgar familiarity to all; maintains a jocular strain, and seems delighted at the notice which he attracts.'

During the official police interview, the accused was very concerned that his wife would absolutely declare his innocence, if only she could see him; particularly if she was accompanied by a clergyman at the time. That thought came crashing down when it was discovered that Maria Manning was quite happy to see her husband blamed for the crime and protested her innocence at every turn. Then, when gunpowder was found in the pocket of his coat, Frederick Manning's fate was sealed. Later, on a train to London, the man asked detectives if he would be able to see his wife soon. They replied in the negative and then reminded him that he was in serious trouble, and anything he said would be taken down and used in his upcoming court case.

Meanwhile, officers travelled to the station where Mrs Manning had left her luggage. There they found two boxes, one containing a gown. On examination of the garment, detectives noticed that the skirt had bloodstains on it, while the body of the dress had recently been washed. There was also a toilet cover and a piece of muslin, both of which were in the same condition as the skirt. Everything was taken into evidence.

The Mannings were now in prison, awaiting their fate. For Frederick, this time was spent swinging between nervousness and depression over his surroundings, and frequently asking for 'trifling indulgences' to make his time more comfortable. His request for cigars was not indulged, but a pen and paper was. He then wrote a number of rambling letters to his wife that were unsurprisingly intercepted by the governor.

Maria Manning was described as being perfectly composed and calm when her husband was on the run, but the moment he was apprehended, she changed. When told that he was steadfastly pointing the finger at her for O'Connor's murder, she could hardly contain her rage. 'The villain!' she screamed. 'It was him that did it, not me.' After that, she spent her days pacing around the cell in what wardens described as an excitable manner, and frequently asked them what the newspapers were saying about her.

The crime of the year finally went to court at the end of October 1849, and an abundance of witnesses were called, including their former lodger, O'Connor's workmates, neighbours and other associates. It was a gruesome story and people crammed into the room in order to hear every piece of evidence. The Mannings sat in close proximity to each other but it was noted that they didn't seem to acknowledge each other at all. Occasionally the husband would glance in his wife's direction, but that was very much the extent of their contact.

During the proceedings, Frederick fidgeted nervously, and his frustration grew more and more apparent as time went on. Maria, however, was as still as a statue in her black dress and gaudy-coloured shawl. Journalists noted that the confidence she had shown at the beginning of the scandal had disappeared, along with a great deal of weight. With a white veil covering her face, it was hard to see her expression, but not once was she seen turning her head in her husband's direction.

As it was not known whether the shooting or the beating had eventually taken Patrick O'Connor's life, Mr Manning was charged with a) 'feloniously discharging a pistol loaded with a mortal wound, of which the victim then and there died', and b) 'causing the death by striking, cutting and wounding Patrick O'Connor on the back part of the head with a crowbar'. Added to those two counts were others alleging that both parties murdered the victim, and then finally one for Maria herself; that of 'having been present, aiding and abetting Frederick

George Manning to commit the felony'. It was then explained to the jury that if they decided Frederick was present but did not actually commit the crime, he must be found innocent. The same went for his wife.

When it came time to plead, Frederick Manning boomed in a very loud voice, 'Not guilty!' His wife, meanwhile, let out barely a squeak, and spectators had to strain to hear her pathetic 'Not guilty.' Things made a slow start when it was revealed that as a Swiss-born woman, Mrs Manning had requested a foreign jury. After a discussion that lasted a full thirty minutes, it was finally decided that because she was now married to a British citizen, she would have the same privileges as him – namely, a British jury.

Once that was sorted out, the trial got underway and the first thing brought forward was the bizarre love triangle between the Mannings and O'Connor. No one was able to identify exactly how and when Marie and the victim had become intimate, but it was predicted that their affair had begun two years prior, in 1847. She had been in the habit of visiting him at his home on a frequent basis, and had even stayed over there when he was out of town. So close were they that she had unquestionable access to his quarters and everyone associated with the man knew who she was.

The case went on for several days and every witness called gave his or her version of events. Finally, everyone had spoken and it was time for the closing arguments to take place. On behalf of Mr Manning, his defence – Mr Serjeant Wilkins – spoke to the jury. He put all blame for the crime onto Mrs Manning, and told the jury that she – and she alone – planned the crime, conducted the murder and then robbed the victim. 'Manning did not possess a single shilling belonging to

O'Connor,' he said. Journalists noted that his speech did more to convince the jury of Mrs Manning's guilt than the entire prosecution side of the case.

Then it was turn for the female prisoner's defence to step up. Speaking on her behalf, Mr Ballantine told the jury that he was sorry Mr Wilkins had taken it upon himself to talk about Mrs Manning in that way. He noted that while the other defence team were probably predicting he would take the same road, he absolutely would not; that he'd prefer to never enter a court-room again than stoop to their level. In taking this road, his closing speech almost turned into one about himself, rather than his client:

'If my duty as an advocate required that I should cast upon the male prisoner the sort of observations and accusations which had been made against the woman, I would feel that my profession was a disgrace, and that the sooner I abandoned it for one somewhat more creditable, the sooner I would be a respected, an honest, an honourable, and upright man, and placed in a position better to respect myself.'

For both defence parties, the emphasis was very much on whether the jury could come to a firm decision as to whether the couple were both guilty, or just one was guilty. If it could not be decided if either of them was actually on the property at the time, then the only decision they could come to would be not guilty. Both counsels seemed fairly confident, but after retiring for just forty-five minutes, the jury came to a firm and immoveable verdict – Frederick and Maria Manning were both guilty.

Justice Cresswell placed a black cap onto his head and demanded to hear from each prisoner as to why they should not be sentenced to death. Maria Manning spoke first, in a far more excitable voice than she had demonstrated at the beginning of the trial:

'My Lord, I have been convicted very unjustly by a jury of Englishmen. If I had been tried, as I demanded, by a jury of half foreigners the result would have been different. I have not received justice, but I have been treated most cruelly in this country. I have had no protection either from the Judge, or from the prosecution, or from my husband. I have been condemned very innocently, although I have got proof that I have property in the Bank of England and that I bought the shares that were found upon me with my own money.'

The speech was long and full of vigour. Why would she want to kill a man who meant more to her than her own husband?

'If I had wished to commit murder, how much more likely is it that I should have murdered that man [pointing to her husband] who has made my life a hell upon earth ever since I have known him, than that I should have killed O'Connor, who would have married me the next month – the next week after I became a widow.'

Maria then took a swipe towards her defence lawyer by claiming that although she had a wonderful reputation with all of the people she had ever worked for, he had not chosen to call any of them to the stand. Then a finger was pointed in her husband's direction as she said that his murder of O'Connor was no doubt caused by a jealous rage, and if that was the case, why should she be found guilty, too?

The entire time she spoke, Frederick Manning stared at his wife intently, never moving a muscle. The speech was long and the moment she took a breath, the judge jumped in.

'Frederick George Manning and Maria Manning, you have

been convicted . . .' He had only got out a handful of words before Mrs Manning began shouting in despair.

'I shan't hear it! I won't stand here any longer!' The convicted woman turned to leave the court, though where she thought she was going is anyone's guess. Needless to say, it was just a matter of seconds before she was brought back, but still she was not finished. 'I have had no law and no justice here!' she screamed. 'Why don't they produce my witnesses?'

Ignoring her completely, the judge started again.

'Frederick George Manning and Maria Manning, you have been severally found guilty of the crime of wilful murder. The jury have felt themselves compelled, upon the evidence that was adduced, to find you guilty, and I must say that if they had returned any other verdict, it would have been difficult to satisfy me that they had not shrunk from the performance of their duty, so satisfied am I with the evidence in support of the charge.'

'The witnesses who were in my favour have not been called . . .' began Mrs Manning once again, whereby the judge completely ignored her and carried on with his comments.

'Under all circumstances, murder is the most dreadful of crimes, but the murder of which you have been convicted is the most cold-blooded, calculating, and deliberate that I ever remember to have read of . . . The law, more merciful than you, will allow you time for repentance, and to prepare for the fate that awaits you. I can hold out no hope whatever for you in this world – as all hopes of mercy here below is past. To the minister who will attend you I therefore consign you, imploring you to give up all hope of mercy on this side and to devote your attention to that which now alone concerns you . . .'

The closing speech was long and peppered with Mrs Manning's cries for more evidence to be presented. The judge waved her away and finally came to his conclusion:

'It only remains for me to pass upon you both the dread sentences of the law, which is, that you be taken hence to Her Majesty's gaol of the county of Surrey, and that you be conveyed from thence to a place of public execution, and there hanged by the neck until you are dead; and that, after death, your bodies be buried within the precincts of the gaol in which you are last confined. And may the Lord have mercy on your guilty souls.'

Even after the judge had handed the sentence and was ready to wrap up the entire sorry episode, Mrs Manning still had much to say on the subject of her 'unfair' trial. As if that wasn't enough, she then picked up various items that were kept just in front of the dock, and started throwing them at her defence counsel. 'Shameful England!' she screamed, while Frederick Manning sat completely unmoved by the outburst. Finally, the two were led away.

'Damnation, seize you all!' Maria screamed. When the guards tried to handcuff her, she made her hands into fists and shook them violently. Her husband, meanwhile, remained completely nonchalant, walking behind her in almost a robotic trance. Strangely, on the way to jail, the female prisoner's mood turned around quite dramatically, and she joked with the guards about the manacle she currently wore. She wasn't going to let the journey go without saying something about her husband, however:

'I showed them resolution, did I not?' she said. 'I had plenty of opportunity to speak to my husband in the gaol and during the trial, but I would not. He did not speak to me, thank God, the unmanly wretch . . .' She kicked at the seat in front of her with some force, and at that precise moment, an advertising van passed by, announcing to all that the full details of her crimes and the trial would be available in a forthcoming newspaper.

This set Maria Manning off into a violent rage and she had to be restrained by the guards. Her anger turned to manic sadness a short time later, however, when she arrived at the prison and was placed in her cell. Crying at the unjustness of it all, Mrs Manning shouted, screamed, stamped and kicked her way around the room until finally she was exhausted and fell asleep. So obsessed was Maria regarding the fact that she should have been tried with a half-foreign jury, her counsel campaigned to see if a new trial could be held under her terms. All this did, however, was delay the inevitable and give the woman false hope for a while.

In contrast, during Frederick Manning's first few days in Horsemonger Lane Gaol, he remained fairly calm, and his guards noted that at times he seemed to be under the deluded notion that perhaps – even at this late stage – his life may some-how be spared. He also spent time writing to his estranged wife:

I address you as a fellow-sinner and fellow-sufferer and not as my wife, since the contract must be considered as cancelled, extending as it does, only until death and not beyond it, and both of us standing as we do on the brink of eternity, we may already consider ourselves as cut off from the world . . . I do beseech and implore of you to be truth-ful in all you utter, and that you may not be tempted to yield to any evil suggestions in the securing of our soul's welfare, to question for an instant the solemn truth that we shall shortly appear before our God in judgement . . .

The letter continued in the same vein, begging his wife to be careful with everything she said so that God may have mercy on their souls. He signed off:

This is the last letter you will ever receive from me. Now let me beg of you to grant me an interview this day if possible. I have a great wish to have one before I depart this world.

Mrs Manning was given the letter on 29 October 1849, and replied shortly after. In the first part, she complained about having to leave her native country, and that she would never be welcomed there again. Then she too spoke about God:

If you live and die unforgiven by God, that these sins will be punished by the laws of men, they are still all registered by the only God. All I have to say is this: I never made any statement of any kind to injure or condemn you in this matter that you well know, from first to last. I am here condemned only by your statement. If it had proved beneficial to you I should have been satisfied . . .

The woman then lamented that all her husband's statement had done, was 'plunge me unmercifully with you to this horrid fate'.

Maria Manning then continued the letter by putting the blame for O'Connor's death onto her husband and a fictional friend:

31

As you know, I was not in the house when O'Connor met with his death. But I was gone to see for him, and during that time he called in my absence and was shot by that young man from Guernsey, who was with you in the back parlour, smoking. That I did not know anything about it until the Saturday; and that it was all settled in the kitchen. I was in hopes you would have brought that young man forward on the trial, but that you did not do; but only blame me as you did from the first day.

The remainder of the letter begged Frederick to admit his crime once and for all. If he did, the woman wrote, she would be happy to meet with him one last time. She then asked God to have mercy on them both.

If Maria thought her husband would suddenly succumb and own up to the full, grizzly murder, she was very mistaken. Still clutching at straws that he would somehow be saved, Frederick spoke in depth to the chaplain and several family members, in order to give his version of events. According to Manning, his wife had told him of her desire to murder O'Connor, a month before the deed was committed. Her motivation was money and revenge over the fact he had not come to lodge with them as planned. The supposedly shocked man tried to change her mind, declaring that such a deed would see her hanged.

In his story, Mrs Manning was not about to change her mind for anyone and said that if she could not murder the man at home, she would do it when he visited friends abroad. She also said very clearly that if the deed was done at Miniver Place, then Frederick would have to help her bury the body whether he liked it or not. He told relatives that he was practically forced to go and buy the lime and the crowbar from local dealers.

Why? So that ultimately no one would ever suspect his wife of murder.

The idea that an innocent man would not baulk at the idea of buying items designed to hide O'Connor's body was ludicrous. However, according to him, it was Mrs Manning who consented to buying the two pistols, and she even asked the shopkeeper to instruct her on how to use them. When she returned, he told his wife once again that he would have nothing whatsoever to do with the illegal and gruesome act of murder, but she waved him away.

After hearing all the testimony during the court case (particularly from the lodger who had been asked about drugs to stupefy or prompt someone to sign documents), it is baffling to see how Frederick Manning could think anyone would believe his tale. To those with a conscience, it surely seemed rather convenient that this confession of his wife's guilt came hot on the heels of her running away with the money. But if anyone did raise questions, the man had an answer for everything. One must wonder why he was so submissive to his wife during this period, but of course he had an excuse for that too. According to Frederick, as a result of his hesitation to be involved with the murder his wife bought a steady supply of brandy into the house and kept him semi-drunk so that she could commit the deed in peace.

'During the whole of this time, I was not in my right senses,' he told his siblings. They were eager to know why he had not gone to the police as soon as he heard of her plans, but Manning was insistent that he could not do this for two reasons: one, he was afraid of his wife and, two, he hoped she would not go ahead with the murder, and so he would have no crime to actually report.

Going by his story, there was literally no chance of Maria ever forgetting the murderous plans. According to Manning, she began digging the grave in the back kitchen with the small shovel she had bought. She then took the earth out to the bin and mixed it with ash from the fire, so that it would all look perfectly innocent. Previously he had told officers about his knowledge of the hole: 'Oh yes, I had seen it, and I believe it was intended for me. I believe she meant to murder me.' The man had told police that his wife was frequently violent; had once followed him around with a knife; and would think no more of killing a man than she would a pet cat. If this was true, not only did Frederick Manning decline to tell police about her plans to murder O'Connor, but he chose to ignore the threats against his own life. At no point did he make any attempt to leave the house or get help; he just went along with everything Maria was doing.

Mr Manning told relatives that, on the night of the murder, O'Connor had been confused as to whether or not to stay for dinner. He appeared, said a few words and then left again. Had he carried on walking, O'Connor may have saved his own life, but unfortunately he turned around and headed back towards the house. Once there, Maria managed to get him to go down to the back kitchen by pretending that a young woman was coming for tea, and he needed to make himself look present-able for her.

'She is a very particular lady,' she said, 'and you should show yourself off to the best advantage.' As he descended the stairs, the man saw that a drain had not yet been fixed, and commented on it. Mrs Manning then took the opportunity to shoot him dead, and he fell almost into the grave she had recently dug.

What was Mr Manning doing as all this was going on? According to him, he was innocently in the front room, getting dressed for dinner. If this was true, then his wife must have given him a blow-by-blow account of what actually happened on the stairway, since he knew every detail of it when questioned. On discussing the events, Manning stated that he did not know there would be a murder that night, due to a lack of time in which to plan things. Furthermore, he claimed to not hear any shots or falls at all. The first he knew about the matter was when his wife appeared in the door of the front room and exclaimed, 'I have done it. He is dead enough.'

Frederick told his brother and sister that he was terrified to hear such news, and announced to Maria that she would no doubt be hanged. Instead of making the woman panic, it just seemed to spur her on. 'If you don't come down and see him, I will serve you the same,' she said, and pointed the gun at his head. Mrs Manning then drunk a neat shot of brandy, and took Mr Manning to the body.

When talking about this particular part of the story, Manning took the opportunity to demonstrate the position of O'Connor by getting down onto the floor. This act was repeated over and over again, as he spoke to his brother, sister and even the governor and chaplain of the prison. However, if this dramatic enactment was designed to gain sympathy, he was quite mistaken.

According to Manning, Maria apparently went ballistic and began hitting at O'Connor's head with the crowbar, calling him names and exclaiming, 'You old villain! You will never deceive me nor anyone else anymore.' The prisoner stated that he took the opportunity of her breakdown to flee upstairs but was met by her in the kitchen shortly afterwards. There she showed her husband the keys to the victim's flat, removed her bloodied clothes and scrubbed her hands clean. Once that was done, she dressed in a clean outfit, grabbed the keys and turned to her husband.

'I will be back directly,' she said, and left the house. It was at this point that Mr Manning went out into the yard and smoked his pipe, while exchanging a few words with the neighbour. His wife then returned with O'Connor's belongings, and after rifling through them for several minutes, burned some in the fireplace and kept whatever she deemed to be interesting or valuable for herself. At some point during this time, the murdered man must have been buried, but Frederick Manning did not mention this part of the proceedings at all. However, he had previously told officers that he had fainted as soon as his wife murdered O'Connor; then when he was revived, the body was already covered.

After giving his confession to his brother and sister, Frederick Manning swore that everything he said was true. The group then got down to pray, though by this time everyone knew that all hope was lost. Even if Maria Manning had pulled the trigger, Frederick was certainly not an innocent party. By his own admission, he knew exactly what the plan was, and then – provoked or not – had helped to hide not only the crime but the existence of the body too. Making plans to try to flee the country was not smart for a so-called innocent man and, as such, no minds were changed and no leniency given.

Because of her tendency to go into violent hysterics with little warning, Mrs Manning was placed on suicide watch. The threat was seen to be so severe that instead of just checking on the woman ever-so-often, three female guards were stationed in her cell to make sure she didn't come to any harm. This wasn't about to faze Maria, however, and in the weeks leading up to her hanging, she let her nails grow long and somehow managed to file them to a point.

She then got into a nightly routine. She would pretend to be asleep but secretly watch the guards in the hope that they would close their eyes. Most of the time they stayed firmly awake, but then in the middle of the night of 11 November, she received her wish. Two of the guards fell into a slumber and Mrs Manning wasted no time in wrapping her hands around her own neck and digging her sharpened nails into her windpipe. She was seen quickly enough by the third guard, and stopped before any serious harm came to her, but that just fuelled her frustration. Maria spent the remainder of the day complaining bitterly about the presence of the guards and trying to convince them that should they leave her alone, she would not try to commit suicide again. Not surprisingly, despite her protests, the guards stayed firmly in the cell.

On 12 November 1849 – the day before the execution – crowds began to file into the area in front of the prison. Reporters estimated that by 10 a.m. there were approximately ten thousand people there. The authorities became concerned, especially when it was noted that the crowds were travelling from all over the county, not just the immediate area. Such was the excitement and curiosity of a married couple being hanged together that barriers had to be placed not only around the jail entrance, but also in the numerous side roads leading to it in an effort to prevent too many people getting to the site of the hanging.

For those managing to get through to the jail, the opportunity of a seat was presented by several residents of Winter Terrace, a row of houses facing the building. They had decided that in order to allow a better view, they would build a stage complete with chairs for those willing to pay a hefty price. This disturbed various journalists including one from the *Bath Chronicle*. 'The systematic and business-like manner in which the whole affair was carried out was most repulsive to all good feeling,' he wrote.

He need not have worried for long, however, as complaints soon circulated that the stage was frankly dangerous and bound to result in death, if allowed to stay. The authorities agreed and the inhabitants of the properties were told they should take the stage down or else pay a £200 fine. The platform was razed to the ground, though a grand price was paid by people wishing to sit or stand in residents' windows.

Inside the prison, Maria Manning could hear the mob from her cell, and told guards that she would wear a veil to prevent people seeing her face on the way to the gallows. After spending weeks talking obsessively about her hate for her husband – including disclosing information that he had once been involved in a train robbery – the woman suddenly asked how he was. The guards, surprised at her compassion, replied that he had become depressed and emaciated.

'I suppose his fat old jowl is thinner,' she quipped.

On her last night on earth, Mrs Manning called the chaplain to her cell. During the visit, she proceeded to give something of a rambling, often incoherent story, repeating her view that a young man from Guernsey murdered Mr O'Connor. According to her, she knew absolutely nothing else about the crime, though when the chaplain tried to get more information from her, she declined to answer.

The minister's next stop was the cell occupied by Frederick Manning. The man was desperate to find out what his wife had said about him and his involvement in the murder, though the chaplain refused to disclose it. He later told reporters that he had frequently been asked by both parties what the other was saying. Given the animosity towards each other, however, he had chosen to treat them both as strangers, rather than husband and wife.

That night, Frederick Manning read the Bible and then decided – for his own curious reasons – to leave his jailers a memento of his life. Scribbling furiously, the man proceeded to write a mini biography, which he presented to them shortly after. The next morning – the day of the execution – he walked in the yard for a while, while the chaplain paid one final visit to Mrs Manning.

The female prisoner had hardly slept at all, preferring to sit and reflect on her life and crimes. She seemed resigned to her fate, and asked the minister to write letters of thanks to several of her friends. By this time, Frederick Manning had gone to the prison chapel, where he asked for one last request – that of seeing his wife for a final time. Unbelievably, the woman agreed to his wish, and appeared in the chapel shortly after. As she sat down beside him, Frederick looked at Maria and smiled.

'I hope,' he said, 'that you are not going to depart this life with animosity. Will you kiss me?'

'I have no animosity,' she replied, and leaned forward to kiss him.

They were then blessed by the chaplain, and Mr Manning embraced his wife. 'I hope we shall meet in heaven,' he said, before the guard told them both that their time had come.

In contrast to the emotion she had shown during her trial, and after almost fainting during the last few moments in her cell, Maria Manning walked towards the gallows with calm and restraint. Blindfolded and veiled as requested, she was composed enough to instruct the guards not to let her walk into the walls. Her only complaint was that the cord around her wrists was so tight it was hurting. Frederick Manning, however, seemed to be in utter terror, supported by two guards, and tottering as if about to collapse. As the bells tolled, the two walked their way to the place of death. While they did so, reporters noted a strange coincidence – they happened to walk straight over the place of their graves, just as O'Connor had done many times in their home.

'Lord have mercy upon me!' Mr Manning cried, as the gallows loomed ever closer. His wife, meanwhile, remained silent except to thank her guards for their kindness. The couple then held hands, before getting into position on the scaffolding.

An estimated thirty thousand people watched as the murderous couple finally met their deaths on the top of the prison building. Before the drop, their boos and jeers were deafening, and reporters described those present as 'the dregs and offscourings of the city of London, the different elements that composed the disorderly rabble crew being mingled together in wild and unsightly order'. They reported that people smoked their pipes, climbed up posts, fell down into the crowds and picked each other's pockets while watching the spectacle.

When death finally came to Frederick and Maria Manning, there was not a sound to be heard from the crowd. However, once the deed was done, their attention turned to each other, and fights erupted throughout the crowd before they were shooed away. Mr Manning's sister was later found wandering around with the public in a fit of madness, her disbelief at her brother's crimes everywhere apparent.

The sights witnessed that day incited nothing but utter horror in the columns of newspaper reporters around the country. Even author Charles Dickens had come out to see 'the inconceivably awful' event, and spent much time gazing upon the horrendous behaviour of the crowd in the run-up to the hanging itself. So appalled was Dickens by the behaviour of the mob that he later wrote to *The Times* revealing what he had witnessed and complaining about the horror of public executions.

Shortly before the couple went to their deaths, Mr Manning had a last request. It was not the kind of request prisoners normally ask for, but something that had bothered him ever since his arrest. 'I have to ask you one great favour,' he told a friend. 'That you will not, for the sake of my family, allow anyone to take a cast of my head to be exhibited at Madame Tussauds.'

The man assured him that if he could possibly prevent such a thing, he would do so. Whether or not the museum actually wanted Manning for its Chamber of Horrors is debatable but, regardless, it is believed that the friend kept his promise and Manning never did end up as a spectacle there. By contrast, thanks to Charles Dickens' presence at the execution, Maria Manning did end up immortalised for ever – as the murderous maid Hortense in his novel, *Bleak House*.

The Dreadful Blackpool Tragedy

Blackpool is one of the most popular British seaside destinations and visitors flock there every year. However, in 1895 one of the fashionable hotels was hit by a terrible scandal – a member of staff was murdered and the culprit went on the run . . .

On Sunday 13 October, 1895, members of staff at the Foxhall Hotel were going about their daily business of cleaning rooms, doing laundry and keeping guests happy. John Toomey was helping in his role as kitchen porter, while Sarah Toomey – cook and chambermaid – was busy readying the food for Sunday evening. The couple had been married for thirty-five years and had worked at the hotel since May. They were a popular team, though at times it was claimed that Mr Toomey could be a little eccentric in his ways. The two had a large family and were seen by other staff members as being extremely happy and content with their lives.

During the servants' midday meal, the couple chatted and then most of the staff – including the Toomeys – retired to their rooms to rest before the early evening rush. The couple were not seen again after that. Later in the afternoon it was noticed that the tables had not been set for tea, and staff thought it odd. It was thought that the couple may have fallen asleep in their room, so two of the waiters – Taylor and Smith – volunteered to go and look.

'Come on, cook, all tickets ready!' one of them joked as he knocked on the door. When nobody answered the call, the men pushed it open and were met by a grisly sight. There on the floor was Mrs Toomey and beside her lay a large knife. The woman's neck had been severely cut to the point where it had almost left the body, and blood poured out of the extensive wound and flooded onto the ground. The blood-soaked clothes of her husband were nearby but he was nowhere to be seen.

The men realised straight away that Mrs Toomey was either dead or dying, so alerted their colleagues. A doctor and the police were called, and once the former had confirmed that she was dead, officers went in search of John Toomey. Not a soul had seen him since the pair retired to their room, and even colleagues resting nearby had heard no altercation at all. The police had an explanation for this. They decided that, given the silence of the victim and the tidy appearance of their quarters, it was very possible that Mrs Toomey had been murdered as she slept.

By this time, curious members of the public as well as hotel guests were wondering why there was such a level of activity in the building. Not knowing exactly what had happened to the woman and trying to avoid a scandal, all staff told them was that Mrs Toomey had died suddenly of natural causes. However, it wasn't long before the truth reached the ears of local reporters, who took glee in announcing – rather questionably perhaps – that this was the first murder to ever happen in Blackpool.

As reporters dug deep into Mr Toomey's background, it was discovered that he had been violent towards his wife on previous occasions, but no charges were ever brought. Also, although described as sober by colleagues, he was known to frequent various clubs around town and had been seen drinking during the lunchtime of 13 October. Journalists wondered aloud if that could have been a trigger to the violence that followed.

Two of the Toomeys' children were interviewed by police in the days that followed the discovery of their mother's body, though neither could shed any light on the circumstances of her death. However, one daughter did reveal that a short time after the killing, she had received a parcel containing money and a watch from her father, delivered via messenger. Where it had come from and why was something that could not be cleared up – yet.

Rumours swirled around that Toomey must have committed suicide after murdering his wife, but police refused to be drawn into the gossip. Instead, they released a statement about what they had found in the bedroom:

Deceased was lying on the floor face downwards, with her throat cut, dead. A half glass of porter and a half-smoked cigar were on a chair near the bed, and the husband of deceased had absconded. A large closing knife was found in the room, smeared with blood and the bed coverlet was saturated with blood. There was a cut on the upper lip, one on the right wrist, and one on the left forefinger.

They also released a detailed description of Mr Toomey and assured the public that if he was still at large, he would be found very soon.

At this point in the proceedings, a man stepped forward with some information. Mr Bickerstaffe, a Blackpool ironmonger, had been working in his store just two days prior to the killing. He reported that a man meeting Mr Toomey's description had come in and asked about a particular brand of knife: an American blade, large and with no closing mechanism. The man had told Bickerstaffe that he intended to go to the United States and wanted to take the knife with him. The shopkeeper explained that there was no such item in stock; the man bought a folding knife, exactly the same as the one used to murder Sarah.

This was a big breakthrough and pointed directly to John Toomey being the killer. There then came another clue. Apparently, the man had visited a pub in Bispham, where he had drunk a beer and smoked a cigar. The landlord confirmed that, during this visit, Toomey had arranged for a messenger to deliver a package to his daughter. After that came a sighting in Fleetwood, where it was presumed he planned to catch a boat to Belfast. Officers stormed to the port but later said that, despite their best efforts, no trace was found and it was presumed John had fled once again.

This was the last sighting of the man, until farmer Robert Bailey happened to see a coat and hat on a beach close to Fleetwood. Closer inspection revealed that along with the clothes was a torn-up note. While it proved to be impossible to reunite all the pieces of paper, one scrap revealed the word Toomey. The clothes were undoubtedly his and it was suspected the man must have drowned in the sea.

A thorough search of the local area was performed, but no trace could be found. Then, out of the blue, police from the St Pancras area of London phoned their Blackpool colleagues to say that a man fitting his description had been found shot in Regent's Park. Toomey's brother lived in London at the time and was sent for, but because it had been so long since he had seen him, he was unable to give any definite identification. An examination of the feet eventually told police that the body was not the man they were looking for. Thanks to an old injury, John had several toes missing, while the body in Regent's Park had a full set.

On 28 October, the real remains of Mr Toomey were found washed up on a beach close to where his clothes had been found. It was said that the body had been in the water for a while and was decomposed to the point where his moustache had disappeared from his face. Despite the gruesome state, the Toomey children were called to identify their father, though in the end they were only able to do so by his clothes and the missing toes.

It was not their last act as children of the deceased. During the inquest, the offspring were called to testify and dropped a bombshell. Over the course of the couple's marriage, they said, their father had been insanely jealous of their mother.

'Did he ever show violence towards her?' asked the coroner.

'Yes,' the daughter replied.

'How so?'

'For eighteen years he has threatened to murder our mother and then drown himself in the ocean.' Sadly, their father had told them so many times of his plans that they had come to believe he would never actually do anything so extreme towards their mother, so had let the story go.

Based on this startling revelation, the jury took no time in delivering a verdict of murder for Mrs Toomey and suicide for her husband. The case was then over, though for the rest of their lives the children had to live with the fact that what they hoped had been an empty threat by their father actually became a terrifying and horrific reality.

The Gruesome Oxford Street Murder

Oxford Street, London, has long been a Mecca for fans of shopping and people-watching. However, in the summer of 1860, it became known for a grislier reason: a horrendous, bloodthirsty murder.

Antoine Dhereng (aka Durrange or Dherand) was an English tailor, born to a French family, educated in France and married to an Englishwoman called Catherine (aka Caroline). The latter was known to be extraordinarily beautiful and, as such, Antoine was incredibly jealous whenever any other man gave her the slightest attention. The two lodged at various locations in London, but in the early summer of 1860, they moved into no. 376 Oxford Street. The building was owned by a confectioner by the name of Carlo De Bolla, who ran his shop on the ground floor and slept at the back of the second floor. The attic was given to Antoine and Catherine, and another lodger by the name of Mr Torreani.

While the Dherengs had been married for around six years, it most certainly wasn't a happy union, and in fact Antoine secretly harboured a deep grudge towards his wife. It seemed that in October 1858 he had met and fallen in love with another woman. Catherine was not about to let the man go so easily, however. To that end, when she found the woman in their home, the disgruntled wife threw the lover out and told her never to return. So furious was Antoine about this episode that he made careful note of the circumstances and the exact date, and wrote about them in a letter to his brother almost two years later.

Antoine Dhereng never forgave Catherine for ridding him of 'this poor little woman, with whom I was happy'. However, if he had loved her as much as he later implied, it begs the question as to why he decided to stay with Catherine over her. One must also wonder why either woman even wanted to have him, as by all accounts he was deeply disturbed, abusive and bad-tempered.

According to Catherine's sister, Antoine was a terrible partner from the very moment the two married. 'She was as good a wife as ever lived,' she recalled, but the husband most certainly did not appreciate her. According to the sister, he would frequently leave Catherine alone with no money to survive, and at one point she even moved in with her sibling after a particularly violent episode. On her return to the marital home, Antoine made it clear that he would never forgive the sister for getting involved.

During the course of their short marriage, Antoine blamed his wife for every single one of his issues and told his brother that she made his life a misery on a daily basis. Things became heated regularly, and on one occasion when he had left to move in with another woman, Catherine apparently threw out his belongings and took his keys. When he returned, they got into a massive fight and once again it became physical. Antoine said that he had 'only' slapped her, but the incident went to court anyway and his wife gave evidence against him. He was sentenced to four months in prison.

Inside his cell, Antoine had many hours to reflect on what had become of his life. He also vowed to seek revenge on his wife: 'The sufferings which I endured in this prison made me hate this woman to such an extent that I always had in my mind to give her on my coming out the just punishment, which she had drawn upon herself.'

When he was finally released, the man seemed to be suffering from even greater anger issues than before. 'I'll never survive the disgrace [of being sent to jail],' he told his brother, George. He also shared the wish to do his wife harm, which his brother was able to talk him out of. However, the rage built up and he had the words 'Death to an unfaithful woman' tattooed onto his chest.

The brutal finale of the relationship between Antoine and Catherine happened when she fell out with one of her sisters, for reasons unknown. On the last Saturday of June 1860, she expressed her wish to visit her sibling's house and 'tear her liver out' over what had occurred between them. Dhereng apparently told his wife that it would be unfair to do such a thing and that she should remain quiet. According to him, Catherine then started shouting and insulting him to such a degree that 'I became quite out of my mind . . . Oh! Mercy, mercy, mercy of you and in the eye of society! I struck her dead . . . All my past animosity flushed into my mind and then, in the heat of passion, I struck her dead.'

While his recollection of the deed seemed pretty straightforward, in reality it was far darker and obscene. Yes, he did strike a blow to Catherine's head, but he did not stop there. He hit her many other times, to the point where pieces of her skull broke away. Next, he slit her throat, and after watching the blood drain onto the floor, the deranged Dhereng cut his wife's head from her body, wrapped it in a black piece of cloth and threw it into the coal cupboard. Finally, he removed her clothes and then tried unsuccessfully to cut off her arms and legs. Eventually he gave up and decided to just let the body remain on the floor of the flat they had once shared.

According to their landlord, Mr De Bolla, the couple had always kept themselves to themselves:

'They appeared to me to live comfortably as man and wife together. I saw the deceased woman alive on Saturday afternoon. On that day I also saw her husband, who said he was going to see the volunteer review. He went out and did not return until about 9 or 10 o'clock in the evening. He had a bottle of ginger beer in my shop and wished me "good night" and went upstairs. I saw his wife the same evening; she was scrubbing the stairs. I did not see either the deceased or her husband after that. There might have been a noise in the deceased's room, but I did not hear it.'

It perhaps wasn't strange that Mr De Bolla heard nothing sinister going on, as he was likely still working in the shop. However, another person who should have heard something was fellow lodger Mr Torreani. Unfortunately, by the time the body was found, he had left for Ramsgate and was never interviewed. Mr De Bolla insisted, however, that Mr Torreani and the couple had no interaction between each other, and he had never mentioned any disturbance in the days that followed.

As the full extent of what had just happened sunk in, Antoine became extremely fearful and distressed. He later described his wife as a 'poor, dear woman', who had her life cut short by none other than her own husband. Of course, in spite of those words, he refused to take any responsibility for the murder, and made it very clear in letters that the deed was all her fault. However, he did find it hard to live with what he had done, and described his life as a burden.

Unable to cope with the guilt, and completely out of his mind, Dhereng claimed to have travelled to Liverpool with the idea that he should commit suicide up there. Why he did not consider committing the act in London is not known, but regardless, if the trip did take place, he did not go through with his plan and was back in the city just a day later.

Three days after the murder, Antoine visited his brother. He was extremely excitable – even more than usual, and George asked why that was. 'I have something very particular to communicate,' he replied and then, while the two men were in a cab, the reason for his agitation came pouring out. Antoine told George about hitting Catherine on the head and watching her fall to the floor. 'I never left her until I had killed her,' he said. 'I cut her throat!'

George could not believe what he was hearing, but as his sibling described how he now wanted to end his own life, his first thought was just how much of the story was actually true: 'He had told me so often he would commit suicide that I did not believe he would do so. I conjured him in the cab to say if what he had told me was really true. He replied he was very sorry to say that it was, but that he would do all in his power to save me and the family from disgrace.'

As the words echoed around the cab, George could simply not see how the family could avoid being dragged into the scandal. In a moment of impulse, he had an idea. 'You must leave the country,' he said. 'That will save the family from disgrace.' Instead of agreeing to that plan, however, Antoine told his brother that he had no intention of going anywhere; as far as he was concerned, there was no way he would consent to give up his life in London. With the confession ringing in his ears, George made his excuses and left. He went home that evening with the knowledge that his brother was quite out of his mind, and swore he would never see him again.

While Dhereng had talked of suicide many times, he was now taking the subject very seriously. The knowledge of what he had done, and the reality that he would be hanged for his crimes, was too much to bear. Added to that, the body of his wife was now decomposing and still located in the flat. It would not be long before his gross deed was discovered, and Dhereng could feel the walls closing in.

The day after visiting with his brother, the murderer sat down and wrote several long letters to him, along with a suicide note. He then walked the short distance to Hyde Park and tried to shoot himself dead. Unfortunately for him, the shot didn't work, so he made another failed attempt before finally cutting his throat. It was this last effort that ultimately killed the deranged man.

The Hyde Park keeper was busy working nearby when he heard the two shots. He ran towards the noise and as Antoine finally came into his view, the keeper was shocked to see him falling backwards onto the ground. Blood poured from a wound in his throat and a knife was in his hand. By this time another man was on the scene and together they took the weapon, tried to help the man and called for assistance. It was too late, of course. By the time a doctor arrived, Antoine was quite dead.

The men then had the gruesome task of trying to find out who the person was. They searched his pockets and found the letters, which just so happened to have Dhereng's full confession and the address of where to find the body. From there, the park-keeper and a policeman by the name of Joseph Brown went to the Oxford Street house, and broke the news to the landlord. He told the men that he had not seen either Antoine or Catherine since Saturday and had become concerned. In fact, during that very morning, just as Mr Torreani was about to leave for Ramsgate, the landlord relayed his fears:

'I said to Torreani, "I should like to see the room," but he said I had better not, as perhaps the Dherengs had gone into the country. I replied that I should like him to be a witness if I went into the room. After Torreani went I bored some holes in the door to see if the things were in the room or whether the Dherengs had run away. I saw that the things were there but they were all upset. I then had stronger suspicions that something was wrong and went downstairs, when I found the officers there from the park . . .'

After it was explained that Antoine had just committed suicide, the landlord shared his suspicions about the safety of Mrs Dhereng. The police officer, landlord and park-keeper then went upstairs, stared through the holes, and agreed that there was no sign of the woman. There was, however, the most horrific smell, permeating from somewhere inside the premises. A crowbar was fetched and the door forced open. All three men then entered the flat.

There on the floor was the naked, headless body of Catherine, covered partially with a piece of cloth. Her arms and legs had deep gashes and the entire room was covered in blood. Several knives were lying around the place, and one of them had a large amount of blood and hair all over it. There was no sign of the victim's head, but on opening the coal cupboard the inspector was greeted with a ghastly sight. There it was, wrapped up in a towel.

Catherine's shocked sister was asked to identify the body, and then a post-mortem was carried out. Mr George William Bridgeman was in charge and gave a full disclosure in court:

'I am a surgeon and reside in Margaret Street, Cavendish Square. I was called to the house in Oxford Street by the previous witness [a chemist]. I found the body of a woman lying on her stomach. There were four wounds on the shoulders and hip joints. There were two cuts over the ankles. The head was found in the cupboard, and on it there were several cuts. I have since made a post-mortem examination.

'There was an extensive fracture of the skull, which was done during life. I have no doubt the wounds on the head were inflicted during life, and that the throat was also cut during life or immediately after. The cause of death was no doubt the injuries to the head, as they were amply sufficient. The cutting of the head and the injuries to the arms were done after death. I attribute the death of the woman to the injuries to the head and the cutting of the throat conjointly. The large shears produced were such an instrument as would have produced a fracture of the skull. There were marks of blood upon them.

The other injuries could have been inflicted with the knife and saw now produced.'

The news of the murder and suicide was shared far and wide, and newspapers reported the story in all its gory detail. *The Maidstone and Kentish Journal* described it thus:

> In our last edition, we noticed the determined suicide of a Frenchman in Hyde Park. From further particulars relative to the affair, there is scarcely a doubt that the man, in addition to having committed suicide, had also perpetrated one of the most horrible murders that for many years have taken place in this country – the murder being attended with circumstances of peculiar atrocity.

Amusingly, this newspaper and several others were quite concerned with the discovery of a tattoo on Dhereng's arm, believed to be of Napoleon. They were interested not because they thought there was anything significant about the inking, but because they all agreed that it was a very good likeness. In court, however, it was revealed that the picture wasn't of Napoleon at all, but actually the figure of a woman.

The inquest into the death of Antoine Dhereng was held in early July 1860 at St James's Workhouse, and as could be expected from the nature of the death, it was a packed house. Catherine's body lay in a room within the building, and each newspaper described how its presence had 'presented a shocking spectacle'. Antoine's body lay in an outhouse, and while the jury were taken to see it, the sight was barely mentioned by the press at all.

A variety of people were called to testify, including George Dhereng, the murderer's brother. He could barely contain his emotions as he spoke about his sibling.

'I have seen the deceased frequently,' he said, 'and he appeared latterly to be – as he had often been – most eccentric in his ways. I believe that his mind was not right, for he often told me he would commit suicide.'

George explained that Antoine had bought several pistols from a store in Paris fourteen years before his death, and then bought another when he had left prison, twelve months ago. He then told the story of the meeting he had the day before his brother's death, during which time the man had confessed to killing his wife. At this point in the proceedings, however, there was an almighty scream, and one of the jurors started having a fit in the jury box. He was carried out by several staff members, but this incident only resulted in upsetting George even more than he was already.

Catherine's sister, Jane, had identified the body and agreed with George Dhereng about the pistols. According to her, Antoine carried them frequently, and had threatened to cut his own throat on a variety of occasions. He was a terrible husband, she said, and as a result she had not seen Catherine since February 1860.

A man called Charles Sudikatis was next to be called. He gave a long and descriptive account of his memories of the murderer:

'I have known the deceased since he was a boy of eleven years of age. His name was Antoine Dhereng and he was about thirty-four or thirty-five years of age. He was a tailor. I saw him last Thursday week. I was in the habit of seeing him three or four times a week. He was always in good health, and a sober hard-working man. He was married about six years ago, but did not live happily with his wife. Last April [1859] he was sent to prison by the magistrate at Marlborough Street police court for four months for striking her. Long ago I advised him if he could not live on terms of affection with her, to consort with some other woman, and I believe if he had done so this shocking affair would not have happened.

'When he came out he said he would do something to her. On the evening of Thursday week, when I last saw him, he was excited, and not in his right mind. I talked to him about half an hour in French. He said he could not live happily with his wife and that I should very soon hear of his finishing his career. I advised him to make up his mind and go and live with another woman. He said he could not do so. I then wished him "Good night" and we parted.'

The man was asked if Dhereng has ever appeared excitable before, to which he replied, 'Oh yes at different times. I could see it in his features.'

Another friend stepped forward and gave his memories of the murderer:

'My name is Lucien Heagarty, and I have known the deceased well for the past eight years. He is very excitable and I always believed him to be insane. He was in the habit of going to see houses where serious tragedies had been committed, and he was also in the habit of going to see people hanged.'

At that point, the judge stopped the man from talking and gave the disclosure that Dhereng was not alone in watching hangings; many others did the same. Still, Heagarty continued his story and told the jury that his associate was quite clearly a madman. 'His wife had often told me that he would kill her someday,' he said.

The testimony of Lucien Heagarty brought up further memories from George Dhereng, who requested he be allowed to provide more evidence. When admitted to do so, he told the court that his brother had been in the habit of visiting Dr Kahn's Museum, where he studied the arteries of the neck and throat. 'He especially familiarised himself with the position of the jugular vein,' he said. 'He used also to say that if he cut his throat, he would not do it in a vulgar manner by severing the windpipe.'

Various items were shown to the jury, including the large, bloodstained knife. The sight of such an item sent cries and gasps around the courthouse, though far more interesting were the letters that were found on Antoine's body. Some of the documents were in French, others English, but all were covered in blood and written in an excitable and frantic hand. A translator very carefully deciphered each one. First of all, there was the suicide note:

'Mercy, mercy, my agony is extreme. I have suffered for what I have done. No mortal being can tell. Adieu, Adieu to all that is dear to me.'

Then there were various letters addressed to the murderer's brother; all showing utter contempt towards Catherine Dhereng:

My Dear George – You know that since I came out of this infernal, infernal prison I became mad and furious for having been made the victim of this incomparable woman. You know that she had the wickedness and ferocity to premeditate everything in order to send me to prison.

And it is this idea which upsets me and which renders me more than mad. I have been cruelly sent to that house of sufferings and degradation by the hands of my own wife. Oh! When I think of it my head bursts. There is no more

happiness upon earth for me, who have been so cruelly
treated by this cursed woman.

Finally, after all the evidence had been presented, the judge
turned to the jury and directed their attention to the fact that
there could be no doubt that the man had killed Catherine
Dhereng. 'This is strengthened still further by the way in which
he committed the crime of self-destruction,' he said.

The jury listened carefully, adjourned to a neighbouring
room and then came back with their verdict. It was of absolutely no surprise when they announced that Antoine Dhereng
was guilty of the murder of his wife and had committed suicide
while in a state of extreme insanity. However, shortly after the
court had emptied, things took a surprising turn when several
members of the jury refused to sign the declaration that claimed
insanity at the point of death. Instead, they insisted that because
the man had attempted to dismember the body and hide the
evidence, 'insanity' was not the correct word to describe his
state of mind.

They asked that the word be taken from the verdict and his
final act be described as a case of straightforward suicide (known
at the time as *felo de se* – felon of himself). It took a full hour of
discussion before they finally agreed to the original verdict, and
the word insanity was officially recorded. Judging by his letters,
the stamp of 'insane' wouldn't be how Dhereng wished to be
remembered:

Now that I am no more, you will pity me and say, like me,
that I do not die a villain, but a poor unfortunate victim of
having so unfortunately met with a most violent woman,
like myself, which is the only cause that now I am obliged

to sacrifice my own life instead of being happy in the world and be respected . . .

The Sad Case of the Scorned San Francisco Woman

While Victorian women were expected to be gentler than their male counterparts, there is little doubt that, once something within them was triggered, they could be just as brutal. Take Louise Kopp, for instance. She and her husband Charles lived a relatively quiet life in San Francisco with their fourteen-year-old daughter, Amanda. He was a retired restaurant owner, and between them they owned a considerable amount of property, including a large building containing six apartments.

In 1898, Louise Kopp was diagnosed with a wasting disease from which she was unlikely to recover. Knowing that her husband and daughter would need support after she was gone, Louise took the decision to sign over all her worldly goods to Charles, then she and Amanda went on a restful trip to Indianapolis. However, once there, the woman discovered that she was unable to return to California due to her husband's reluctance to send her the necessary travel expenses. Once she did manage to get home – a full nine months later – she soon realised why Charles had been anxious for her to stay away. It seemed that her husband had grown bored with his life of domesticity and was now on the lookout for some excitement.

Charles had become frustrated with her illness and disliked having to take care of Louise, his third wife, himself. After she had left town, he developed an obsession with a widow by the name of Madam Monti, who was a new tenant in his building. This rather fancy name wasn't her real one, of course. In reality she was Mrs Bertha Beck, but that wasn't good enough for her profession of fortune-teller, so she had changed it to Madam Monti after her husband's death.

The woman did not seem to mind the attention from Mr Kopp at all, and was frequently seen coming and going from his apartment during his wife and daughter's absence. The two were also spotted shopping for home furnishings together, and he would frequently cook for them both in his family home.

By the time Louise returned, the affair was in full swing, but that did not stop Charles having the bravado to introduce the two women. By this time, rumours swirled around the building that a relationship had taken place between the two, and it wasn't long before Louise heard the whispers and became extremely worried about the situation. When the stories of his infidelity gathered pace, the wife felt that she had no option but to ask outright if there was anything going on. Unbelievably, Charles straightaway admitted that he had been carrying on with Madam Monti while she was away.

'I cannot live without her,' he told Louise. 'I intend to love her until my death.' When asked why he had such a fascination for the woman, he merely replied, 'I like her because she is good looking and interesting.' He then brazenly announced that he had signed over the deeds to much of the couple's property to his lover, including the items Louise had given him before she went on her trip.

While Charles made it clear that he had no intention of remaining married, he continued to live in the marital home. Sensibly, however, Madam Monti decided to move out of the building and take a house nearby. As if his betrayal wasn't bad enough, Charles then refused to pay anything towards the upkeep of the Kopp house or financially support his family in any way. As the weeks wore on, Louise's health continued to deteriorate, and she did not have the funds to feed and clothe herself and her daughter.

Shortly after the separation, the scorned woman turned up at Madam Monti's home and stayed until 1 a.m. During her time in the house, Louise cried and begged her rival to look elsewhere for a man to love. 'Please don't take my husband's affections away from me,' she sobbed. 'I am sick. I need his comfort.'

Faced with an awkward situation, Madam Monti denied ever looking at Charles, and claimed he did not love her at all. Louise did not believe the story and then went into a long rant about how her marriage had broken down, and now Charles was extremely cold and unfeeling. She then explained that her husband had taken all of their money from the bank; a crime she had repaid by breaking the windows of their house during a fight earlier that evening.

'If my husband does not put back the property in the same condition that it was,' she told Madam Monti, 'he shall not live to enjoy it.'

Things had become desperate, and Charles was now extremely abusive. According to Louise, on an almost daily basis the man would hold her by the neck against the wall and throttle her until her coughing caused her lungs to bleed. In an effort to scare her husband into leaving her alone, Mrs Kopp bought a .38-calibre pistol. During one attack, she took out the weapon and threatened him with it. On that particular occasion, he was able to wrestle it from her hands, but a few weeks later he would not be so lucky.

In the final week of June 1899, Louise tried to regain control of her life, and made steps to protect her home from being given to Madam Monti by her husband. She also told tenants in the building that if her husband did not put the deeds of the property back in her name, she would divorce him and name Monti in the suit.

On 28 June, Louise was walking past a restaurant, when who should be sitting in a window seat but Charles and Madam Monti. Since Louise had been struggling to feed herself and daughter Amanda since her husband had financially deserted them, the sight caused even more distress and sent her into a rage. Louise was not going to take the humiliation lightly and, instead of walking on, she went straight into the restaurant and sat at a nearby table. When the couple were finished eating, she then followed them out onto the street and had a huge fight with her husband, right outside the restaurant.

'Charlie, how could you have the heart to do this?' Louise demanded. Then she started questioning Madam Monti, too.

'You're crazy,' was all the woman had to say, before turning her back.

After the argument, both parties stormed off. By the time she arrived home, Louise's estranged husband was already sitting in his favourite chair, reading the paper and smoking his pipe. It seemed as though he didn't have a care in the world, but that was soon to change. Louise confronted him about the earlier sighting and the two quarrelled like so many times in the past four weeks. She asked Charles if he intended to ruin everything they had worked for, just so he could be with Madam Monti.

'If you were as nice as her, I might take you out places,' he replied, before heading to the kitchen.

While he was there, Charles could be heard rummaging through the freezer box. Unsure what was to come next, Louise grabbed her gun and put it into her pocket. Moments later he returned, and after he had cursed the woman and told her he was leaving once and for all, Louise took the gun from her pocket, aimed carefully and, before he could do anything about it, she shot Charles Kopp straight through the forehead. He died instantly.

Having witnessed everything that had just happened in the parlour, teenager Amanda Kopp was – understandably – in a great deal of shock and anguish. She had been innocently reading a book when she heard the deafening sound and looked up to see her father falling. Her mother stood close by with the gun in hand.

Instead of panicking about what she had just done, Louise remained perfectly composed. She examined the body, made sure he was dead, then locked up the house and calmly walked with her daughter to her sister's. Once there, she asked her brother-in-law to kindly report her crime to the police, which he did. She was arrested and taken away for questioning, during which time she told detectives that her husband had squandered all of their money on Madam Monti.

An inquest was heard almost straightaway, and the jury decided that Louise Kopp had been driven to desperation by her husband's brazen affair with his lover. They decided the event had been justifiable homicide, though the judge did not agree and arraigned her for murder. Mrs Kopp pleaded not guilty, and a court date was set. Meanwhile, an obituary appeared in the newspaper with funeral details, announcing to the world that Charles Kopp was the beloved husband of the very woman who had killed him.

In July 1899, Louise was brought to court for a preliminary trial before a police judge to see if she would be given a full trial. People were aghast that while jurors in the coroner's court had declared the deed justifiable homicide, it was as if their views had not counted for anything at all. The proceedings excited reporters, however, as they were given their first look at the now infamous Bertha Monti, who sat and smiled sweetly. In complete contrast, Louise Kopp wept frequently, especially whenever she looked towards Monti, and when her daughter gave her version of what happened on the fateful night.

The journalists in court had absolutely no patience for Madam Monti at all. While wearing mourning clothes, they noted that the woman seemed to have taken the news of her lover's death very lightly indeed. She also gave various conflicting answers, but when asked why that was, replied that she must have just misunderstood the question. Monti also denied ever having an affair with Charles Kopp; she said he had absolutely not signed over any property to her and had only ever given her one dollar in cash, no more, no less. Had they frequently dined out together? Only once was the reply.

Another witness by the name of Joanna Laconte then testified to say that Louise was deeply jealous of the other woman in her husband's life, and worried constantly that he had – or was about to – sign the deeds to her home over to Madam Monti. Once that witness had left the stand, a patrolman told his story that a few days before the death, Charles Kopp had come up to him on the street, asking about a warrant for the arrest of his wife. However, the testimony was not allowed to be heard in court after an objection from the defence team, and the man left without finishing what he had wanted to say.

During the next day, there was great excitement in court when the proprietor of a local restaurant came forward to say that she had witnessed Mr Kopp and Madam Monti frequently dining in her establishment. Monti was called back to the stand in order to answer the question of why she had told the jury she had only dined with Kopp once before. The startled woman replied that she thought the question only applied to the period after Louise had returned from Indianapolis, not the entire period of their 'friendship'. The restaurant proprietor then stood up to inform the court that Madam Monti was lying; that she had been seen there on at least two occasions over the past few weeks. There then followed an argument between the two women and great whooping from the public, before finally the judge brought the matter under control.

Several neighbours and tenants testified, and each told stories of how Charles Kopp had been intimate with Madam Monti during his wife's absence. One – Maria Carlo – shocked the court by telling a tale of Kopp striking his wife twice with a hammer; an incident which only stopped when Amanda intervened, and Louise broke furniture in retaliation. Louise's sister then disclosed that she had recently asked Charles to be kinder to his wife. 'I'm in love with Madam Monti,' he answered. 'What of it?'

Finally, Louise Kopp took to the stand and gave the story of her marriage, stifling sobs and with her voice almost no more than a whisper. Madam Monti was frequently seen straining her neck to hear the full testimony. The entire court was transfixed as the scorned woman told a tale of a good man who suddenly turned abusive and neglectful. 'I lost a good husband,' she was heard to cry at one point.

During her time on the stand, the woman confirmed the story about being hit with a hammer, recalling: 'I was afraid to stay in the house. Once he struck me on the side of the head . . . Another time he hit me with a hammer on the shoulder.

I bought the pistol to frighten him, so he would not choke me anymore. I thought maybe if he were frightened, he would give up Madam Monti. I never intended to kill him.' She was asked if it had all been an accident, to which the woman replied, 'Oh no, I pulled the trigger, but I did not think it would go off so easily.'

Louise then revealed that while arguing that evening, her husband had pulled out a pocket knife and toyed with it in his hand. This was dismissed, however, when the prosecution questioned the story and she admitted that Charles had been using it to cut tobacco. The questioning was finished, and the defence gave their closing statements, saying that poor Mrs Kopp was extremely ill with consumption, and if it was decided to send her to a full trial, the stress would lead to her death. Not so, said the prosecution. 'Should jealous women be allowed to slay and not be punished? If there is such a law in California, then it must be changed.'

When she was called back into court several days later, Judge Conlan had made his decision. The woman would have to go to trial, purely for the reason stated by the prosecution. However, the charge would be reduced to manslaughter and the trial would only take place should the woman recover suitably from her consumption. This was unlikely to happen, since her health was now deteriorating rapidly to the point where she had to be carried into court. The judge gave a speech to explain his feelings:

'My duty as a committing magistrate is to ascertain if a crime has been committed, and, if so, whether there is cause to believe that the defendant committed it. Both of these questions are answered affirmatively by the evidence. Under the circumstances, while it is true my sympathies are with the unfortunate woman, I would not like to assume the responsibility of restoring her to liberty. In a case like this I cannot render judgement as dictated by my feelings . . . The bail will be the lowest possible amount ever known to the law in one of these cases, namely, $1000.'

Mrs Kopp did indeed live long enough to see her manslaughter charge brought to trial, but the evidence was very much regurgitated from before, and nothing new was brought to light. In fact, by that time the woman was so ill that she could hardly speak and claimed to have no memory of the actual shooting at all. By the end of it all, the jury couldn't decide whether she was guilty or innocent so another trial was brought, which ended in just a few hours with the acquittal of Mrs Kopp. The woman passed away less than six months later, on 5 June 1900, leaving her possessions to her daughter, Amanda. Interestingly, before she passed, Mrs Kopp was able to regain the right to the two properties her husband had apparently promised Madam Monti, and these too were passed to her daughter.

This should have been the end of the story, but a strange twist came in April 1901 when it was revealed that Madam Monti was currently destitute and in hospital. Several days before, the ill and upset woman turned up at the home of her old landlady, Mrs Reimer. Suffering from nervousness and what appeared to be amnesia, the woman gave her name as Mrs McClure and stated that she had recently been married. She then told various conflicting stories, which included one of living off the estate of her dead husband. This changed later when she claimed she had no money at all, since her supposed dead husband was actually very much alive and now married to somebody else.

Mrs Reimer asked what had happened between her and the husband, but Mrs McClure didn't seem to know. All she could share was that he had run away to San Diego, and she had not heard from him in many months. While Mrs Reimer listened, Madam Monti continued to talk in circles, going around and around with subjects that made little or no sense at all. Concerned for her mental and physical state, the woman called for an ambulance. When it came, however, Monti refused to leave and so stayed the night with Mrs Reimer. The following morning she was taken to hospital, admitted with severe exhaustion and administered sedatives.

It didn't take long before the story of her breakdown leaked to the newspapers, and reporters hurried to the hospital. They eventually spoke to various friends and were able to figure out what Monti had been doing since the trial. Apparently, after the death of her lover, she had carried on her fortune-telling business, where she had met her now estranged husband. However, on hearing about the desperate death of Mrs Kopp, the cocky and overconfident woman now suddenly had an attack of conscience. She told friends how sorry she was that she had caused such a lot of grief in the life of Louise, and accepted that her presence in their lives had contributed to the death of Mr Kopp. In the months after, friends noted Madam Monti's spiralling depression, which eventually led to her husband's estrangement and her complete nervous breakdown. 'She is completely without means,' one friend told a reporter.

It should be said that the journalists seemed to be rather happy to hear about the woman's downfall. 'Retribution has come in a hurry,' was the *San Francisco Chronicle*'s sarcastic reaction.

The Dreadful, Late-night Murder at Battersea Bridge

Sarah MacFarlane was a widow in her mid-forties, living in
1840s London. To all who knew her, she seemed to be a respectable woman who looked after children, took in needlework
and washing, and worked hard to raise a son by herself. She
even rented out the lower rooms of her home as a chapel for
Baptist Methodists, and looked after the premises on their
behalf. However, when she became involved with a neighbour,
her reputation and finally her life were both put in danger in
the most horrific of ways.

Sarah had known Augustus Dalmas and his family for a
great many years and, according to the 1841 census, the
families lived next door to each other. The neighbours were so
close that when Dalmas's wife passed away in June 1843, Sarah
was at her side. She also took his teenage daughters into her
house to be cared for when the man suddenly ran away. His
official story was that he could not cope with the loss of his
wife and contemplated suicide. However, rumours abounded
that the actual reason for his departure was because he had
become involved in several dodgy business deals and had fled
with all the money.

'I am tired of life,' he wrote in a letter to his eldest daughter
while he was away. 'My body can be found by the river.'

The local community showed great sympathy for his teenage
children, and a reward was offered for the return of their father's
body. But it turned out that the letter was not a genuine cry for
help. It was a dramatic gesture on Dalmas's part; something for
which he would get quite a reputation in the months ahead.
The man did not commit suicide after all, and following a few
months of seclusion, he began visiting his family at Sarah

MacFarlane's house, before he finally moved back into his own home.

By this time, Sarah had secured work placements for all of his daughters and, according to Dalmas, was keen to begin a relationship with him. He claimed that the woman had made a play for him from the moment his wife died, but since he ran out on the family almost immediately, this was perhaps an exaggeration. However, by the time the two were living as neighbours once again, the affair did become physical and Sarah even made a secret entrance from her house to his, so she could come and go without being seen by her sister, who lived nearby.

Dalmas felt a huge amount of guilt for having a sexual relationship with Sarah MacFarlane, likely because of the short space of time since his wife passed. In letters, he revealed that the woman seemed to have some kind of spell over him, and he was unable to say no. Rather dramatically, instead of calling off the relationship, he chose to flee his house once again, and this time headed to Liverpool. He also abandoned his business and made plans to commit suicide, though these were thwarted when one of his daughters managed to locate him and talk him into returning to London.

On his return, he moved into a boarding house where he gave the false name of Chaplin, and then remained there for the next eight months. An excited Sarah heard that he was back in the city and persuaded Dalmas to renew their sexual relationship. According to him, she exclaimed that since losing her husband she had held no feelings for anyone until she met him.

The two became engaged and were due to marry at a Kensington church in January 1844, a mere six months after the death of his wife. However, in the end, the marriage never did take place. Dalmas, though, began referring to himself as Sarah's husband from that moment on, even though they lived apart. He even wrote a handwritten contract, which he gave to his lover:

I hereby declare that I have made a solemn promise to Sarah Andrew MacFarlane, widow, to marry her, and that the banns of the said marriage have been duly published in the church of Kensington; but that unforeseen circumstances forcing me to postpone the solemnisation of marriage for the present, to guarantee the said Sarah Andrew MacFarlane against any breach of the said promise on my part, I hereby bind myself in the sum of five hundred pounds not to marry any other person during the lifetime of the said Sarah Andrew MacFarlane.

He finished the contract by declaring his wish to leave all his worldly possessions to the woman, including two French homes he had inherited from his aunt.

Sarah signed the contract and seemed to be a keen participant in the relationship. However, whether she was actually in love with the man is unknown. Certainly her sister Ellen disliked Dalmas with a passion. The feeling was mutual, and he described her as a fiend and blamed her inhospitable manner for him fleeing his house and contemplating suicide. Interestingly, during the inquest, Ellen said that it was the family's dislike of Dalmas that prevented Sarah from officially marrying the man.

Still, the relationship continued and, according to Dalmas, he supplied Sarah with a great deal of money for gin, took her on theatre trips three times a week, bought suppers and provided private cabs. He also claimed that the woman asked him for a rather substantial loan so that her son could start his own business. While he was initially keen to help, he ultimately decided not to go ahead with the investment, which – according to Dalmas – led Sarah to steal part of the money from him.

It would be no exaggeration to describe the couple as having a rather turbulent relationship. This was due to many factors, including the negative reaction from the family and resentment felt by Sarah that, even though Dalmas's daughters were now grown, they still turned to her for food and lived with her on various occasions. Added to that, since the man was spending money at a rapid rate, he soon got into a host of financial difficulties. Letters show that when discussing the issues with Sarah, she did not give much – if any – sympathy.

There was also another matter that caused concern. For a long time it had been rumoured that Sarah was having an affair with a married man called Meredith. Dalmas refused to believe this, but then friends told him that she was also known as a highly skilled prostitute and this was how she earned the majority of her money. If she did conduct herself in such a way, she did so quietly, as none of her friends mentioned anything of that nature during future testimony. Furthermore, a search of the Old Bailey proceedings reveals that if this was the case, she was likely never brought to court for it. However, while Dalmas was loath to think she could possibly earn her living this way, he became more and more suspicious as time went on. For now, though, he remained quiet.

Dalmas was a huge fan of writing long, rambling letters. In January 1844, he sent one to Sarah, which talked about the making of a bonnet by his daughter, Caroline. He began the note with the words 'My dearest', and ended with 'Your ever faithful and affectionate husband'. On 15 April he wrote to her again, this time to ask if she would give a good word to a man by the name of Dr Morrison, whom he hoped would be able to save him from the financial misfortune that had arisen:

Pray, my Sarah, do not fail, as on you alone depends the success of my application to Dr Morrison, and you will then be indeed the saviour of my life and the means of promoting my future welfare . . . I want you to tell nothing but the truth, as I represented you to Dr Morrison as a most respectable, good and charitable widow, enjoying the respect of some of the most religious ladies in Battersea and Clapham.

On 18 April 1844, another letter arrived. Describing her as 'Dearest and beloved Sarah', the man wrote of his heartbreak at hearing she too was in such dire straits financially that she was now considering opening her house as a boarding lodge. Later he would change this sadness into rage, when he became sure she was converting her home into a brothel where she could entertain men.

In the letter, Dalmas lamented not ever making their relationship official, and put the blame on Sarah's sister, Ellen. Speaking of leaving his house because of her attitude towards him, he declared that the woman would not be happy until she saw him dead, and that if such a thing happened, it would be on her head. Describing Sarah as his only friend, he begged her to go to church with him that Sunday, and to contact him when she had a moment. He then asked her to 'pray for your affectionate husband', before finally signing off.

On 20 April 1844, Sarah and Dalmas spent the day together, and during that time he asked her son, William, if he would sharpen a knife for him. The lad thought nothing of it, did as he was told and returned the instrument to its owner. The next day Dalmas wrote to Sarah again, this time describing how one of his daughters – Augusta – had been relieved of her duties as a servant and had fallen on hard times. He begged his lover to meet him in Trafalgar Square the next evening, to receive the girl into her care and act as her mother once again. Rather strangely, he also wrote that there was something important he needed to discuss, just in case something terrible was to befall him.

While it is not known exactly what Sarah had to say to Dalmas in return, it certainly wasn't positive. In his next letter, dated 23 April, he berated her for sending such a cross message, and then spoke of his daughter, Augusta, several times. If we are to read between the lines, it becomes clear that Sarah must have baulked at the idea of having the girl live with her again, even though Dalmas confirmed in the note that she would be suitably compensated. 'See you I must,' he wrote, before signing off once again as her affectionate husband.

By now Dalmas had decided to confront Sarah about the persistent rumours of her having an affair with Mr Meredith. Instead of denying it as he hoped, the woman not only admitted the dalliance, but told him that she intended to carry on. When he asked what her sister thought of the affair, she answered that all of their meetings took place at the home of a friend, so her sibling could not find out.

Dalmas was fast becoming broke due to his vast overspending and living a life beyond his means. He wrote that during this time, Sarah lost all interest in him, insulted him in front of friends and began calling him Mr Kiss My Ass to his daughter. 'She has driven me mad, mad, mad,' he said. 'She has murdered me.'

In the days ahead, the man found himself in a state of uncontrollable rage. During that time, he wrote several letters that were later found in his room. The content of these notes was considered to be so vile that when the matter went to court, women were sent out of the room before they could be read. The notes were never actually sent to Sarah herself, but they do offer a glimpse into the state of affairs between the couple, and how Augustus Dalmas had finally begun to believe the rumours circulating about the nature of Sarah's business.

Addressed to 'Mrs MacFarlane', the first undated letter was a rambling mess of over one thousand words. In it, he described his former beloved as being a 'profligate prostitute of the lowest order', and accused her of ruining his life.

I know all your artful deceptions. You are little aware who watched you when you were carrying on your criminal intercourse with your paramour. You used to send my daughters upstairs, and under pretence of bringing the tea-kettle on the wash-house fire, you artfully examined the passage and the stairs to see that no one was listening or watching, then locked yourself in the back chapel room, and prostituted yourself for hours together. You have dishonoured the names of your father and husband, and have the effrontery to boast of it. Well might the gardeners, when they used to pass your dwelling, say, 'This is the house of that whore MacFarlane, who used to live in the gardens; she keeps a chapel and a brothel.'

Dalmas then went on to berate Sarah for having sex with him on countless occasions.

Your obscenity with me ought to have opened my eyes, but under a spell, I mistook your profligacy for affection. All you wanted was to satisfy yourself at my expense, and when you found all the money gone, like other prostitutes, you laugh at me for a fool, and insult me in the most disgusting language, fit only for a Westminster whore.

In the letter, Dalmas laid all blame for their affair firmly at her door. According to him, he was an entirely innocent man who had been lured into a life of sin by Sarah. The pathetic man then made a gruesome threat that the deed would not go unpunished, and vowed to take his revenge by writing to her family about everything she had done. But that was not all. He also accused Sarah's son of being a thief; he claimed that Sarah overcharged any expenses brought about by the care of his children; and that his daughters had to keep house while she wore French shoes and silk stockings and stayed in bed until late morning. He then accused Sarah of living solely off his money for a matter of four months, and gave a long list of items he had paid for by himself.

Dalmas also used the letter to list every single event that he found to be vile or disgusting. Among the most descriptive was that Sarah had relieved herself in a chamber pot in front of his daughter, and also shared a bed with her own son. 'These are the actions for which you ought to be horsewhipped out of Battersea,' he wrote, 'and wherever you go there ought to be a post and a lantern with the words, "beware of a prostitute".'

Another letter was found in Sarah's home and showed that while the man had tried to gain her attention by insults, now he tried emotional blackmail and had returned to calling himself an 'affectionate husband'.

'The time is approaching fast,' he wrote. 'I will not delay an hour if it is within my power: therefore do not disappoint me tomorrow; for it would lead me to believe you no longer entertain any friendship, regard or love for me. Such gloomy ideas would prompt me to despair, and perhaps, to crime and perdition.' He then begged Sarah to make her love him more than he already did, by meeting him at 3 p.m. the following day.

Despite any attempts on his part to completely reconcile, the relationship was effectively over. However, that did not stop the couple making love until the early hours of 28 April 1844. Then, still in bed but overcome once more with guilt, Augustus blamed Sarah for the indiscretion.

'My mind is in such a state, I feel as though I should cut my own throat,' he said.

'Don't do it here,' she answered. 'It will make such a mess.'

Despite any negative energy between the two, the couple were seen later that day at Dalmas's boarding house, where the owner's daughter described them as being 'very quiet and comfortable together'. The next day, Sarah's sister, Ellen, saw her at home around 1 p.m. No doubt happy that the relationship with Dalmas was on the rocks, she said that her sibling was 'as well as I ever saw her in my life'. Nothing about her demeanour led Ellen to think that she was anything but content, but unknown to either of them, this would be the last time the two women would ever see each other.

In the early evening, Sarah helped Dalmas's daughter, Augusta, to move out of her house. The girl had obtained a job as a servant in Chelsea, and since it provided living quarters, she would no longer have to rely on Sarah for accommodation.

Having looked after Augusta on and off for nearly a year, one cannot help but think that this news would have provided Sarah with a little relief.

Around 8.30 p.m., they were met by Augustus, who continued to help his daughter move into her new room.

'How are you?' he asked Sarah.

'Very well,' she replied.

The man then thanked her for bringing Augusta to her new place of work; she acknowledged him and then went into the house.

'My father was walking up and down outside, waiting for her,' Augusta later said. 'She stopped about ten minutes when I wished her good bye and the housekeeper went up with her, and let her out. I have not seen her since . . . the deceased and my father were on very intimate terms.'

When Sarah exited from the girl's new house, Augustus was still waiting for her. What conversation transpired between them is unknown, but around 10 p.m. he was alone and seen by another daughter, Caroline. During this meeting, the man behaved in what she felt was a very odd way. At one point during their conversation, he shouted, 'I'm mad! I'm mad!' Then he grabbed at the girl's shawl, pulled it down and began feeling her neck.

'Father, what are you doing?' she demanded.

'I am only examining a mole,' he replied. Caroline thought this was extremely strange, particularly since she did not have any moles on her neck at all.

Once he had bid his daughter farewell, Augustus somehow met back up with Sarah, and at 10.30 p.m. they were seen by various witnesses at Battersea Bridge. One woman overheard Sarah telling her lover that she was unable to stay out late that night. Another heard Dalmas saying the words, 'And so you won't,' but she was unaware as to the context in which the sentence was being said. No particular attention was paid to the couple because from the outside they looked just like any other taking an evening stroll. The truth, however, was far more sinister. Augustus Dalmas was about to show the world just why he had felt his daughter's neck earlier that evening. Instead of looking for an invisible mole, it had actually been a creepy dress rehearsal for what was coming next.

Reaching into his pocket, Augustus took out a knife he had been hiding. Then, when there was a quiet interval with no witnesses around, he pulled down Sarah's shawl and sliced his lover's throat. As the shocked woman tried to understand what had just happened, Dalmas ran quickly away. However, he did not go far and remained on the bridge for at least the next few minutes to see what would transpire. He was then seen running down the road in an agitated manner, crying, 'Police! Police!' as he did so. When asked by one witness what was wrong, he replied, 'A woman has cut her throat on the bridge.'

Passer-by William Parkins had been on Battersea Bridge when he heard some kind of exclamation coming from the other side. Seconds later he saw a woman heading in his direction in such a way that he presumed she was intoxicated. It was Sarah, excitable and in a deep state of distress.

'Will you be good enough to take me to the toll house?' she asked Parkins and grabbed hold of his hands. Still thinking she had been drinking, the man was undoubtedly suspicious.

'What for, my good woman? What do you want to go to the toll house for? What is the matter with you?'

At that point, Parkins realised there was something far more sinister afoot than a mere case of too much alcohol.

'Someone has cut me,' answered Sarah. The shocked man grasped hold of her and the two headed to the toll house, where they were greeted by the collector, Thomas Hall. 'See how someone has been ill using me,' she spluttered, and Hall noticed blood trickling down the front of her dress. He held her up, recognised her as Sarah MacFarlane, and called out to his wife for help.

Having handed the woman over to Hall, and not realising just how injured she was, Parkins headed back along the bridge. However, he didn't get far as he soon noticed that his hand felt wet and odd. Stopping for moment, he took a good look and saw that it was completely covered in blood. Stunned, he started to run straight back to the toll office.

At the same time, James Andrews was coming along Battersea Bridge in a cart. At one point, he drew up next to a man whom he later presumed to be Dalmas, leaning over the railings. Andrews was startled and called out to the man to refrain from jumping off. His concern may have lasted longer, if not for the fact that when he reached the toll house on the other side of the bridge, he was met by the anxious collector, shouting at him to get down off his cart.

'I saw a woman lying on the ground by the toll house door bleeding from the neck,' he said. 'Saw no-one else with her but the toll collector. I went to her, and having pulled the strings of her bonnet asunder, I loosened her boa and opened her shawl. Whilst doing that two policemen came up and asked what I was doing. I answered, "See how she is bleeding." Her throat was cut on the right side. All I heard her say was, "Oh dear, oh dear."'

By this time a small crowd had gathered, and Sarah was carried carefully to a passage in the Swan and Magpie Tavern by Parkins and several others. There, she was placed on the floor, where a policeman knelt down to speak with her.

'Mrs MacFarlane, who has done this?' he asked.

'Dalmas,' she replied, very faintly. The policeman did not quite hear, so looked at the landlord of the tavern for clarification. He repeated the name to him and the officer leaned towards Sarah once again.

'Did you say Dalmas?' he asked.

'Yes, yes,' she replied.

'Was there anyone else involved?'

'No,' she said.

Parkins left the scene for a moment in order to wash his hands, and on his return he saw a great difference in Sarah's appearance. Whereas before, she had her eyes open and was able to say small words, now the woman was deathly quiet. He removed her bonnet and then felt for a pulse. There wasn't one. She was declared dead shortly after.

Surgeon William Conner was sent for, and arrived to examine the body. He discovered the woman had a wound on the right side of her neck, measuring three inches in length, and an inch in depth. The large muscles of the neck were divided and the two jugular veins were separated. 'I found no other wound or injury,' he told the coroner. 'The injury was sufficient to destroy life, and deceased died from the infliction of that wound on her person.'

Conner decided very early on that the likelihood of the wound being self-inflicted was none; that it was most certainly done by someone standing behind her. When the coroner later asked if he was sure that it could not have been done by Sarah, Conner was adamant. 'It was impossible she could have done it,' he said.

Meanwhile, Augustus Dalmas was walking aimlessly around outside his daughter Caroline's place of work; a large home in Knightsbridge, where she was employed as a servant. At one point, the man let out a cough as he walked past Caroline's window. This had been a long-standing signal between father and daughter, so she went out to meet him on the steps of the house. She noticed straightaway that he looked haggard and rather ill.

'Father, how are you this evening?' she asked. Augustus failed to reply. Instead, he looked her in the eye, reached into his pocket and took out a notebook, which he then handed to her. 'I thought there was something extraordinary in this,' she later said.

'Dear father, what is the matter?' she asked. She was still met with silence, and by this time Caroline was deeply concerned. Asking once again what was wrong, she then refused to take the man's notebook.

'But you must,' he replied. 'I have poisoned Sarah MacFarlane.'

Caroline was beyond shocked. She fell down onto her knees.

'Oh father, what have you done?' she asked. Sensing his daughter's despair, Augustus then changed his story.

'No, no,' he said, 'I have not done it. I have attempted it.' The woman then calmed down slightly.

'Very well,' Caroline replied, 'I will take the pocket book and see you in the morning.'

'Very well,' Augustus said, and took his daughter's hand. This innocent gesture very strangely resulted in the woman having her hand cut.

'He had something in his hand, which cut my hand in three places,' Caroline said, 'and it bled very much. He ran away instantly, as on my screaming, the ladies at the next house came to the windows.'

As Augustus's daughter watched her father depart, she feared he was about to commit suicide. Interestingly, when the case went to court, Caroline denied all knowledge of the cut hand, or any mention of Sarah MacFarlane. Even though her testimony was on record, she swore she never said it at all, before later changing slightly to say, 'What I have before stated, I stated when in an excited state of mind.'

While Sarah's body was moved to her home, a search was carried out to try to find the man she had named as her killer. Officers and her son arrived at the boarding house where Dalmas resided. While they did not locate him, they did find the aforementioned disturbing letters, as well as a suicide note. Blaming the woman completely for everything that had happened in his recent life, he told his family about Sarah's affair, her alleged prostitution and spending of his money. He signed off with a dramatic 'Farewell forever!' before asking that the children take revenge for his death.

While police were poring over Dalmas's bizarre letters, Sarah's belongings were returned to her family. Her brother took one look at her boa and bonnet and immediately destroyed both. The boa was so saturated in blood, he said, that he could not bear to see it.

As expected, newspapers up and down the country were filled with stories relating to the crime. 'A murder of the most diabolical character, committed under circumstances of peculiar aggravation, took place on Monday night,' wrote a reporter for *Lloyd's Weekly Newspaper*. The articles were so terrifying that many readers refused to cross Battersea Bridge alone, and some even ruled out going there at all. It was, they said, just too dangerous to attempt.

While the public discussed the murder in the safety of their homes, an inquest was opened at the Swan and Magpie Tavern, where Sarah had passed away just days before. Once the jury had been sworn in, they all trekked down to the victim's house, where her body had been moved after her death. Once there, the gentlemen all took a good look at the poor woman's remains, and then returned to the inn, where a number of witnesses were called. These included two of Dalmas's daughters and many people who knew the couple. Remarkably, the coroner refused to allow the man's letters to be used in evidence, since he did not consider them to be in any way threatening towards Sarah MacFarlane. In fact, he said, Dalmas's words seemed to threaten his own welfare much more than anyone else's.

Meanwhile, the police were still searching for the man, and when no trace could be found it was widely believed that he had either thrown himself off the bridge or taken his own life in some other way. However, his daughters refuted this, insisting that he had such a love for himself that he would never dream of taking his own life, in spite of what he had written in his letters. Their thoughts turned out to be correct.

The man had not done anything at all to threaten his own welfare. Instead, he kept his head down and went about his business as best he could, living on the few shillings he had in his pocket at the time of the murder. When these were gone, he then travelled to the Bloomsbury shop of a Mr Wells, and pawned a frock coat and handkerchief. Dalmas gave his name as John Mott of Compton Street, in order to avoid being recognised. This would have been far more effective, however, if he had not stored the falsely named receipt in his pocket.

For several days, Dalmas seemed quite happy to avoid detection. 'The commissioners of police have spared neither exertion nor expense, or considered the toil imposed upon their constables in the endeavour to trace out Augustus Dalmas,' reported *Lloyd's Weekly Newspaper*, 'but it would seem that, like the miscreant Good, he in his turn is likely to keep the public in a state of feverish suspense for some time to come. That he will ultimately be apprehended, there can be no doubt.'

They were correct; the man was found, but not through any tip-off to the police. In the early hours of 4 May, Dalmas had finally had enough of hiding and decided to give himself up voluntarily. Police Constable William Cumming was on duty that evening, and remembered a man coming to the locked door of the station. Just as he was wondering what he was doing there, another officer arrived. When the officer unlocked the door and came inside, the brazen Dalmas followed and approached the desk. When asked what he wanted, the man very calmly gave his full name, and then stepped back to see the reaction of the officer.

Cumming was stunned. He had heard the name Augustus Dalmas many times over the past few days. However, just to make sure his imagination wasn't running wild, he took a quick glance through the log book. Sure enough, it confirmed his thoughts. Cumming told Dalmas that there was a very serious charge against him and that whatever he said would be told to the magistrate.

The constable worried that after hearing such a disclaimer, the man would make a run for it. Instead, Dalmas very calmly replied that he wished to hand himself in. However, he assured officers that it was certainly not because he wanted to admit his guilt. He explained how 'haunted' he had been by the 'untrue' stories that had appeared in the press. He merely wanted to set the record straight, he said, and get the truth out there – but his version of the truth, of course. Dalmas was placed in a cell, under the supervision of Police Constable Taylor.

'I believe the authorities of Scotland Yard have determined to spare no trouble or expense in my apprehension?' Dalmas asked. The officer ignored his question and enquired as to whether he would like some bread and cheese. 'No,' the prisoner replied. 'I am so agitated on account of this affair tonight, that I can't eat.'

It goes without saying that Dalmas's innocence was not believed by anyone in the constabulary, so he was charged with the murder of Sarah MacFarlane and sent to court. When his trial began, crowds gathered around the doors of the building in the hope of catching a glimpse of the 'unfortunate fellow', but they were left disappointed. Only a few were allowed into the room, and the rest were forced to admit defeat and return home.

Witnesses were called, and among them was Dalmas's daughter, Caroline, who was so upset by the proceedings that she fainted. When she revived, she went into such hysterics that she had to be escorted from the building. Throughout it all, Dalmas sat calm and unflustered, staring at each and every witness as they took to the stand. Unsurprisingly, when it was his turn to be questioned, Dalmas denied murdering Sarah MacFarlane. Instead, he described how the two had been walking together on the night of her death, and she had spent the time complaining bitterly about what she considered to be his ungrateful children.

According to the murderer, Sarah said that if one of his daughters continued with such behaviour, she would not be allowed into her house again. The couple then argued about the situation and MacFarlane ended up pulling out a knife and slicing her own throat. After that, she staggered all the way to the toll house in order to get help. This unbelievable story was pooh-poohed by a doctor who saw Sarah moments after her death. According to him, given the direction of the wound, it would have been impossible for her to inflict it upon herself.

All kinds of details about the relationship with Sarah were revealed, and subsequently published in the press, including the gross letters Dalmas had written to her and to others. Some of the witnesses provided crucial evidence, while the testimonies of some were struck off due to their random or insufficient recollections. For instance, a waitress in a coffee shop told a story of a man waiting for her to open on 30 April, then coming in to order coffee. According to her, the customer turned his head away when he saw a police officer enter the premises. By that gesture, she decided that he must be Augustus Dalmas, though when asked to identify the man in the courthouse, she admitted she could not. The frustrated judge demanded the testimony be scored from the record, and sent the woman on her way.

When it was all done, Dalmas was not surprisingly sentenced to death. However, his family and friends did not take this news lightly, and campaigned for weeks to stop the hanging going ahead. Subsequently, a great deal was made of the fact that the man must surely be insane to have carried out such a terrible deed, and a number of stories were told to strengthen this case.

For instance, first of all it was revealed that Dalmas had experimented with chemicals that had altered his personality. Then it was said that he had received a huge blow to the head some eleven years before his crime, and since then had gone through various episodes of memory loss and violence. On one occasion, he had attempted to strangle his daughter, but the very next day apparently had no remembrance of it. Doctors had been so concerned about these periods that they advised friends and relatives to remove all razors, knives and pistols from his home.

While Dalmas was in prison, awaiting hanging, his memory loss was said to be severe. He complained to a warden that a young woman kept visiting his cell, sometimes three or four times a night. He asked the man if he would please arrest her when she next visited, but then later had absolutely no memory of the conversation or the mysterious woman.

Finally, just days before he was due to be hanged, two doctors came to the prison in order to examine Dalmas closely. They could not see him straightaway, however, as he was busy praying in his cell with two of his daughters and the prison chaplain. When the man finally did make his way to the magistrate's room, the two doctors noted that he seemed to be in excellent health, wore a hat and smart clothing, and walked 'with a firm and light step'. He took a small bow and then sat down to be questioned.

The interviews were conducted over many hours and several days, during which time the prisoner seemed rational and calm. However, after talking to the prison wardens, chaplain and others, the doctors eventually decided that his mind had been greatly affected. They took their report to the Secretary of State for the Home Department, who reprieved the death sentence but insisted Dalmas be confined for life. A messenger was employed to take the notice to Dalmas, who apparently expressed great cheer and declared himself satisfied. He was then moved to another prison, but not before thanking the wardens for all the kindness they had shown since his incarceration.

Newspapers that had once called Dalmas evil now suddenly softened and described him as 'an unfortunate man'. However, some continued to question the issue of his insanity, and made it clear that the prisoner could very well be faking his mental problems just to avoid the death penalty. The authorities were wondering the same thing, as during this time they sent doctors to visit him on an almost constant basis. The man was either a brilliant liar or extremely ill, because by the time the visits came to an end, they were of the opinion that he was so insane that he must be confined to an asylum.

The public were outraged by these new developments, and some gave their opinions that a master criminal had avoided the death penalty by his fantastic acting. These comments had more weight when, after eight months in the asylum, doctors told the authorities that Dalmas had not shown any signs of insanity at all. In fact, he had been remarkably calm and lucid for the entirety of his stay.

The Secretary of State had heard enough about Augustus Dalmas, and ordered that he be removed from the asylum and placed back in prison. This time, however, he wanted the man gone for good; not by death penalty, but by his permanent removal from the country.

On 13 May 1845, he was released from prison and shipped off to Australia with 220 convicts, arriving in his new homeland on 25 August. Just over a year later, his eighteen-year-old daughter Augusta passed away, and his other daughter, Caroline, decided to leave her London home and travel to be with her father. Once in Australia, she began a campaign against her father's conviction. This eventually saw Dalmas become a free man with no sentence to his name whatsoever.

The murderer then lived for another thirty years before eventually passing away on 26 October 1874. Poor Sarah MacFarlane was long-since forgotten, and aside from a small time behind bars, Augustus Dalmas had effectively managed to get away with murder.

The Manslaughter of a Birmingham Wife

In 1891, thirty-year-old brass dresser John Patchett had been married to his thirty-two-year-old wife, Harriett, for ten years. Together they had six children, but in spite of their seemingly good relations in the bedroom, their relationship was fraught with fights, arguments and – more than anything – alcohol.

The couple lived at 14 Cumberland Terrace in Birmingham, England, a road that had been lived on by their families for years. Harriett had actually been born on the street, and John's mother and brothers lived opposite the marital home. When they married in 1881, the groom told everyone that he had a good wife and he was very happy. Their relationship was fairly ordinary and neighbours did not have any concerns.

Just two years later, Harriett fell into the company of 'dissipated companions' and began inviting them back to her house. By this time, the couple had two children, but the care and attention needed by them did not go well with Harriett's new love of alcohol and unsavoury individuals. Her habits turned what was once a happy household into one consisting mainly of alcoholics and degenerates.

John was, according to newspapers at the time, a hardworking young man. He had kept the same job for his entire adult life, and was a good provider for his wife and children. Every week he handed over housekeeping money to Harriett, and anything he had left would be spent on buying new clothes for his growing family. He wanted desperately for them to be dressed well, and neighbours noted that his main concern in life was a wish that his children were well cared for.

Harriett Patchett was the complete opposite. She neglected the children in favour of buying alcohol with her housekeeping money. When that ran out, she would not only pawn the children's clothes, but those of herself and her husband too. She would then drink the proceeds and pass out on the sofa, while John scrambled to obtain new outfits. It was a never-ending circle, and when he discovered that Harriett had pawned the children's Christmas presents, he admitted to giving her 'a good hiding'.

By 1889, alcohol and violence had completely ruined the marriage, and to make things even worse, John began drinking too. Neighbours told reporters that while he occasionally became inebriated, he was 'driven to drink by the intemperate and dirty habits of the wife'. Harriett responded to this new development by drinking more herself, which resulted in more arguments and pawning of belongings. But while the couple were preoccupied by their problems, the family continued to grow. The two-bedroomed house was now far too small, and while some children slept in a room next to their parents, the older ones ended up dossing in the attic.

In late February 1891, John damaged his hand and was unable to work on a regular basis. He and his wife were still drinking, and the family relied on their few savings in order to get by. His employer of eighteen years, William Bibb, recalled that on at least one occasion, John appeared at his office in the hope of borrowing a sovereign. Until then, however, he believed Patchett to be a 'steady man generally, sober and industrious'.

The couple's fights became ever more frequent and grew to the point where, on 30 March, Harriett moved out of the family home with her youngest child, and went across the road to live with John's mother. There she stayed for the next three nights with her mother-in-law's blessing, since the older woman believed that if the couple were not living together, they would not have cause to fight.

Every day when she saw John leave, Harriett would return to the house to see the children. However, it would seem that very little attention was given to their needs since there was virtually no food in the house, and for most of the three days she visited, they all went hungry.

On Thursday 2 April, Harriett was on one of her home visits, and intended to go back to her mother-in-law's later that evening. The couple were still not on speaking terms, so rather than stay home with her, Patchett decided to head to the local pub. There he enjoyed several beers but apparently remained quite sober. On his way home, the man bumped into a friend and, in the midst of their conversation, Harriett walked by, ignoring her husband but calling out 'goodnight' to the friend.

After announcing that he was going to turn over a new leaf and go back to work, John called into a local shop to buy some ham and bread. He knew Charles Summerfield, the shopkeeper, very well, and the two became involved in conversation.

'You are looking after yourself, John?' asked Summerfield.

'Yes,' he replied. 'I am obliged to. She won't.' At that very moment Harriett walked past the shop, and was pointed out by the grocer. Patchett gave thanks for the information, and exited the store. What happened next remains sketchy, but it would appear that Harriett decided to follow John back to their home.

Dora and Samuel Garrett lived next door to the couple, and heard voices at around 11.15 p.m. They later claimed to have never seen Harriett drunk during the time they had lived in the house, but both had seen Mr Patchett drinking on various occasions. The wife could not recall hearing them fight, though Mr Garrett said he heard the occasional shout, but not to a degree that was concerning. On the evening of 2 April, both were anxious to see what was going on outside their window, so pulled back the curtains for a closer look. They could not see anything at all, but could hear the voices of Mr and Mrs Patchett very clearly.

'Be off! I have done with you!' exclaimed John Patchett. 'You shan't sleep in this house no more.' In spite of that, however, the two certainly ended up going into their bedroom together. About an hour later, the baby was heard crying and then suddenly stopped. Another neighbour then heard what she believed to be a chair falling over, and then Patchett's heavy footsteps headed across the bedroom floor. No further sound was heard after that.

In spite of the relative quiet in the house that night, the couple did get into an altercation. However, instead of arguing as they had in the past, this time John took his pocket knife and thrust it deep into Harriett's neck, even though she was holding their small baby at the time. The woman fled towards the stairs and either fell or stumbled down, collapsing dead in the hallway seconds later. What exactly happened between the pair remains a mystery to this day, but the killing must have been swift, since the neighbours reported hearing nothing suspicious or concerning at all.

After striking the fatal blow, Patchett calmly left the house and wandered down to Sherlock Street, where he found Acting Inspector Alfred Conduit out on the beat. 'You are the man I want,' he told the officer. 'If you will take me back to my house you will see what I have done. I have stabbed my wife.'

The shocked inspector asked where the knife was, to which Patchett explained that it was still at home, upstairs on the side of the washbasin. Conduit was suspicious and asked if the man had been drinking. 'I have been drinking for six weeks,' he replied, though the officer came to the conclusion that at that moment in time, Patchett was perfectly sober and coherent.

The two men went back to the house, stopping briefly at the local police station to alert more officers. 'It's true, I have stabbed my wife,' Patchett told them. 'You'll find it's true when you get there.'

The men headed to Cumberland Terrace, and once inside, they found Harriett on her back at the bottom of the stairs, with her baby still held tight in her right arm. He was crying hysterically, and though covered in blood, was thankfully unhurt. John sat down on a nearby chair and began to whistle to himself. 'Is she dead?' he asked, to which a policeman answered that, at that point, he was not sure.

After a thorough examination of the still-warm body and confirmation that the woman was in fact gone, a blanket was placed over her. A policeman then made a search of the premises, where he found the murder weapon in the bedroom, along with a broken chair. In the middle of the scene, the couple's two-year-old boy sat in a pool of his mother's blood. The four other unsuspecting children were asleep in the attic, and were awoken by the officer. Together, they filed down the stairs one by one, to where their grandmother was now waiting for them.

Having been called to the home just moments before, the old woman saw the sight of her daughter-in-law and sobbed.

'Oh, John, whatever have you done? What did you do this for? Why ever didn't you settle in another road?' she asked.

'How could I help it, when there's not a rag of clothing in the place?' he replied, referring to the fact that Harriett had – by this time – pawned almost every single item of clothing they and their children owned. The devastated grandmother then left the house with her grandchildren, assuring the eldest that everything was going to be all right. When a doctor arrived to do the obligatory examination of Mrs Patchett's body, police noted that John watched it all without emotion, before calmly handing himself over to be handcuffed. 'I did it in bed,' he said. 'She ran downstairs.'

On the morning after the terrible event, reporters swarmed to the couple's house and spoke to the neighbours, savouring every drunken, terrible story. According to one associate, the house had been furnished more than once, since Harriett had sold the chairs, table and everything else for drink money. The reporter jotted it all down and then stared into the window. 'At the present time it is fairly well furnished in every room, considering the class to which the people belong,' he wrote.

Inside the house, police found no fewer than twenty-two pawn tickets in Harriett's dress pocket, dating from April to the present day. They did not relay this information to the reporters, however, and so the press took it upon themselves to make up elaborate tales of what might have happened in the house. 'The general opinion is that Patchett and his wife must have gone upstairs to bed some time about one o'clock and that then they quarrelled,' wrote one reporter for the *Daily Post*. 'It may be that while his wife was undressing Patchett began to eat his bread and ham, cutting it with his pocket knife. Then after his wife got into bed, possibly she aggravated him to such an extent that he struck at her with the knife in his hand . . .'

The inquest into the death was held just days later, on 6 April 1891. There the evidence was laid out and doctors told the court that Mrs Patchett's liver was a little diseased, which could have been caused by drinking. Interestingly, they commented that the only person who was able to give evidence of the woman's drinking was her mother-in-law. Everyone else in the neighbourhood had never seen her intoxicated, but they all had stories of the drunkenness of her husband. Taking everything into account, the jury brought back a verdict of wilful murder, and John Patchett was committed for trial.

In early August 1891, the case went ahead, with everyone from his boss, to his mother, to his friends, giving evidence. Shopkeeper Charles Summerfield said that he had known the accused for many years and had always found him to be a 'straightforward, quiet man'. He frequently bought the children sweets from Summerfield's store, and even if it was clear he'd had a few beers, he was never excitable.

After all the evidence was given, Judge Hugo Young spoke to the jury. 'From the evidence it would be insulting to the common sense of the jury to say that the case was not either murder or manslaughter,' he said. 'The issue is whether that is the most serious offence man can commit, or whether a more merciful verdict cannot be arrived at.' After giving that speech, the judge urged the jury to think long and hard before coming to a decision, and to know that they must not exercise any mercy if the facts led them to the most serious conclusion.

He then reminded them that John Patchett had been – until the night of the murder – a man whose nature seemed to oppose killing. To him, it seemed as though the crime was spur of the moment and not something the man had thought long and hard about. 'We cannot tell what transpired in that bedchamber, but the evidence seems to show that there was a struggle, and in the heat of that struggle the one blow might have been struck.'

The entire speech to the jury was in total sympathy with John Patchett, and the judge made clear his feelings that perhaps he was eating the newly purchased bread and ham, and only took the knife with him to the bedroom in case his wife wanted some too. 'Unfortunately sometimes if a woman has been vexed she will not forget and forgive when others want to offer conciliatory words. The deceased might have said angry words and continued the quarrel, which probably ended in a struggle, and in the heat of the moment a blow was struck with the knife . . . Don't forget, the accused told police, "I've stabbed my wife," not, "I have killed my wife."'

Judge Young's speech seemed to go on for ever. He tried extremely hard to convince the jury that while they had to come up with a verdict to serve the crime, they also had to decide if it was worth punishing him by death, which is what would happen should he be found guilty of murder. The jury listened, retired for a full five minutes, then returned to the courtroom. 'We find the defendant guilty of manslaughter,' said the spokesperson, and the judge nodded his head. He then broke into another speech, during which time he said he completely understood the jury's decision.

'That Patchett killed his wife, the mother of his children, the woman who for eleven years he had been bound to protect and honour, was undoubtedly true . . . But he probably had great provocation . . . There was so much misery as might be inflicted upon a man by a drunken, extravagant, unfeeling wife. It was constant; it was inevitable; it could not be escaped from. It ate out of the man's life, heart and soul, everything he cared for in this world . . .'

After the elaborate speech to the court, Judge Young finally sentenced John Patchett to prison, where he remained for the next fifteen years. When that year's census was conducted, John was already in jail, giving his occupation as a brass dresser, and his status as married. However, by the time the census was taken in 1901, his status had been quietly changed to that of a widower. On his release from prison, he remained in Birmingham but lived on his own, cleaning windows in order to make ends meet.

While incarcerated, John's children moved across the road to their grandmother's house, and by 1901, his eldest daughter, Ada, was working in a children's home. With memories of her sorry existence still fresh in her mind, she remained in Birmingham and became a housekeeper for a lawyer who specialised in the Poor Law.

The Hot Springs Church Murder

In 1884, the town of Hot Springs, Arkansas, was hit with a scandal involving two men and their love for the local minister's daughter. Leon Dishowan and Pete Lewis were both crazy about the woman, and each wanted to become her sweetheart. The trouble was the minister's daughter could not decide which one of the men she liked most, so when Dishowan and Lewis both asked if they could walk her home from church, she agreed to the requests.

While she was happy to have both men in her life, they clearly weren't and each made plans to become her only sweetheart. While attending church one hot, June morning, Dishowan quietly placed himself in the girl's pew. There, he was in a good position to gain her attention as soon as the sermon was over. Unfortunately for him, Lewis was keeping a close eye on proceedings, and as soon as he saw his rival in the pew, headed there himself.

By then emotions had hit boiling point. The two men began to quarrel, and Dishowan pulled out a pistol. Not to be outdone, Lewis reached into his pocket and took out his own. They then exchanged gunfire, and though no injuries were incurred, the noise and commotion were enough to cause bedlam in the chapel. Screams and shouts could be heard from all around, and a great majority of the congregation threw themselves out of the church windows.

One person brave enough to stay was the clergyman, who disarmed the two young men and told them to fight it out with the power of fists, not firearms. They agreed and a battle commenced in a local wood. However, what poor Dishowan did not know was that the minister's daughter had suddenly decided she liked Lewis better than him. Shortly before the fight took place, she had words with her would-be lover and slipped a tiny gun into his boot. The two men then went into the woods, began their fistfight, and then seconds later Lewis reached for the revolver. He took aim again, and this time shot his rival straight through the chest.

The congregation – still dusting themselves down from having jumped out of the church windows – rushed to the clearing in the wood, and saw Dishowan lying on the ground, blood pouring from the wound. He managed to tell them that he had been winning the fight, but Lewis had decided to shoot him. Almost as soon as his story was spluttered, the man expired, leaving his killer to run from the scene.

While the murder made the small columns in several newspapers, not a word was ever said about whether or not the murderer was arrested and tried. Reporters surmised that the reason for this was that the Hot Springs townsfolk were averse to such an outcome from a simple romantic entanglement, and did not wish the scene to create headlines. Instead, some suggested that the matter was dealt with quickly and quietly by locals, who either let the man disappear or else lynched him in utmost secrecy. The girl, meanwhile, was kept completely anonymous throughout the subsequent media interest, and no mention was ever made as to whether or not she was punished for her role in the murder of Leon Dishowan.

The Kentish Town Tragedy

In 1891, the Kentish Town area of London was going through something of a bloody crisis. Just a few months before 1890 ended, a young woman by the name of Mary Pearcey had murdered the wife and child of her lover. The brutal crime had shaken the neighbourhood badly enough, but then further shockwaves rippled through a short time later, when a man murdered the daughter of a local pub landlord. When another person committed suicide in the area not long after that, it felt to some as though a curse had been put on the neighbourhood.

Things certainly seemed that way to William Else, who lived with his wife, Jane Maria, and their five children: Ellen (aka

Nellie, fourteen), Alice (seven), Mable (three), Albert (two) and baby Archibald. At one point, the family would have been described as rather ordinary: they attended church, the parents did not drink and were known to friends as being rather affectionate towards each other. William worked as a cab driver and Jane Maria cared for their growing brood.

At the beginning of 1891, the man was involved in an accident, where he fell from a hayloft and broke his leg. This would have been a terrible time for anyone, but for someone with such a physical occupation it was absolutely catastrophic. After the accident, William was confined to the Merchant Taylors' Convalescent Home for four months. His wife remained at their home – 11 Jeffrey Street – in order to care for the children, but when William returned in late May 1891, life did not get any easier. The man was still on crutches and unable to work. His recovery would be a slow one, though it was difficult for him to accept that.

In the days after the cab driver's return home, circumstances grew rapidly worse. William Else suffered headaches and, although he had savings, he still worried about running out of money. His brother-in-law stated that the man was – at times – behaving strangely; sober but excitable. On the last occasion of their meeting, Else kept repeating that he had 'come up the lane', and had 'bitten fingers'. On looking at the man's hands, there were no bitemarks to be seen, and the brother-in-law decided that neither remark was true or made sense.

A definite change in personality was noted during the two weeks after his release from confinement, and some neighbours whispered that the fall seemed to have affected William's mind. As if that wasn't enough, his wife Jane Maria was struck down with influenza and it was left to the cab driver to look after his five children throughout the day and night. He was still exhausted from his own injuries, and the headaches grew rapidly worse.

On the evening of 1 June 1891, Jane Maria was still very ill, so William stayed with the children to allow her to rest. Baby Archibald was particularly restless and, according to daughter Ellen, her father paced the floor with the child for most of the night. When he wasn't caring for the baby, William was attending to his ailing wife, placing a flannel on her forehead and making sure she was otherwise okay.

The following morning, Ellen woke up with a start. Her father was standing over her, complaining that his head was sore. Although still half-asleep, she could sense that William was acting rather strangely. When he bent down, first to kiss her and then to ask if her throat felt all right, the girl was even more disturbed. When she saw the glint of a knife hidden in his hand, she became hysterical.

Getting out of bed, Ellen tried desperately to flee from the room, but her father pursued and grabbed her nightdress. After a short struggle, she eventually managed to escape. Heading through the hall, the girl saw a trail of blood on the floor. She ran as quickly as she could to the room of a neighbour, Mrs Lockwood, and told her what had happened. Mrs Lockwood was terrified and raised the alarm, summoning the help of painter Walter Deacon, who was working nearby.

When Deacon entered the property, he found Jane Maria lying on the bed in the front parlour. Her throat had been cut to the point where it was almost severed from her body, and there was blood all over the bed and running onto the floor. Deacon explored the rest of the house and found young daughter Alice behind the door of the kitchen, her throat also cut and most certainly dead. The three remaining children were all safe and well, though the murderer was nowhere to be found. Unarmed, the brave man continued to walk around the premises, but his search was cut short when he entered the outside toilet. There was William Else lying on the floor with his throat sliced from ear to ear. The bloody knife that had been used to perform the crimes was underneath him.

Deacon ran straight to the Kentish Town police station and summoned help. Inspectors rushed to the property and saw for themselves how William Else had murdered two members of his family, before committing suicide in the garden. There were no signs of struggle in the bedroom, which led investigators to believe that Mrs Else most likely remained asleep during her ordeal. While none of the neighbours heard any disturbance from the house, poor Alice was still in her nightdress though not in her bed. It was impossible for anyone to know exactly what had happened between her being asleep and being found dead behind the door.

As word spread that there had been yet another grizzly event in the area, crowds of people flocked to Jeffrey Street and milled around waiting to see what would happen next. The fact that Mrs Pearcey had murdered her victims a street away less than a year before was discussed thoroughly. Reporters jotted down the whispers so that they could report the strange occurrences in the newspapers the next day. Even the arrival of a funeral cortège for one of the Elses' neighbours was not enough to dispel the crowds. They continued to gather, while across the road the mourning family tried to conduct their business in private.

William, his wife and daughter were all laid to rest on 8 June 1891 at St Pancras Cemetery. An inquest was held by Dr

G. Danford Thomas, and the murder–suicide charge was confirmed. The reason, it was decided, was that William Else was in a state of unsound mind.

Sadly, the remaining children had now lost their parents and sister and were consequently raised as orphans. Ellen – the girl who had survived the attempt on her life – went into service, while the others were sent to orphanages. The 1901 census shows that Archibald Else, the baby who had been restless on the evening of his parents' deaths, was living in a boys' home in Twickenham. Because of the callous act of his father, he would never have any memories of his mother or the sister who died alongside her.

A French Girl's Sad Suicide

Marie Jolivet was a woman desperately in love with her chef boyfriend, Edward Vignon. For eighteen months, their relationship seemed to work well and the two lived in Paris together as man and wife. However, eventually the union began to sour and when Vignon was offered a chef's job in London, he jumped at the chance. Promising that he would allow his lover to visit 'if business allows', he travelled to England in early January 1899. Marie was left in Paris, hurt and wondering if she would ever see him again.

When asked if he could come back to Paris on a visit, Vignon told her that he could not. 'My occupation will not allow it,' he said. Incensed, on 1 February, the woman sat down to write him a long, passionate letter. 'My dear Edward,' she wrote. 'I cannot stay any more alone here. I must see you, and I leave Paris happy in thinking that I shall be near you after this long month, in which you have given me such a blow in the heart.'

That evening she visited the apartment of friends Mr and Mrs Olivier, and caused such a scene that the next day she was prompted to write a letter to them, too. Without actually mentioning exactly what she had done, it was clear by the note that she felt guilty for behaving in such a way. 'I ask you a thousand pardons for the bad conduct I have shown you at your home yesterday evening,' she said. 'I thank you a thousand times for kindness shown me in Paris and in London. I hope you will not take notice of the trouble I have caused.'

Very shortly after this episode, Marie managed to get herself to London and tracked down her wayward boyfriend. No record exists of his initial reaction to her appearance, but within days the pair arrived at the boarding house of a Mrs Annette, who lived at 28 Marlborough Street. There they falsely told her they were a married couple, and she then showed them to her upstairs back bedroom. The woman noted that Marie could not speak a word of English, but that she was 'a very nice woman, not at all excitable and made no complaint'.

For the next few weeks the couple lived in Mrs Annette's home without causing barely a stir. However, Vignon was growing frustrated with the relationship and told Marie that he thought it best she return to Paris and live with her parents. The woman replied, 'I will never leave you again. I came to London to be with you. I will never stop.'

This seemingly obsessive reaction irritated the man even more and he told her that she must leave him alone. Edward Vignon stormed out of their room at 4 p.m. on Tuesday 17 February and told Marie that he would come back 'on some other occasion'. That time just happened to be three days later, when he hoped that his girlfriend had calmed down, or possibly even taken his advice and gone back to Paris. He arrived at the boarding house at 4 p.m. and went straight to the room. However, it was firmly locked and no matter how much he knocked, there was simply no answer.

Vignon went downstairs to get help from the landlady and ended up forcing open the door to gain entry. There in front of him was Marie, lying on her back with a handful of letters in her left hand. Her right hand was flexed and next to her was a revolver. Further investigation revealed that she had a gunshot wound to the head and was quite dead.

The police arrived on the scene and discovered that the letters the woman was holding were all addressed to her lover. On the dressing table was a note to her parents, begging them 'a thousand pardons for what I am doing. In this life there are moments which are so painful to pass that I have not the strength or the courage to support them . . . Forgive me.' Marie's body was handed to Police Surgeon Dr Percy Edmunds, who came to the conclusion that she had been dead for around ten hours.

When the inquest was opened just days later, Edward Vignon denied ever abandoning his girlfriend, but did admit that he had told her to move back to France. When the woman's letters were read out to the court, they revealed her sadness at being left alone in the room:

'My dear Edward,' she wrote in the first note. 'I have always said that when all is finished between you and me, life will be finished. After all the words and promises exchanged between us, you must be happy – that is all I desire. From her who adores and who dies for you, Marie.'

The second note, however, revealed a much angrier woman. 'Edward, you are a wretch,' she wrote, and then went on to say that all she ever wanted was to work with him, but she had now come to realise that he had never loved her and he wished she were dead. 'Now you can do what you like with my body. Take the ring from my finger and never part with it.'

The coroner delivered the decision that Marie Jolivet's death was one of suicide, brought on by a temporary lapse of sanity. 'There can be no doubt the deceased was passionately fond of Vignon,' he told the court. 'She destroyed her life because she could not have him with her.'

The Gruesome Murder of Edith Poole

Waitress Edith Poole lived and worked at the Temple Bar in the Strand, London. She was a young woman – just nineteen years old – and had known barman Alfred Highfield since she was in her early teens. The two were engaged and due to marry in August 1900 and, to all intents and purposes, they seemed perfectly happy and well suited.

During a rare day off, Poole and Highfield visited Crystal Palace and had a massive falling out, which resulted – according to Poole's sister – in the woman being assaulted. Since Highfield later refused to answer questions on the matter, not much is known as to exactly how or why it happened. However, it was noted that their joint account had been cleared of the money the couple had been saving for a house, and it was widely believed that Poole may have spent the cash through a clothes club to which she was subscribed. Despite what transpired between Poole and Highfield, the barman believed it all to be only temporary. However, it was taken far more seriously by his fiancée, and she vowed never to see the man again.

The day after the break-up, Highfield appeared at the door of Edith's mother, Elizabeth. He had scratches all over his face, but he laughed them off when questioned. 'I had a bit of bother at the brewery,' he said. 'One of the chaps scratched my face.' Elizabeth told the man she thought it was a strange thing for anyone to do, and the subject was dropped.

Alfred Highfield tried to win Edith back through a series of letters. One asked if she would meet and forgive him for what had gone on between them. Blaming drink, he added that he would never have said such things if he'd been sober. In another letter, written almost a month after the break-up, Highfield explained that he had been due to start a new job at a brewery, but had received a very bad reference from his previous employer.

This ambush had been unknown to the man until his new manager wrote to inform him that the job was off the table unless he could explain why his character had been described as very bad. The letter confused Highfield, but he found another job at a new company, and hoped he would be able to start there soon. With the possibility of new employment fresh in his mind, Highfield asked Poole if she was sure they should be parted, but his letter went unanswered.

After being ignored by his lover for so many weeks, Highfield decided to emotionally blackmail the woman. He sent a note that said simply that he would not be writing to her again and that he was 'a broken-hearted man'. He also advised that he wanted to say goodbye in person, since he could not last much longer. When that did not work, Highfield decided to pay the family a visit. On Sunday 13 May, he went to the home of Poole's brother James and sister Lorena and asked to see his former fiancée. She was not keen to speak to him, but he was determined to find some answers.

'Why is it that you have not seen me?' he asked. The woman did not reply and so the family – including Highfield – settled down for tea. Afterwards everyone busied themselves around the kitchen while the couple spoke once again.

'You are not wearing my ring,' the man said, to which Poole replied that she may not be wearing it, but it still remained in her possession. This was a lie. According to her mother, the woman pawned the ring as soon as the two split up. 'Do you ever intend to go out with me again?' Highfield asked. His former fiancée thought for a moment and then replied that she was sure they were better off apart. The news did not sit well with the barman and he immediately stood up and declared himself 'done'. When Poole's brother asked if he was okay, Highgate sharply replied, 'No!'

In an effort to get out of the house and away from the jilted lover, Edith Poole agreed to go out for a walk with her sister and brother-in-law. However, while no one had invited Highfield, he decided to tag along regardless. They all headed to the pub, where they met a mutual friend, Mrs Negus. The party of five then had a drink and Poole and Highfield were seen chatting to each other perfectly amicably.

When the group left the establishment, three of them walked ahead, while the former couple trailed behind, apparently arm in arm. They walked for a few minutes, before Mrs Negus turned around to see if the couple were still behind her. They were, but instead of being jovial as they had been before, Poole was now lying on the ground while Highfield was on top of her. Mrs Negus thought he may be punching her, so ran back and pulled him off. It was at that point that she saw the man had sliced her friend's neck open with a cut-throat razor.

'Why did you do this?' shouted Mrs Negus.

'She has blighted my life,' he replied, 'and I have blighted hers.'

By this time the entire group had run back to the scene, and as Edith lay dying, her shocked sister tried to get her to speak. It was no good; the victim was unable to say a word. Lorena turned to Highfield, who made no attempt at all to leave the scene.

'What have you done? You have killed my sister! You have killed my sister!' the woman screamed at him.

'I know what I have done,' replied Highfield. 'And I don't care if I die for it.'

As the young woman's friends and family gathered around, Highfield knew he was done for. However, in a bid to hide the evidence, he threw the weapon into the gutter, where moments later a cab driver by the name of Robert William Atto found it and slipped it in his pocket. He later presented the blood-soaked razor to police at Bow Street Station, and it was used as evidence against the jilted lover.

A crowd had gathered around, but Mrs Negus kept a firm hold on Highfield, though he still did not seem in any hurry to get away. An old man came past, surveyed the scene and told Highfield that he was a scoundrel. Ever defiant, Highfield shouted back, 'You don't know what she has done to me!' The police were called and on the arrival of PC Frederick James Stringer, Highfield was determined to make his statement and leave the scene quietly. Meanwhile, Edith Poole was taken to King's College Hospital, where doctors tried frantically to save her life.

On the way to the station, Highfield suddenly became talkative. 'I did it and I don't disown it,' he said. On his arrival at Bow Street he produced a razor case, a photograph and six letters to his former fiancée. Then when he was installed in his cell, he told an inspector that three weeks prior to the stabbing, he had lost his job, thanks – he said – to his relationship with Poole. 'She aggravated me tonight and in a fit of madness, I did what I did,' he said.

At King's College Hospital, Edith lay in a terrible condition. Doctors examined her and discovered three wounds to the neck; one of those was four inches long and between one and one-and-a-half inches deep. The cut at the front of the neck divided the larynx from the windpipe and her hands were covered in small cuts where she had tried to defend herself. Unbelievably, despite her deep wounds, the woman hung on, and Highfield appeared in court charged with attempted murder. His defence – like so many others – was that he had committed the crime in a fit of madness.

Edith Poole fought for her life during the next few days, but her cuts eventually led to septic pneumonia. Once it had reached her lungs there was no hope and the young woman passed away on 17 May 1900. 'The wounds were the cause of her death,' the surgeon told the court.

The charge against Alfred Highfield was amended from attempted to wilful murder and the case went to court on 25 June 1900. The family of Edith Poole were all questioned, and each gave their stories of what had happened leading up to the fateful stabbing. It was decided that the attack had taken place as a result of Highfield's excited frame of mind and the loss of his work. However, when the barman's former boss, Herbert Lee, was called to the stand, he dropped something of a bombshell.

According to him, the terrible reference he had sent to Highfield's new employer was not meant to be negative at all.

He explained to the court that he had written 'Highfield is honest and can work' but the telegraph clerk had mistaken the word honest for lowest and can for can't. Thus the positive reference had become a negative one in the eyes of the new employer. It was clear on the stand that Lee felt terrible that this mistake had happened, and had written a much better reference to another prospective employer. However, this one did not arrive until after the stabbing, so at the time Highfield attacked his former love, he still believed his character may be in ruins.

The jury had no option but to declare Highfield guilty, but because of the stress caused by his job situation and break-up, it was recommended that the court show him mercy. This was swept aside by the judge, however, and the prisoner was sentenced to death.

The representatives of Alfred Highfield, dubbed 'The Drury Lane Killer', tried to get the Home Office to overturn the sentence. While the Home Secretary was sympathetic to the plea, he decided that Highfield needed to be punished accordingly. As a result, the young man was hanged at Newgate Prison three weeks after the trial. He had – apparently – been extremely remorseful during his incarceration and went to the gallows without uttering a single word.

Don't Put Your Daughter (or Son) on the Stage

WHILE THE EVER-PRESENT scandals of the movie industry were a long way off, there was still a significant amount of raised eyebrows when it came to actors in the Victorian age. Stories revolving around so-called loose morals, children born out of wedlock and even the odd murder or two can all be found in the nineteenth-century press. The men and women who treaded the boards were no strangers to scandal and in many cases even gave their twentieth-century counterparts a run for their money.

Take Edward Forshay, for instance. He was an American theatre manager and actor, madly in love with actress Edna Stokes. In 1901 the pair acted together in Chicago, when a huge argument broke out in their hotel room. Forshay ended up beating Stokes around the head to such a degree that she received large cuts and bruises, and refused to see him ever again.

Determined that she should forgive his terrible behaviour, the actor begged Stokes for one more chance. By this time, the actress had told hotel security to keep him well away from her room, but unfortunately she did not give the same instructions to the manager. He saw Forshay waiting for her in the foyer and directed him to the parlour without a second thought.

'Miss Stokes will see you when she comes downstairs,' he said.

When the actress finally appeared, the couple spoke for ten minutes before suddenly the actor pulled out a gun and shot her at point-blank range. Edna died almost immediately and the murderer was arrested as he tried to run away. Inside his pocket, police found a farewell letter to his mother.

'I intended to kill myself as I cannot live without Edna,' the deranged man said. 'But I lost my nerve at the last moment.'

Another rather scandalous tale happened in November 1883, when the Ward Dramatic Troupe arrived in Vicksburg, Mississippi, to appear at the local theatre. Actor and manager David R. Allen had an argument with Frank E. Starke, a member of the company, and fired him. He presumed he'd never have to cross paths with him again, but he was wrong.

On the evening of the show, a furious Starke decided to confront Allen and his wife in their dressing room, as they were readying themselves for their appearance on stage. Brandishing a pistol, he was disarmed by Mrs Allen, and she threw the man out into the hall. Unfortunately, Starke managed to grab the gun from her hands as she did so, and as David Allen followed him out, the ex-employee fired four shots, killing his former boss instantly.

In the days that followed, Starke was arrested and awaited trial. Still, he pleaded his case and insisted that the charge should be reduced to manslaughter, since – according to him – Allen had threatened him with a huge chair. There were numerous court appearances and for a time the public seemed to be on his side, urging the sheriff to consider that the killing was done in self-defence. However, when the charges were reduced to manslaughter, there was a complete turnaround in opinion. Now the public insisted the charges be changed again to murder, which they eventually were.

The stories of the deaths of Edna Stokes and David Allen were not unusual and certainly not restricted to the United States. The Victorian press recounted dozens of similar stories from around the world, ranging from the outrageous to the truly heartbreaking. Here, then, is just a selection of stories confirming why showbiz was possibly not the safest of Victorian professions in which to be.

Richard Archer Prince and the Murder of Swashbuckler William Terriss

Richard Archer Prince (real name Richard Archer), was born on 11 May 1858, on a farm in Scotland. His mother told a story of taking the baby to work in the fields, and leaving him to one side as she harvested the crops. When she returned, the baby was blue and there was a noticeable difference in his eyes. A doctor told her that the baby had suffered from sunstroke, and, from that point on, he had a constant squint and was considered by many to be mentally weak.

It would later be heavily discussed as to whether or not the sunstroke could have rendered Prince so ill. Since two other brothers had been admitted to asylums, the consensus was that while the sun did not benefit the boy at all, there was no denying that he came from an emotionally weak family. Regardless of the episode in the field, it was decided that the boy was almost destined to have problems.

As he grew into a teenager, Prince developed quite a temper and disliked playing with friends, declaring himself much better than anyone else. He had dreams of becoming a great actor, and delusions that his talent was far superior to even professional actors. After finishing school, he gained manual work during the day, but every night headed straight to the local theatre, where he worked as an extra while pretending to be a great star.

David Simpson was Prince's boss at Gourley's Iron Works. While he freely admitted that the man was a good, attentive worker, he had to confess that he was also jealous, obsessive and strange. His fellow workers took an instant dislike to him, calling him names behind his back and trying to keep out of his way. Robert Beveridge, a colleague at the theatre, remembered Prince similarly. To Beveridge, the young man was particularly stage-struck and 'very peculiar'. He constantly spoke about how wonderful he was as an actor, and held himself above absolutely everyone else in the theatre.

As he grew older, Prince's temper increased and he suffered bouts of paranoia. So much so that his parents eventually moved to London without him, in an effort to gain some peace. When he followed them there, they packed up once again and moved back to Dundee. By this time, Prince was taking on small roles at the Adelphi Theatre in London, and touring sporadically with different theatrical companies. He began dressing in an eccentric style, with his trademark outfit being a huge stand-up collar, felt hat and extremely long coat or cape.

Instead of using cufflinks, he would use ribbon or even string. He was quite a sight, and people would often stare as he walked past them. Prince did not seem to care, and decided that nobody knew how to dress in a good style except him. He remained confident that they were only looking because he was putting on quite a show.

William Terriss – the man who was to accidentally become the arch-rival of Richard Prince – was born William Charles James Lewin on 20 February 1847. The son of a barrister, and nephew of an author and historian, Terriss had a good childhood. He was well educated, enjoyed many activities and had a love of the theatre. He also developed a strong, positive personality, as his friend, Joseph Hatton, later described: 'He took care and worry with the same philosophy, interpreted by the commonplace remark, "What will it matter a hundred years hence?"' This was an attitude he took with him through life and when he left the Lyceum Theatre in 1885, the cast had a similar quote engraved onto the bottom of a goblet for him.

Always on the lookout for adventure, the young Terriss joined the merchant navy before he became an actor. The unpredictable nature of the sea attracted him, and he showed great courage while on board the ship. At least twice he saved fellow sailors from drowning at sea, and was awarded various medals. His view of life, and the way it should be led, grew strong during this time, and he decided that your fate is fixed at birth and you must live knowing that you cannot avoid or outrun whatever is meant to come your way.

'He was a fatalist,' explained Joseph Hatton. 'He spoke with such a cheerful kind of optimism about death that sometimes you doubted whether he had thought seriously or spoke at haphazard. Anyhow, he did not fear death. He had faced it often enough without flinching during a singularly adventurous career.'

'I am not the first of my race who has met with adventures,' Terriss told a reporter. 'My grandfather Thomas Lewin was secretary to Warren Hastings in Calcutta, and on his way home he was chased by privateers, with a price on his head of two thousand pounds, dead or alive. Nevertheless, he bore his despatches to England in triumph. He had been a gallant of the French court in his youth, and danced with Marie Antoinette, who gave him a ring, which is still in the possession of the family.'

After toying with various professions around the world, Terriss eventually decided to try his luck at acting, and in 1868 he made his debut on stage in Birmingham on a salary of eighteen shillings a week. Terriss was the first to admit that he was so nervous he made barely a ripple. However, he soon found his feet, and started to develop quite a following, moving back to London and taking an engagement for a much better fifty shillings a week. Despite that, his roving nature required him to try a variety of other obscure professions, including sheep farming in the Falkland Islands. When he decided to return to England, he found himself shipwrecked for days in an open boat. After more acting engagements, he headed to the United States and became a racehorse owner. Eventually, however, his love of the stage could not be denied, and he returned to London to become a full-time actor.

A good-looking, charming man, he could have any woman he wanted, but fell in love with Isabel Lewis, whom he met in the theatre and married in 1870. Together they had three children, two of which – Ellaline and Tom – went on to have successful theatre and film careers. While it was widely reported that he took a mistress later in his marriage, his reputation as a family man and love for his children ran deep. Friend Charles Wyndham described him as having an 'unceasing love, care and devotion to [his daughter]'. Although dedicated to his work, there were times when he would beg a night off due to her having a temperature or some other childhood disease.

While Richard Archer Prince was busy believing himself to be a legend, William Terriss was actually living the dream. After his death, it was reported that while his triumphs were many, he had no failures whatsoever. That was an enviable achievement. Wherever he went in the country, people flocked to the theatre and did not seem to mind standing outside for hours just to catch a glimpse of the legendary actor. He was also a regular performer on the Lyceum stage in London, where he starred successfully for six years.

Terriss's kindness seemed to know no bounds. On his way to New York by ship, he went out of his way to help those passengers confined to the steerage hold. However, his place in the hearts of the public was truly cemented on 13 August 1885, when the actor was on holiday in Deal. While sailing with his son, he noticed three boys in the water, one of whom was bobbing under and shouting frantically for help.

Without even taking off his clothes, the actor dived into the sea and swam straight for the boy, who by now was sinking fast. When he reached him, the child was so relieved he threw his arms around Terriss to such an extent that the man found it impossible to swim back to the boat. Thankfully his son was just as quick-thinking as he was, and threw a rope into the water, hence managing to get both his father and the boy onto the boat.

The rescue may not have been revealed if not for a nosey local who had seen the incident from the clifftops and contacted the local press: 'This so interested me that I thought I would make every inquiry and I found the gallant preserver who risked his life so unconcernedly was none other than the well-known actor of the Lyceum, London, Mr William Terriss. I hope he will pardon my having given publicity to so gallant and unselfish example of pluck.'

The story caused a great deal of excitement in the newspapers. 'Courageous Conduct of a Well-known Actor,' said one, while another described it as 'heroism'. So welcome and extraordinary was the news that, just a month later, Terriss was awarded a bronze medal from the Humane Society. The ceremony was conducted just after the curtain had gone down on his successful play, *Olivia*, and special mention was made of his son for throwing the rope into the water.

When Terriss left the Lyceum in December of the same year, there was an overwhelming outpouring of grief from his fellow actors and stage crew. A glittering ceremony was held, and a heartfelt speech was given by friend and colleague, Mr Howe. 'Your cordial, manly, and cheery nature, together with the invariable good temper of your disposition, the sympathy you have always shown for the misfortunes of those around you, have endeared you to us all. The public have acknowledged your humanity in saving life at the risk of your own; and do we not ourselves know of the unpretending sympathetic kindness and the various acts of assistance and good heartedness you have conferred on those below yourself in position?'

While everybody was busy honouring William Terriss as a man of great virtue and heroic powers, Richard Archer Prince was bitterly waiting in the wings to bring him down to earth.

It is unknown as to the exact date when he became manically jealous of William Terriss, but it would be a good guess that it all started in the mid-1880s, when they worked together on various theatrical productions.

We may only be able to roughly pinpoint when the jealousy began, but we can almost certainly work out why. For starters, while Prince was now begging theatres for work, Terriss was a huge star, with a dressing room fitted with an almost unheard-of electric light, and filled with medals and trinkets related to his good nature. While Prince had to resort to telling everyone that he was a great actor, Terriss had no need to – people could see for themselves just how wonderful he was every time he walked onto a stage. Finally, while Prince dressed elaborately even in private, Terriss wore a simple Turkish robe and still managed to look suave. In short, Terriss was everything Prince wanted to be, and everything he could never be.

This theory is backed up by an interview actor Percy Baverstock gave to the press after William Terriss's death. 'The most singular side of Prince's character was exhibited in his constant denunciation of Mr W. Terriss,' he said. 'When asked upon what this dislike was based, he would reply in a mysterious way that Terriss had taken the place he ought to have filled, and that he had always been successful in getting engagements, whereas he [Prince] could not.'

In 1888 the pair worked on a play called *The Union Jack* at the Adelphi Theatre, London. Terriss received star billing in every advertisement for the show. Richard Prince, however, was not even mentioned in the smallest of print. It would take five years for him to be mentioned on the bill, and only after William Terriss had left the production. Even then, Prince only managed to come eighth on the cast list.

It was while working on *The Union Jack* with Terriss that Prince became increasingly paranoid. He began thinking that people were trying to poison him, and this bizarre notion was repeated by him in a letter he wrote some years later:

> Through William Terriss, a person or persons unknown to me during the time I was with J. F. Elliston in *The Union Jack* company administered poison to me at Chester, Greenwich, and Plymouth. From Greenwich we went to Parkhurst Theatre, and I had to go to the Northern Hospital, where the head physician said I was suffering from poison. I did not say anything, as I wanted to save my aunt from any disgrace or scandal. I followed the same course in other places.

For eight years Prince's parents had not seen him, until finally the actor showed up in Dundee and insisted he move back in with them. Life at home was not happy. Prince would sometimes go off on acting jobs, but his behaviour towards others with whom he worked ensured that nobody was his friend. During one evening, he had to be escorted from the star's dressing room, which he had sneaked into without permission. Once again, he told everybody that he was the greatest actor the world had ever seen, which only led to the other cast members laughing behind his back, and calling him 'Tripe'.

For a while he went on tour with a production of *Rob Roy*. However, even that did not go without incident, and one evening Prince decided to shout insults to the actors on stage from the middle of the dress circle. He was booed by the audience, and ended up being physically carried out of the building. When word spread that his behaviour was out of control, virtually no director would entertain him. Very disturbingly, after being told he was unsuitable for a particular role at the Dundee Theatre, Prince pulled out a gun and threatened the attendant and manager.

With his acting career in tatters, the highly strung man was forced to work at the shipyards and engineering works. This did not please him because he truly believed that he should be a big star. As far as he was concerned, this was the very least the world owed him, and the displeasure at having to work a manual job made Prince even angrier than usual. Workmates complained that his paranoia was everywhere apparent.

On one particular evening, while employed at Gourley's Iron Works, a boat trip was arranged for all employees, including Prince. While out on the vessel, the failed actor took it upon himself to entertain everyone with his singing, but his renditions were appalling. Workmates were patient to a degree, but when he was eventually told to be quiet, the man completely lost his temper and began foaming at the mouth. He then became so threatening and out of control that he had to be locked in a compartment until he eventually quietened down.

After that, Prince began rumours that the employees of the iron works were trying to have him fired, and complained bitterly about it to his boss. Unfortunately, the fact that he was easily roused often meant that colleagues would go out of their way to torment him, and he would end up getting into trouble as a result. 'He always had a way of reciting to them, and he was always considered a sort of butt,' remembered his boss, David Simpson.

Around this time, Prince started to accuse his innocent mother of poisoning his food, just as he had accused William Terriss and several others. He also told her on more than one occasion that he was Jesus Christ and she was the Virgin Mary. While he was not violent towards her, his behaviour certainly gave cause for concern, and he would get into frequent fights with his brother. One day he accused the man of poisoning his tea, and then told him he was going straight to hell. When he wasn't shouting, Prince would stare into space for long periods, unblinking and completely emotionless. Then he would swear and blame others for his inability to have a happy life.

Whether or not Prince had told his mother about the real reason for his frequent 'resting' periods seems unlikely, but she would have surely been very naive if she did not work it out for herself. But despite his unemployable status, Prince continued to frequent local theatres and companies. He was turned down over and over again, and when Dundee theatre manager, Robert Arthur, refused to employ him any more, the man went berserk. He spread rumours that Arthur was preventing him from working as an actor, and told everyone that he had blackmailed him. Of course, neither tale was true.

When people stopped listening to his cries against the manager, he then began adding others into the mix – actors were trying to blackmail him, then people he knew at the shipyards were preventing him from getting theatre work. At one point, he even accused his niece's friend of spying, and his brother of scheming with Robert Arthur against him. He also attacked the man with a poker and knife. Police were called, and told Prince to calm down. It took three hours, but he eventually stopped the violent outburst and no charges were brought.

When he wasn't in a fit of rage, the failed actor would be 'entertaining' his family with acting recitals and singing frenzies. One neighbour complained that she would often hear the man singing from 7 p.m. until the early hours of the morning. When he finally discussed the situation with other neighbours, their reactions were unsurprising. 'Oh, that's Mad Archer,' they said and then the discussion led onto the eccentric clothes he wore. 'He was dressed as a mad man,' the neighbour told officers. He only ever spoke to Prince on rare occasions, but whenever he did, the conversation would always revolve around how he was one of the best actors in the country – in his own opinion.

Prince continued to try to make it in the theatre, and wrote to William Terriss to ask for a character reference. He wrote back favourably and told the man that he would be very happy to see him in another acting job, and that he should feel free to use his name. Quite bizarrely, instead of being happy to have Terriss's approval, Prince was absolutely furious with his reply. He decided – once again – that the actor was out to get him.

Given the amount of vitriol put forth by Prince towards his fellow actor, it is a wonder the man was never sued. While William Terriss was a man of great dignity, he also had a tough side, especially when it came to his career. In 1890, for instance, he sued a journalist who dared say his reception in New York was 'noticeably cool'. Terriss took great exception to this, particularly as he had not yet set foot on the stage when the piece was printed. He demanded an apology at once, but when none was forthcoming, he took the matter to court and won £200 damages.

Court appearances and the threat of legal action apparently meant nothing to Richard Archer Prince, and soon his list of 'blackmailers' had grown, with the addition of theatre manager J. F. Elliston. Elliston had employed Prince in small roles at various intervals over the years, but had eventually decided not to work with him again. The reason for this was because of his behaviour and refusal to take on roles that he felt were beneath him. Eventually Prince became so disruptive that it was impossible to give him acting parts, and he was downgraded to a baggage handler. This made the man incensed, and he refused to touch any bags whatsoever.

While Prince had left the company on particularly bad terms, he now assumed that he was owed a good reference, and began bombarding Elliston with letters. The manager threw all of them away, until eventually he received one which was so disturbing that he finally had to take notice.

In the letter, Prince berated Elliston for remaining silent, and demanded he reply to his request for a reference. 'No more blackmailing for me!' he wrote. There then followed a few garbled sentences in which the actor accused Elliston of blackening his character and taking away his living. He then added that the manager deserved to be horsewhipped, and that if he did not supply a reference, Prince would fight for it in London.

Another letter was received shortly after, only this time it was fairly long and began with the words, 'You hell hound! You Judas!' It transpired that Prince was now blaming Elliston for not being able to secure a particular acting job, due to not having a reference. He claimed to have previously saved Elliston's play, *Alone in London*, from being a disgrace after he stood in for an ill actor. Then he accused the manager of going out of this way to lie about his abilities. 'I have suffered worse than death!' he said.

The letter went on, and Prince told Elliston that the next time they saw each other would be in Bow Street police station, where he would make him tell the world about the blackmail he had dished out. The failed actor then added that the note should be taken to Scotland Yard, where his own innocence would be confirmed, and he could tell his story to every newspaper in London. 'Victory or death is my motto, and the fear of God,' he wrote.

Elliston was concerned enough by the contents of the note to decide to hand the paper over to the police. They apparently had words with Prince, who apologised and – for the moment – stopped writing the disturbing communications. Shortly after being warned off Elliston, he tried to drown himself in Regent's Canal, London. He did not succeed, however, and this only seemed to add to his fury.

In March 1896, Prince was out of acting jobs and forced to obtain work at the Wallace Foundry in Dundee. While he seemed to be a steady worker, his boss, Alexander Husband, remembered that he was exceptionally obsessed with William Terriss and J. F. Elliston. One day, the man brought the letter he had received from Terriss, in an effort to prove that the actor was keeping work from his door and blackmailing him. 'I will bring an action in the court of law against him and Elliston,' he told the stunned manager.

Husband presumed that Terriss must have injured Prince in some way, therefore making it impossible for him to gain acting work. When he questioned it, however, the failed actor went into an obscure rant and was forced to admit that the only thing Terriss had done wrong was to provide a friendly letter rather than an official job reference.

In November 1896, Prince sat down to write a garbled note to Percy Baverstock, with whom he had acted some years before.

Sir,

When I met you first, I thought you were a gentleman. Afterwards I found you out to be a thief. For the sake of Mr Elliston and the honour of the company, I saved you from a Scotch prison. The lady in Falkirk spoke the truth. I remember now I saw a chain in your pocket when Mr Percival lost his watch and chain, and I had to go for the police. You can take this to the police station at once, or your manager. Your Irish bloodhound – Richard Prince.

Baverstock was confused. The last time he had heard from Prince, it had been in a fairly friendly and polite manner. Now though, the tone and contents were exactly the opposite, and the actor had no idea why. If anyone should have been angry, it was Baverstock, not Prince. He later explained that the content of the letter referred to an incident in Falkirk, where he was questioned by the police in connection with a theft from his landlady. Who was the person who had contacted officers and pointed the finger at the innocent actor? His room-mate, Richard Prince.

In the early summer of 1897, Prince was in Dundee and once again living at his mother's house. There he continued his obsession with blackmail, spies and poison. The next-door neighbour told a story of seeing the man pour the entire contents of a teapot straight down the sink in the belief that his mother was once again trying to kill him. Prince's mother told the concerned friend that it was a frequent occurrence and she was not to be worried about it. Still, the neighbour made a mental note to keep an eye on the man, and later described him as 'very excitable and wild'.

In late July 1897, Prince left the Wallace Foundry after securing an acting job. It was fairly short-lived, and on 23 October, the man travelled to Newcastle to try to gain work for himself with another theatrical company. The manager of the theatre, Ralph Croydon, recalled that Prince entered the room and eccentrically introduced himself as Mr Macgregor from Scotland. 'My feet are on my native heath!' he declared in a dramatic manner. When asked about his theatrical experience, Prince scoffed, 'My experience justifies me in taking very much better parts than the one you are offering!'

When questioned further, the man told Croydon that he had once played in *The Union Jack* at the Adelphi, 'and I would have been there now if it had not been for one man!' he said. That man was almost certainly William Terriss, though all evidence suggests that the actor did absolutely nothing at all to prevent Prince from working at the theatre. In fact, his family and friends were steadfastly sure that he had only ever tried to help Prince, just as he did other strug-gling people. 'I can speak to many acts of kindliness and sympathy that were the outcome of a naturally generous nature,' said Terriss's friend Joseph Hatton. 'He hated tyranny, and resented it either for himself or others. He was always bright and pleasant, and he carried into his work on the stage, cheerfulness of a genial nature.'

Despite Prince's rather elaborate behaviour during his initial meeting with Croydon, the man decided to employ the actor, but only to play small parts. The next day he introduced the newcomer to the company over afternoon tea, where once again Prince told everyone about his experiences of blackmail and wrongdoing. He put over the opinion that had it not been for the Actors' Benevolent Fund, he would have starved. During the whole conversation, the tone of his voice was one of anger and disgust. Then when Croydon's wife brought out a knife to open a can of sardines, Prince recoiled. 'Put the knife away,' he demanded. 'I do not like the look of it.'

The next day, the company travelled to the first theatre on their tour, but during rehearsals it was found that Prince was completely incapable of remembering any lines. When asked to explain the problem, the actor replied, 'My brain is gone.' The rehearsal was called off and the man was asked to leave. Bizarrely, he turned up at Croydon's front door the very next day, demanding payment for his services. When told that no money would be forthcoming, Prince returned to his rant about William Terriss. 'He is a dirty dog!' he exclaimed, to which Croydon replied, 'You must be mad to speak like that.'

Prince headed straight back to London, where he went to the home of Mrs Charlotte Darby, a landlady in Eaton Court. She specifically remembered that he had only a brown paper parcel with him and no other belongings. 'I have come from Newcastle,' he said. 'I left some of my luggage on the boat.'

Prince tried to strike a deal whereby he could pay just two shillings for a room, but Mrs Darby was a hardened business-woman who told him that a week's rent of four shillings in advance was required. He gave her three, and promised to give the other shilling at the weekend, which he did. Mrs Darby found Prince to be a gentleman who kept himself to himself. However, while he may have been private, his enquiring land-lady did her best to discover everything she could about his day-to-day life.

During her strict observation, the woman found that Prince received a lot of letters, but did not seem particularly social. He never asked for meals; instead, he would eat bread and drink milk in his room. He had a habit of lying in bed until late in the morning, then he would be in and out of the house for the rest of the day and into the evening. The man also kept a knife in his room, which the woman examined and presumed was used to cut bread. 'I attached no importance to it,' she said. As far as she was concerned, Prince was a decent man.

One thing Mrs Darby did find strange, however, was that every time she visited Prince's room, more and more of his clothes had gone missing. She didn't know it at the time, but the man had been unable to find work, and was in such dire straits that he had begun pawning his belongings to pay his way. Still blaming William Terriss for his lack of employment, Prince went to the stage door of the Adelphi Theatre where the actor was once again working, and asked the doorkeeper, Henry Spratt, to deliver him a letter.

Spratt took the note and returned shortly after with a message: 'The answer to the letter is all right.' Prince nodded and left the building, but came back six times in the weeks ahead, looking for William Terriss. He was out of luck, however, as the actor never used the stage door. Instead, he used a private entrance a short distance away.

While the obsession continued, so too did his unemployment. He wrote another begging letter to theatre manager J. F. Elliston, and then visited agent Charles Dexton, who had known him as an actor over a decade before. The two had once shared a dressing room at the Adelphi, and the man remembered that Prince had a real problem with anyone who managed to gain bigger roles than he did. Furthermore, he also had a bad temper and was very quick to lose it, especially when jealous of other people.

Dexton had not seen or heard from Prince since, until he arrived in his Maiden Lane office in November 1897. The man was used to down-on-their-luck actors walking through his doors, but when Prince arrived, he was surprised by his appearance. He looked as though he had fallen on exceedingly hard times, and so Dexton promised to do all he could to help. After that meeting, Prince would arrive at his office every day, looking for news. However, when Dexton offered him a week's theatre employment in a pantomime he was producing, Prince turned him down, blaming a lack of wardrobe. Despite that, the agent said he would continue to look for something suitable.

Unwilling to take on the pantomime role, eventually Prince had no option but to tell Mrs Darby that he was going through some financial difficulties. He explained that his rent would be late, but assured her that he would pay as soon as possible. Despite the promises, he fell into arrears. Prince knew there was no way he would be able to survive without help, so he applied once again for assistance from the Actors' Benevolent Fund.

Secretary of the fund, Charles Colston, later explained that when Prince arrived at his office, he was told he would need to produce a letter of recommendation. The actor then proceeded to hand over the note from arch-enemy, William Terriss himself. 'I have known the bearer, Mr Richard Archer Prince, as a hard-working actor for many years,' the letter said.

'It was Mr Terriss's generosity that made him call the man an actor,' said Colston. 'He was a super [an understudy or extra]. He played at the Adelphi, but a long time ago. He had been helped pretty often – before Mr Terriss recommended him as well as since; he had been relieved from time to time ever since 1892. Not long ago I gave him a pound because he wanted to go to Scotland, but he did not go. He's mad . . . His manners are those of a madman. He gave me the impression of an anarchist.'

Prince told the committee that he had been out of work for twelve months, and had lost the Newcastle gig through no fault of his own. He assured the fund members that if he were only able to have enough money to live for the next few weeks, he was sure to find work. They listened to his pleas, and on 10 November gave him £1.

However, the money was not enough to support Prince, and the out-of-work actor sent letters to the fund over and over again. He told the committee that he had asked everyone he knew in London if they could give him a job, but nothing was forthcoming. Then he believed there would be a position for him in South Africa, but that had fallen through. He wondered about returning to Dundee, but decided he could not afford the fare. Finally, he had gone to the Prince Richard Theatre in the hope of acquiring a position there, only to miss the last bus and have to walk the eight miles home.

'If the fund does not help me,' he wrote, 'I shall have to starve or die.' Over the course of the following weeks, the Actors' Benevolent Fund sanctioned a further three payments, but still Prince returned regularly to ask for more. He even sent a rambling letter, which read,

> Dear Sir, I don't know how to thank you and the gentle-men of the Committee for your great kindness. It's worth ten years of one's life to receive such favours by one in the poor position I have always had of my art. But I hope to Almighty God my luck will change in a manner to pay back such kindness. Thanking you, sir, for the gentlemanly way you have received me at the Actors' Benevolent Fund – you do it the greatest honour. If it's ever in my power to do any good, I will.

When Prince's landlady, Mrs Darby, reminded him once again that his rent was due, the actor seemed forlorn. 'Can you wait till Thursday?' he asked. He then showed a photograph of his sister, and began complaining about her bitterly. 'I have a sister who is well to do, but she will not assist me. She keeps her servants, while I am in a small back room. I am expecting a letter from her soon. [The rent] will be paid . . . one way or the other . . .' The landlady had no clue what the man meant, and asked him to explain. 'That is best known, to God and man,' he replied, and that was the end of the conversation.

While he had previously seemed quite cheery, now Prince spoke in riddles, and Mrs Darby saw that he was a troubled man. 'He seemed depressed and worried about his rent,' she said. 'He had no clothes left.' Incidentally, while the actor seemed to hate everyone he came into contact with, he held a great deal of regard for his landlady. During the later inquest, he interrupted proceedings to declare, 'May I explain I am sorry this lady is mixed up in this affair? She is a perfect lady, at any rate, she acts like one.'

Shortly after telling Mrs Darby that he would pay the rent, 'one way or the other', he wrote to his mother in Dundee. The letter was full of his usual dramatic flair, only this time it also included a great deal of darkness, revealing that his experience in London had been a miserable one. 'Is there any use in coming home at Christmas?' he wrote. 'Because if not, I might just as well die in London.'

On 11 December 1897, Prince turned up at the Drury Lane theatre and asked for admission. When asked for identification, the man showed a card bearing the words, 'R. A. Prince, Adelphi Theatre'. He was given standing tickets and admitted inside. On several occasions in the past, he had stood up and shouted at the actors during performances, but this time he remained quiet. So much so that his attendance did not cause any kind of murmur until almost a week later, when his name suddenly became notorious.

By 15 December 1897, the man's rent was once again due, and he was now two weeks in arrears. Mrs Darby knew that he was seriously worried about the situation, but what she did not know was that, privately, Prince was blaming William Terriss more than ever before.

That evening, Prince arrived at the Adelphi Theatre and hung around the stage door, as had become his regular pasttime. He seemed impatient and agitated, and was eventually asked to leave by one of the stage staff. 'Mr Terriss comes up this way, doesn't he?' Prince asked doorman, Henry Spratt. 'Yes,' he lied, in an effort to protect the actor's privacy. He need not have bothered, however, as Prince was about to work everything out by himself.

Prince had hung around that stage door enough times to know that the actor never went in and out of it. There must be another way into the theatre, he decided, and after wandering around for a few minutes, he suddenly discovered the private entrance in Maiden Lane. William Alger, Mr Terriss's dresser, just happened to be coming out of the door shortly after Prince arrived there. He noted that the man was watching people come and go, though at the time he did not think anything of it. He walked past, unaware that Prince was plotting the worst revenge on the man he felt was the cause of all his problems.

While Prince was obsessing about Terriss, the great man himself was making plans for the future. Sir Henry Irving, an actor and close friend, told reporters that they had been discussing a revival of a play entitled *The Corsican Brothers*, which he had previously worked on at the Lyceum. 'We think of him in all the vigour of his attractive personality,' he said. To Irving, his friend would always be the epitome of a 'buoyant happy nature'.

On Thursday 16 December, Mrs Darby saw Prince leave her establishment at 2 p.m. From there, he visited the offices of the Actors' Benevolent Fund, where he was still a frequent and unwanted visitor. This time he was met by a clerk, who recognised him on sight. 'We will not be able to entertain any more applications from you,' he said abruptly. Prince made no reply and turned to leave.

At 3.45 p.m., he was back at his lodgings and knocking on the door of Mrs Darby's room. The desperate man explained that he simply had no money at all, and would be unable to pay his rent. He asked what he should do, to which his landlady replied, 'I don't know, Mr Prince. I am very sorry for you.' He then asked for some hot water, but when told there was none, the man went on his way. That was the last time Mrs Darby saw her lodger as a free man.

Unknown to the landlady, the knife she had found in his bedroom just after he moved in was now hidden in Prince's coat. In the early evening, he left his lodgings for the last time and headed towards the Adelphi Theatre. On his way there, he happened to bump into his sister and her husband, and once again asked for financial assistance. She told the man that she would rather see him dead in the gutter than give him another farthing. With his mental state disintegrating rapidly, Prince took this rebuff to mean that she was in league with William Terriss. 'If she had given me ten shillings,' he said, '[what I did] would never have happened. It is all through her.'

Prince then reached Maiden Lane, where the private entrance to the Adelphi Theatre was located. There, he called into the office of agent Charles Dexton once again to ask for work. The man had been unable to secure any further positions for Prince, so told him there was nothing he could do and sent him on his way. A few minutes later, William Terriss's understudy Frederic Lane was coming out of the private entrance at the Adelphi, and saw Prince standing in the shadows. Strangely, he had dreamt of Mr Terriss being stabbed just the night before, but had forced himself to put the vision out of his mind. 'I passed Prince without speaking,' he said, 'but a few minutes afterwards, I heard a great noise . . .'

William Terriss had spent some of the afternoon at the Green Room Club, where he was seen by his friend, Charles Fulton. 'He was in the very highest of spirits,' Fulton later said of the visit. 'In fact he was nearly always chaffing. Even when he seemed inclined to be serious he would turn it off in a bantering way. He was very fond of saying things as, "Shadows we are and shadows we pursue." At the club yesterday, he was playing solo whist, with a deal of noise and laughter. There was something about his personality that had a great attraction for me; and he was beloved by the club. Nothing I could say would make you realise how much he was loved and respected in this club.'

Terriss left around 4 p.m. and then spent time with his friend, John Henry Graves. Around 7 p.m. they left the actor's home and headed to the theatre. Arriving at the private entrance, the actor fumbled around for his keys, found them and slid one into the lock. Out of nowhere, a cape-wearing Richard Archer Prince came charging across the road and plunged his knife deep into the back of William Terriss, not once but twice. Shocked and confused, at first Graves thought the man was simply patting him on the back, though he did admit to finding it all a little 'rough'.

The moment the knife struck the second time, Terriss swung round and Prince took the opportunity to stab the actor firmly in the chest, almost pulling him downwards as he did so. 'My God, I am stabbed!' cried Terriss, before slumping down onto the ground. Upstairs, dresser William Alger had been busying himself in the actor's dressing room when he heard a commotion outside. He looked out from the first-floor window just in time to see the fatal blow to the chest and hear Terriss cry for help. 'I am stabbed,' he said again, 'arrest that man.'

Prince backed away from the door and onto the road, before walking slowly away from the scene. Graves was right behind him, however, and the man was arrested some distance from the theatre. 'If it had not been for the police,' recalled Terriss's understudy, Frederic Lane, 'I believe the man would have been lynched. I can suggest no motive whatsoever for the crime.'

While Lane and everyone else could see no reason for such a dreadful incident, Terriss's friend John Henry Graves was determined to find out for himself. During the walk to the police station, he asked Prince why he had performed such a terribly cruel deed. The man very calmly replied, 'Mr Terriss would not allow me to have any employment. I did it in revenge.'

Prince then added that he had been blackmailed by the actor for some ten years, though the message was garbled and nobody could make any sense of it. Unbelievably, the man still had possession of the murder weapon in his back pocket. It was only when he was asked at Bow Street station that he finally surrendered it, though even this was done in a dramatic fashion. Throwing back his cape, he took the bloodstained knife and handed it over with a flourish. 'This is what I stabbed him with,' he said, before going on to blame Terriss for his inability to gain further assistance from the Actor's Benevolent Fund. 'He had due warning,' he said.

Back at the theatre, William Terriss was lying on the ground, with friends and passers-by gathered all around. They each encouraged the man to hold on and assured him that it would be okay. A doctor tried to work on his failing body, but it was too late; the knife had gone in a staggering five-and-a-half inches, and a rib was broken. There was no chance at all of making a recovery, and by the time Graves arrived back at the scene, Terriss was on the brink of death and passed away very shortly afterwards.

His frequent co-star and rumoured mistress Jessie Millward was said to have kept a stoic stance during his dying moments, but after Terriss passed, she – and the others present – completely broke down. 'Grief reigned alone where, only a short time before, there had been the busy preparation for the evening's entertainment,' wrote one reporter for the *Peterhead Sentinel.*

The information was relayed to officers at Bow Street, and Prince was charged with murder. 'All right,' he replied, totally unfazed. He then asked an officer to tell his sister about his predicament. When word came back that she wanted nothing more to do with him, he told the policeman that she had joined Terriss in blackmailing him. She, meanwhile, packed her bags and left London in an attempt to keep herself well away from the murder inquiry, and her brother.

Inside the theatre, the audience was still waiting for Terriss to arrive on stage. One of the crowd, Dick Milton from Hove, was a huge fan of the actor and had followed every one of his plays for the past ten years. He wrote to the *Stage* newspaper and described sitting in the theatre, waiting for the man to appear. 'Whilst we awaited the rising of the curtain, poor

Terriss lay dead, back-stage, having half an hour before been foully murdered, the victim of a madman's rage and delusions.'

An announcement was eventually made; the theatre closed and shocked members of the public filed out onto the Strand. At first whispers abounded that there had been an attempted murder, but then ripples of the truth began to wind their way round the streets. The result of this was that while theatregoers would normally have just gone home, now they hung around the area, trying to hear a slither of truth, rumour or hearsay. For some, the goings-on behind the scenes were far more exciting than anything they could ever dream of seeing on stage. Their interests were piqued even more when they saw the tearful parade of celebrities running in and out of the stage door. This would remain the focal point for a long time and, even today, a blue plaque hangs at the theatre, advertising the fact that Terriss 'met his untimely end' there.

When reporters caught up with Adelphi manager Fred G. Latham, he was bombarded with questions. 'Do you feel able to make a statement on William Terriss?' asked one.

'Oh my dear boy, we cannot! We are in such a state!' he replied.

'Can you say what arrangements will be made to fill Mr Terriss's place and carry on the performances?'

'We do not know yet,' said Latham. 'We are too upset. But we don't open tonight. That's all I can say. We will send round to the press as soon as we have settled what to do in consequence of this shocking affair.'

At other theatres around the West End, the news of William Terriss's murder spread quickly. Herbert Beerbohm Tree, one of the actors at Her Majesty's Theatre, recalled that the news actually leaked out while he was on stage. 'It took all our spirit out of us,' he said. In the moments after the story broke, the actor looked out into the audience and could have sworn he saw the ripples of rumour and speculation spreading throughout the crowd. 'That may have only been fancy,' he said, 'but I think not.' Chillingly, the actor revealed to reporters that he had received a letter from Richard Prince just a few weeks before the murder, offering congratulations on his performance in several plays.

At Prince's lodgings, Mrs Darby was surprised to find detectives banging on her door. When she let them in, they headed straight for the actor's bedroom and discovered many letters, a list of subscribers to the Actors' Benevolent Fund (which included Terriss) and some manuscripts. The letters were mainly to associates in Dundee, and were so garbled it was virtually impossible to decipher them.

At Bow Street Police Court, Richard Prince was officially charged with the murder of William Terriss. Prince arrived at court dressed in a shabby cape – possibly the one he had worn during the murder – and carried a cap. The *Daily News* described him as 'a man slightly above the middle height, with brown hair and dark eyes, which have a somewhat sinister expression. He shows a powerful build, especially about the forearm and hands, which have the appearance of possessing great strength.'

He walked confidently and briskly to his seat, and took a look at the crowds of reporters, artists and agents, many of which were making quiet booing noises. A smile slowly snaked its way across the murderer's face and he turned his chair to face them. He had finally achieved the level of fame he had long-since been denied, and Prince fully intended to make the most of it. Unfortunately for him, the judge saw exactly what he was doing, and the actor was directed to move his chair back forthwith. He then spent the entire court appearance smiling, twirling his moustache, listening intently and occasionally glowering in annoyance. When Terriss's friend, John Henry Graves, described the scene of the murder, Prince had the audacity to question and comment on the authenticity of his words. 'I do not think the statement is quite correct,' he said. 'I did not rush behind him. I met Mr Terriss and this gentleman, face-to-face. [Afterwards] I simply stood where I was. I did not attempt to run away. The policeman was only two seconds in coming. I went peacefully and quietly to the police station. When I saw Mr Terriss, I made a motion to him to ask him to speak to me, but he said, "No."'

Several minutes later, a police officer spoke of how he arrested Prince, 150 yards from the theatre, and how he had told him of plans for revenge against Terriss. Once again, the prisoner shot forward.

'What the constable has said is right, except that he took me about three yards from the stage entrance. I did not say anything about revenge. I said he had blackmailed me for ten years.'

'Did he say anything about blackmail?' asked the judge, to which the officer replied that the prisoner had told him Terriss had blackmailed him out of money from the Actor's Benevolent Fund. At this point Prince opened his mouth once again, and completely contradicted himself.

'I could not possibly say that!' he shouted.

'The wisest thing you can do is to hold your tongue,' the judge replied.

'Then I suppose I can contradict that afterwards?' asked Prince.

'Certainly,' was the reply.

During his entire appearance, Prince smirked incessantly and often volunteered information without being asked. When a police officer said he could not make out what address was printed on the murder weapon, Prince shouted out, 'The address is 48, Brompton Road!' Then when he discovered his sister had skipped London and gone into hiding, he lurched forward and shouted, 'I don't see why she shouldn't be here. If she had been innocent she would have been here of her own accord.' His interruptions and laughter became so extreme that there were frequent jeers from the public gallery and, at one point, a Terriss fan even threw a notebook at him.

By the time the hearing had finished, the judge referred the matter to the Treasury and ordered the accused to remain in prison. However, even the end of proceedings weren't enough to keep Prince quiet, and he showed displeasure that he did not yet have a solicitor. 'You can see about getting a solicitor in the meantime,' the judge told him. Prince then left the dock with the same confident air he had shown on his arrival, despite a loud hissing and booing from the public gallery.

In the days and weeks that followed, the newspapers were full of stories about both Terriss and Prince. These ranged from long-lost interviews with the fallen star to articles on how much money he was worth at the time of death. Rumours swirled that his fortune was around the £60,000 mark, though in actuality it was worth £18,809. There were also tributes from those who knew William Terriss, including an emotional one from actress and co-star, Ellen Terry:

Oh, it is too shocking! I have been completely prostrated ever since I heard the dreadful news. It will evoke the profoundest feelings in the heart of every member of the profession. Poor Terriss! He was such a kind-hearted fellow! He was a fine actor, with the prospect of such a grand career before him, and then to be butchered to death in that cruel way. It is too horrible to think of. I am perfectly unnerved at the very thought of it.

Friend and colleague George Alexander summed up what all of Terriss's friends thought about the man and the murder: 'He was one of the best fellows that ever breathed and one of the dearest friends I ever had,' he said. 'He was present at a performance of *The White Heather* not long since, and occupied the Royal box. I did not know that he had an enemy in the world. I can only suppose that the murderer was mad.'

Perhaps the strangest story to be published after his death was a short interview with William Terriss's son, Tom. He did not provide a tribute as such, but concentrated on the subject of what he was doing on the night of his father's death:

My brother Will and I were playing chess, and the dog was apparently quietly dozing on my mother's lap; and it startled us all considerably as it bounded up and down the room with frantic snaps and snarls. My mother was very much alarmed and cried out, 'What does he see? What does he see?' convinced that the dog's anger was directed at something unseen by us. My brother and I soothed her as well as we could, though ourselves considerably puzzled at the behaviour of an ordinary quiet and well-conducted pet. Yes, the incident occurred at the very hour of my father's death.

The funeral of William Terriss took place shortly before Christmas 1897. It was estimated that around fifty thousand fans lined the route from his home in Bedford Park to his final resting place in Brompton Cemetery. House blinds were kept closed and flags flew at half-mast. Men took off their hats on seeing the cortège approach, and everyone bowed their heads in respect. Even Queen Victoria sent a message of condolence, stating that the death of the actor had deprived the English stage of 'one of its brightest ornaments'. Her son, the Prince of Wales, sent a wreath of white lilies and orchids, with the words 'With deepest sympathy' printed on a card.

The coffin was carried to the cemetery in a flower-filled carriage, with hundreds of other wreaths carried by four florist's vans. Newspapers estimated that there were at least one hundred coaches following the hearse, all filled with friends, family and colleagues. Terriss was laid to rest alongside his mother and his baby granddaughter, in a brick-lined grave. 'To my darling old father, from his devoted, heart-broken daughter, Ellie,' read a card from his daughter, Ellaline Terriss, while his son-in-law wrote, 'To my dear, dear father-in-law, the best friend I have ever known.'

Always an avid letter-writer, Richard Archer Prince's notes did not stop with his arrest and detainment at Holloway Prison. From there he wrote a series of twenty letters to the wife and family of William Terriss, the contents of which were described as 'extraordinary', though they were never made public. Other letters went to his friend, Mr. G Astley, during which he complained bitterly about William Terriss. 'Had he only spoken to me, he should have been alive now,' he wrote. He then begged the man to come and visit him, and to bring the best doctor he could find.

Astley promised to help, but when he did manage to track down a doctor and make the visit to Holloway, Prince had forgotten to ask the staff for a visitor's pass. Astley was turned away at the door and several days later received another letter from the actor, this time apologising for the mix-up and begging for some new underwear and clothing. 'I don't want a doctor now,' he wrote. 'Come by yourself.'

But whether he wanted a doctor or not, one was assigned to Prince's case. On 31 December 1897 and again on 6 January 1898, the man was visited by Dr Henry Charles Bastian. Then on other occasions, he was assessed by Theophilus Bubbly Hilsop, a lecturer on mental diseases at St Mary's Hospital, and Holloway's resident doctor, James Scott.

Bastian interviewed the prisoner extensively, and studied the letters written while in custody. Over again, Prince told the doctor that he had been blackmailed by William Terriss and theatre manager, J. F. Elliston, and that wherever he went in the country, the latter was one step ahead of him, poisoning his tea in an effort to kill him.

Prince also claimed that Terriss found out about every place he was to appear on stage, and personally told scandalous tales to his new colleagues and even his landladies. Elliston was accused of similar, but this time it was an attempt to have him act with people intent on ruining his career. When the doctor tried to make the actor see how ludicrous his suspicions were, he was met with a blunt rejection. 'I could not shake him [of the theory],' Bastian said.

This paranoid belief was also demonstrated in a letter Prince wrote while in prison:

During the time I was with the *Alone in London* company, they sent people, scum to ruin my character if they could, and kept me out of an engagement for two years. During this time, Mr Terriss sent blackmailing money to [unnamed men] in Dundee, and sent men who worked in Camperdown Shipyard and Waller's Foundry in Dundee, dressed as swells, to my sister's house in London to disgrace me and keep me out of an engagement.

One thing Prince did deny to the doctor was the purchase of the knife for the purpose of murder. As far as the actor was concerned, he had only bought it to cut bread in his room. He did not, however, admit that there was a kitchen knife supplied by his landlady for that very purpose. Furthermore, he denied all accusations of having purposely killed William Terriss. As far as he was concerned, he merely wanted to scratch the actor, in an attempt to get people to hear his blackmailing charges in court.

'I solemnly declare that I am as good as Terriss before God and man,' he wrote, 'although I could never make his money per week. It was a cowardly act for me to have done what I did against Terriss, as it was the last of my thoughts to kill him.'

Through his garbled exchanges and excitable attitude, it didn't take long for all three doctors to decide that Prince was of unsound mind. They noted that despite showing remorse for the murder on paper, the man showed very little in person, and at times he even blamed God for making him do it. 'I was carrying out his will,' he said. At other times, he remained fixated on the idea that he had never meant to kill Terriss, but just wanted to talk to him.

This was all rather dubious, especially considering the evidence given by William Terriss's friend that the murderer had stormed across the road while the actor's back was turned, putting his key into the door. However, regardless of his confessions, his aim was certainly to wound William Terriss. Additionally, it was very much apparent that the man was not capable of exercising self-control, and the doctor decided it would be better in the interests of both him and the public at large if he was confined to an asylum.

In January 1898, Richard Archer Prince appeared at the Central Criminal Court, charged with the wilful murder of William Terriss. The man pleaded guilty, though still insisted it was under great provocation. His representative, Mr Sands, wasted no time in putting forward the idea that Prince could not be held responsible for his actions.

'That Mr Terriss was killed by this man is indisputable. I submit, however, that the prisoner was not, at the time he committed this terrible act, in a state of mind to realise what he was doing. I shall call witnesses who will speak to lapses of memory and strange behaviour on the part of the prisoner, before this act was committed. It will be shown that he suffered from sun stroke and delusions as to his enemies and the failing of his capacities.'

The opening speech gave way to the questioning of a variety of key players, among them William Terriss's son, Tom; Prince's landlady, Mrs Darby; officers who witnessed the aftermath of the murder; old employers; and the doctors who assessed him in the days and weeks after the murder. Things did not go altogether quietly, however. When Dr Bastian explained that the prisoner had not shown any remorse for such a bloody act, Prince interrupted proceedings by crying out loudly, 'Why should I?'

The evidence was pretty much the same as that given during former appearances at the police court and the inquest, and the jury soon retired. Despite the severity of the case, it took them only thirty-five minutes to decide their verdict and return to court. 'We find the prisoner guilty of wilful murder,' said the spokesperson, 'and we say that he knew what he was doing, and to whom he was doing it. On the medical evidence we say he was not responsible for his actions.'

'You say that he was insane at the time according to law?' asked the judge.

'On the medical evidence, yes,' came the reply.

The judge then sentenced Richard Archer Prince to be confined to Holloway as a 'criminal lunatic' but, once again, the man himself wasted no time in interrupting him.

'Shall I not be allowed to make a statement of thanks? I wish to express my thanks to all those gentlemen who have assisted in the case. I did not bring my defence properly forward after the medical evidence, because I did not think it necessary, because I should not have been believed. All I can say is I have had a very fair trial, and that . . .'

At this point the judge cut the murderer off, and insisted that no further statement could be made. Richard Archer Prince was then led away from the court and onto a new life at Holloway and then Broadmoor. The public remained outraged for years that one of England's most notorious killers seemed to have been given a soft sentence, especially when it was rumoured that he spent his days happily conducting the asylum's orchestra. He outlived his victim by almost forty years, eventually passing away in Broadmoor, though rumours of an early release and subsequent visits to West End theatres were persistent.

And what of the memory of William Terriss? Paying tribute to his love of the sea and time spent as a merchant marine, a building was erected in his honour in the seaside town of

Eastbourne. The foundation stone was laid by the Duchess of Devonshire on 16 July 1898, and a memorial jar was placed in a small cavity, which included local newspapers and programs describing the day's events. Terriss's son, Tom, was in attendance, as were some of his friends and fans. Daughter Ellaline could not be there, but sent a heartfelt note:

> I am deeply grateful to her Grace the Duchess of Devonshire and the public who have so generously come forward to erect this splendid lifeboat house in memory of my dear father, and nothing would have been of more consolation to me than to have witnessed this loving tribute today, did I not know that the strain would be more than I could bear.

The building is still there today, and houses the RNLI Eastbourne Museum and Shop. The plaque on the wall reads:

> This life boat house has been erected in memory of William Terriss with subscriptions received by the *Daily Telegraph* from those who loved and admired him, and who sorrowed together with all his friends and fellow countrymen at his most cruel and untimely end. 1898. Shadows we are, and shadows we pursue.

An Actress is Arrested

Olga Nethersole was a successful English actress, who toured the world with plays she both starred in and produced. Such was her popularity in the United States by 1895 that she received daily letters from women around the country. If the actress did not receive these letters, she said, it was a very depressing day.

However, while fans loved her, reporters declared her popularity to be a fad, especially when hairdressers began to offer a special 'Nethersole' style inspired by the actress's beautiful waves. Even her collie dog gained column inches, when it was revealed that he travelled the world with her, ate at her table and always took his rightful place next to Nethersole during carriage journeys – whether the other passengers liked it or not.

On the outside, Olga was a staunch supporter of women's rights and never shied away from showing her independence. Underneath the outward sparkle of her career, however, Olga was a very sensitive person, who had lost her father when she was four and her mother when she was in her early twenties. This sadness was recognised by anyone who met her and, by her own admission, the actress had very little confidence.

'I feel that I have no genius,' she said in 1895. 'I am completely used up by my performances, and do not want even my maid to speak to me. She is devoted to me, and has become used to all my little oddities.'

While Olga's self-confidence was already fragile, it was hit beyond anything she could imagine when she decided to produce and star in a play called *Sapho* in February 1900. The piece was considered to be relatively risqué, and Olga played Fanny LeGrand with a great many nudges and winks. Many of the scenes caused raised eyebrows, but the main ones involved the heroine (Olga) kissing one man, before ogling another (Jean, played by Hamilton Revelle) at a party. Once they had become acquainted through a waltz or two, they were next seen in a Paris house scene, where Jean carried Fanny upstairs and presumably to bed.

In the second act, the two were seen together in Jean's apartment, where it was revealed that Fanny's real name was Sapho. She had been a lover to a great many men, all of whom had written her letters, describing how her naked arms felt around them . . . As if all this wasn't scandalous enough, there was also an illegitimate child, a former lover in prison, and a violent make-up scene between Fanny/Sapho and the main male character. The latter apparently involved Fanny grovelling at her lover's feet, begging him to let her be his slave, and asking him to kick her like a dog. All this inevitably led to mixed reviews, especially from Victorians of a more conservative nature.

In February 1900, the play arrived at the Wallack's Theatre in New York. However, it could not have received a colder welcome. Several members of the public complained that it was far too risqué to be played to an audience, and film critic Sewell D. Collins wrote a rather abrupt review:

The first act is a riotous and noisy carnival, and the guests there, from what they say and the way they act, are not the most respectable people in the world. They were a crowd of artists, bohemians, people of very loose morals, singing and dancing and drinking. I remember there were a great many of the lines very suggestive.

When a reporter by the name of Robert Mackey went to see it, he claimed to be absolutely appalled. Declaring that the whole play was 'imbued with an immoral tone and endangers public morals', Mackay complained bitterly about the storyline, but particularly Olga's acting technique. According to him, the actress accentuated all the lines to make them even more lewd and offensive, and when she was carried up the stairs by her co-star, she behaved in an indecent manner.

The reporter took his complaints to District Attorney Gardiner, who felt disgusted enough to ask Magistrate Mott for an arrest warrant. The magistrate was confused. He had heard that the police had been to the show and saw no reason to complain at all. He asked the DA about this, and the man shrugged. 'This does not alter my position,' he said. 'I still believe the play to be immoral and offensive to public decency.'

'The people do not have to see this play if they don't want to,' suggested Mott. After that disclaimer, the two men went back and forth for a while, before finally the magistrate succumbed and an arrest warrant was drawn up. The authorities then headed to the theatre and arrested Olga Nethersole, her manager, the theatre manager and the leading man, for 'offending public decency'.

Of course, the outcry and arrests just gave the play more publicity than it probably ever would have received if Mackay had kept quiet. Newspapers went crazy about the 'disgusting' play, though seemed to love reporting every sordid detail in their rags. Suddenly, the public and various church groups claimed that they too were horrified by the blatant sexual references and violence it contained. They did not care if they hadn't seen the material – if it was wrong, it was wrong, and that was that.

Meanwhile, all this publicity led to cheap, bootlegged paperbacks of the play script being touted by various New York salesmen. One – Benjamin Morris of Jersey City – made quite a good income from the cheap copies, until one day two students saw him harassing a woman into buying one. Together they dumped his books in the gutter and rolled the man down the muddy street. Not surprisingly, he was not seen in that area again.

Another theatre company then decided to perform the play themselves, but were contacted by Olga's representatives, who claimed they had stolen the rights to her story. A lawsuit was threatened and the performance was shut down, though not before the company retaliated by claiming that Olga had probably stolen the story from another source, and had no right to say it was her own.

Despite being on parole, Olga Nethersole decided that the show must go on. The theatre opened and of course people piled inside to see for themselves exactly what this immoral play looked like. Before they watched, however, they were greeted by Olga, who read out a statement to explain her current predicament.

'Allow me to appeal against the persecution begun by one New York paper and continued by another, and which has resulted in a warrant being issued. I believe I am innocent of corrupting the morals of the public by this performance. I am informed that these papers are what are called sensational journals. I am their victim. I believe in all truth that neither of these papers has made its attack on the play from a sincere motive. I believe their persecution is actuated only by a base motive – to make a sensation and thus increase their sales. I am, I hope, an honest woman, and as such I ask only justice from the American public, as I know I shall get it from the American courts.'

Not many listened to Olga's pleas, and there was a steady call for the piece to be banned completely or suppressed by legal means. If that could not happen, the detractors said, then certain scenes should be toned down or taken out altogether. One outspoken reverend found himself in serious trouble when he spoke publicly and negatively about the actress. He was threatened with a lawsuit, which was only revoked months later after he apologised and promised not to do it again.

When it was rumoured that the magistrate who initially ordered the arrest of Olga had sneaked in to see what all the fuss was about, the public – and media – were outraged. The man was forced to release a statement, which said that he had been nowhere near the theatre on the night in question; he had been home the entire weekend. However, few believed him.

Not everyone took offence at the play though, and the suffragettes were firmly on Olga's side. But perhaps the biggest support came from rather a surprising quarter. In the midst of all the outrage, Reverend Hugh O. Pentecost gave a sermon about 'Immoral Amusements':

'The attempted suppression of the play, *Sapho*, by legal means, is ill-advised, impolitic, uncalled for and foolish. I do not believe that any good can come of the movement. Let it go undisturbed; this or any other play of a similar character. Interference with the amusements of the people by the process of law is wrong.'

Olga's predicament rumbled on for weeks, with court appearances to decide if the matter should go to trial, then others to decide on the dates and times. Finally, the main trial was held in front of the grand jury. From the very first, Olga's lawyer was determined to receive a quick and thorough hearing. 'We are confident that there can be but one verdict, and that is acquittal. The interests at stake are enormous, and we are entitled to an immediate trial.'

Many witnesses were called, among them theatregoer W. O. Inglis, who said that 'my moral susceptibilities have been shocked by the performance of *Sapho*'. He was supported by

Mr Almon A. Hensley, who when asked what she thought of the play, described it as, 'Most objectionable.'

An unlikely supporter (and one of the chief witnesses for the defence) was Police Inspector Walter L. Thompson, the man who had arrested Olga and her colleagues. He caused shockwaves when he stated his belief that the play was not immoral and that the arrests should never have been made. When asked how many times he had seen the play, the man excitedly shouted, 'Twenty times! I have omitted only four nights since 1st February.' At one point he also seemed to forget himself and actually shouted towards Olga, 'We'll win! We'll win!'

There was great merriment in court when the policeman was asked to recite passages from the play. 'I wish I could,' he said. 'If I could I'd get more money than I'm getting now.' In the end, Olga Nethersole recited them, and afterwards Thompson made those in the public gallery laugh when he announced, 'I couldn't do as well as that.' He also caused titters when he said that it was perfectly all right to take a sixteen-year-old girl to see the play, but refused outright to say whether he would like his wife and daughter to go. 'I decline to answer that question,' he replied. 'That is my business.'

Speaking afterwards, Thompson's boss said that it was unprecedented to have the arresting police officer appear as a witness for the defence, especially since it was his decision to do so. Then the President of the Board of Police Commissioners waded in to say that if it was found that Thompson had acted contrary to the rules of the department, he too would find himself under investigation.

One drama critic who was quick to defend *Sapho* and its actors was Arthur Gordon Weld. He told the court how he had taken his wife and sister-in-law to see the play twice, and had seen absolutely nothing immoral at all.

'Is your wife a churchgoer?' asked the prosecution.

'Well not aggressively, no,' he replied.

His testimony was going in Olga's favour, but when it transpired that he had seen the play only in Milwaukee, and never in New York, his opinion was thrown out. So too were any reviews and ticket-sales statistics that weren't related to the theatre where it was now showing.

'I have not any business to take that into consideration,' said the judge. 'It is what they did here and what they are doing here in this city and that is all.'

During proceedings, the four defendants were described by the prosecution as being 'persons of wicked and depraved mind and disposition and not regarding the common duties of morality and decency, but contriving and wickedly intending, so far as in them lay, to debauch and corrupt the morals as well of youth and other persons, and to raise and create in their minds, inordinate desires'. The play itself was described as 'lewd, indecent, obscene, filthy, scandalous, lascivious, and disgusting'. The characters, actions and words were labelled in exactly the same way.

Every time Olga appeared in court, she caused a sensation. Often wearing a long fur or silk cape over a glamorous dress, she would also arrive with a beautiful velvet hat perched on her head or sometimes a veil over her face. The court would be abuzz with news of what she was wearing on that particular day, and often witnesses (even those who had previously complained about her moral fibre) would not be able to give their testimony without staring at her wistfully. One day, while telling the court how disgraceful he found the play to be and

how he had been brought to a state of collapse by her performance, one theatregoer was so obsessed with staring at Olga that
he quite forgot himself.

'When Sapho saw Jean [the main male character],' he said
excitedly, 'she grabbed him with her feline embrace!'

'Strike the word feline,' the unimpressed judge told the
court, while those present burst into laughter.

Still, the obsession with Olga and her clothes continued, and
even reporters seemed under her spell. When one day she wore
a purple cape and hat, one described colleagues seated beside
her as being 'tinged with a delicate lavender tint'.

The strain, however, was certainly taking its toll on the
actress, and she had called in sick to the theatre on several
evenings since the arrest. 'This experience is racking my nerves,'
she said. 'The tension is horrible.' Whenever she left court,
Olga was accompanied by her bother Louis, and would be
harangued by the throng of reporters outside. When asked why
she often wore a veil, the actress revealed that it was to protect
her face from the weather and the stares from the crowd.

While she was feeling a great deal of anxiety about the situation, it also played on her brother Louis's mind too. He had
been touring with his sister for a long time, and Olga had
described his dedication to her several years before: 'My brother
was a lawyer and doing well in his profession, but he gave it up
for me. Dear fellow, he is so much to me. I am not his only
sister, for there are two others married, but we have always been
chums, and he knows me better than I know myself.'

At the time, Louis had laughed about the stresses that came
with his job, saying, 'The American tour has added ten years to
my life. For the first time in my existence, I look my age!' He
had laughed at that comment at the time, but little had he

known just how much more stressful his situation would become. Doctors told reporters that the actress had a terrible temperature and was 'completely prostrated'.

Even though the shadow of the trial hung over Olga for some time, in the end it was very quickly wound up. This was – in part – thanks to Judge Fursman, who refused point-blank to listen to any evidence he did not deem necessary to the day's proceedings. This behaviour was most apparent when critic Sewell Collins was called.

The man who had complained so bitterly about *Sapho* was at first unable to find his way to the front of the court when called to testify. The whole room was disturbed by his inability to get to the aisle, and several seats had to be moved to create a space. By the time he finally arrived on the stand, the judge was in no mood to have his time wasted any more.

'I would not take any girl in good society to see the performance,' Sewell said. 'I don't believe mothers would sanction it. I think the play is very immoral in tone, and it teaches no moral whatsoever.'

The judge stopped proceedings just a short time into the testimony.

'There's no point repeating all this,' he boomed. 'It's a waste of time. I won't admit opinions as evidence.'

The man was then dismissed from the bench, only to find himself lost once again. This time he caused more titters from the courtroom when he mistook Judge Fursman's room for the exit. As he opened the door, a court attendant came rushing over and sent the man in the right direction. The judge looked on, unamused.

Shortly after this, he shocked the defence by reiterating his desire not to hear from any witnesses who had seen the play in any other region than New York. At this point, Olga turned quietly to her attorney and whispered in his ear for some minutes. Finally, he turned to the judge and declared that Olga was now resting her case on the evidence so far submitted.

His partner then stepped forward and gave a flowery speech on why the case should be dismissed altogether, which included reciting the original indictment. This did not impress the judge, who tut-tutted and told the attorney that all his speech did was show that the person who wrote the summons 'had a very large vocabulary'. This rebuff caused laughs from the room, and a large gentleman then collapsed in excited hysterics and had to be carried out.

After the court had settled down, the judge told Olga's defence team that while he had his own personal views of whether or not to proceed, perhaps he did not share the same opinions as the jury. He told everyone to go home and return the next day, when the jury would deliberate and give their verdict.

Sure enough, on 5 April 1900, the attorneys gave their closing statements. For a full hour, they went on, pleading with the jury to do the right thing. Olga's lawyer had tears in his eyes as he pleaded her case, and at one point even likened her to Caesar's wife, above suspicion of any foul conspiracy thrown at her. Being in the company of an actress had obviously brushed off on the man, as he turned and pointed a finger at his client, his voice breaking with emotion. 'Ah gentlemen,' he wept. 'Had there ever been a smirch on her pure womanhood? After fame and fortune are hers, now comes a charge that she is trying to subvert public morality, and forsooth she is dragged into a criminal court. Poor, defenceless woman!'

At that point, Olga threw her head onto the desk and wept inconsolably.

By contrast, the prosecution spent a great deal of time reading out parts of the play they believed to be obscene. However, by this point the entire spectacle had annoyed the judge to no end, and he turned to the jury. 'Do not pay much attention to what has just been said,' he declared.

'What a wet blanket,' one lawyer was heard saying to another.

The jury retired to their rooms, while the crowded court waited impatiently to hear the outcome. They did not have to wait long. It took the men just over thirty minutes to come back into court and announce that they found Olga and the other parties not guilty of any wrongdoing. The actress once again burst into tears and fell into her brother's arms as the crowd cheered and were then told to be quiet. Then the jurors left the building and Olga was kissed and hugged by most of the women in the room. Finally, she was taken into the judge's chambers, so that she could fully recover from her ordeal.

'Poor little woman,' said her co-star, Hamilton Revelle. 'She has borne up wonderfully.'

Shortly afterwards, the actress made her way to her lawyer's offices, where she was followed by a crowd of fans and onlookers, all begging her for a speech. Eventually, she stopped, straightened her hat, and then spoke. Praising the judge for all his work on her behalf, she expressed her joy that the jury had found her innocent of any wrongdoing.

'When this attack was made upon me,' Olga said, 'I placed myself in the hands of the judge and he assured me that my interests would be safely conserved. So as soon as my managers are ready with the production, I will be only too anxious to proceed with the play.'

As promised, Olga Nethersole did indeed return to the stage in New York, just a day after her ordeal was over. There, she was greeted by a huge crowd of well-wishers, many of whom had queued all day just to see her perform. Humorously, those present included most of the jurors involved in the case, as well as members of the District Attorney's office and Police Inspector Thompson, who was accompanied by his wife. As Olga entered her dressing room, she was thrilled to see a deluge of British and American flags, hundreds of flowers, and a banner with the words VICTORY emblazoned above the door.

By the time she reached the stage, the actress stood for a full ten minutes, while the audience cheered her courage and threw flowers at her feet. The reception was such that she was forced to give a speech before she could begin her performance.

'I am still suffering from the strain,' she said, 'which will take time and peace of mind to remove. Yet remembering what has been done for freedom of art and literature, what the jury and his Honour have done, I am proud and glad that I have borne the brunt of this battle.'

Olga then got on with her performance, and at the end of the evening she was treated to rapturous applause and a full-house standing ovation. However, as pleasing as it was to return to the stage a free woman, as she had explained to the New York audience, Olga was worn out, deeply emotional and extremely ill. The stresses of being in court all day and on stage every evening had certainly taken its toll, and it didn't help when her manager unexpectedly announced that she owed him thousands of dollars for his services. The actress quit America as soon as she could, and returned to England.

After being fined for bringing her pet dogs into the country from the States, Olga spent the summer resting, and then made the shock decision to return to New York and revive *Sapho*. However, the emotional scars from her last trip were still everywhere apparent, and from the moment of her arrival, things did not go well. Stopped by customs officials in New York, the woman accidentally told them she was an American citizen, then her baggage was searched and fur coats confiscated until she could pay duty on them. It was left to Olga's brother to sort out the situation and get the coats back. When asked why the actress had told authorities she was a US citizen, it was brushed off as just a mistake.

Away from troubles at the port, Olga joyfully told waiting reporters that she had big plans to travel around the United States in a variety of different plays. She seemed extremely excited about the time ahead, and anxious to get back to work. However, illness struck once again and she was forced to drop out of the company. The actress then returned to London, where she underwent major surgery and a long period of convalescence.

In December 1901, she finally felt well enough to go on another tour, but first she spoke with a reporter for the *London Mainly About People* publication. The journalist noted that: 'She rarely laughs, but her smile is so quick and expressive that it changes all the sweet gravity of the face into mirth and pleasure, as fleeting as it is delightful.'

Olga made the decision to bring *Sapho* to the West End, where she received a great deal of acclaim. However, the advent of the First World War put her years of acting into perspective, and Olga decided to quit the stage and went into the health profession. In 1917 she created the British People's League of Health, an organisation to help raise the standard of health for the nation, and in 1936 she was awarded the CBE (Commander of the British Empire) for this work.

Extraordinary Death by Poison

William Wheaton Ball was a thirty-five-year-old actor, who by all accounts was well respected and admired in his field. He had never known the dizzying heights of Broadway or the West End, but nevertheless, he enjoyed a successful career in the United Kingdom and abroad, and had also created a successful property business.

Arthur Dillon was a theatre agent based in Covent Garden, London, and represented the career of Ball. In 1844, he obtained an acting job for him in Blackburn, Lancashire, and on 1 April the man arrived at the Dun Horse Inn, where he intended to stay for the entire run of the play. The innkeeper was a friendly man by the name of John Wilson, and immediately took a liking to Ball. From the moment he arrived, the two men spoke about a great variety of subjects, and the actor would recall stories about travelling to Italy and other European countries.

On the outside, at least, there seemed to be absolutely nothing whatsoever unusual about William Wheaton Ball, apart from the fact that he seemed to go out on a very limited basis. He smoked a great deal, but his drinking was only moderate and gave no cause for alarm. However, his personal care regime left a lot to be desired. While Ball had been described as 'fresh' on his arrival at the pub, as the week wore on he became less and less concerned with the state of his appearance. This was noted by the innkeeper and even mentioned during the inquest.

Unknown to anyone at the time, when Ball arrived in Blackburn, he brought with him a phial of laudanum, a powerful narcotic containing opium. He had purchased the chemical during his last placement in Boston, Lincolnshire, but as soon as the actor arrived in Blackburn he began the search for more. It did not take him long to find the shop of Robert Wilding, where he was seen by an assistant and apprentice on Tuesday 2 April. Unbelievably, neither of the men thought to ask any questions when the laudanum was requested, and when Ball returned on the fourth, they still served him without query or concern.

'It is customary to ask persons what they require Laudanum for,' the assistant recalled. 'It did not occur to me to make that enquiry. I was deceived by the gentlemanly appearance of the deceased. If he had been a mean looking person I should have asked for what the Laudanum was for.'

On Thursday 4 April, Ball had a meeting with theatrical manager William Mills. Together they spoke about the forthcoming play – *The Wife* – and more specifically, his role of Ferrado Gonzago. Ball gave Mills a reference from his agent, which showed how much he expected to be paid, and what he would do at the theatre in exchange. The two met again on 5 April, when they discussed the play and the manager presented the actor with a copy of the script and instructed him to write out his lines in a notebook.

Everything was going well, until Ball suddenly began talking about friends of his who had once known great wealth, but were now so poor they were forced to go into the workhouse. Still, in spite of this rather strange interlude, the meeting was a successful one. When it was done, the two men then made arrangements to see each other the next day, and bid farewell. To Mills, it looked as though Ball was very much looking forward to taking on the role of Gonzago, and he looked forward to working with him. Unfortunately, it was all an illusion.

That evening, Ball parcelled up his copy of the play and went down to the bar. There he asked the landlord, John Wilson, if he would return it to Mills after 9 a.m. the following morning. He agreed and then Ball sat down at a portable writing desk, where he seemed to be feverishly writing several letters. While scribbling away, the actor managed to keep up a conversation with Wilson about nothing in particular – certainly nothing to cause concern anyway. Then at 11.30 p.m., Wilson closed the inn, poured Ball a glass of rum and water, and readied himself to go to bed. The actor placed the letters, pen and ink into the writing desk, and got up to leave with it.

'I hope you will not require the pen and ink early in the morning,' he said to Wilson. 'I should not want to be disturbed by you fetching it.' The man assured him he would not, and then both retired upstairs, bidding goodnight in the process.

Once in the quiet of his room, the actor continued his letter writing. There was one to the landlord, enclosing money for his room and board; then another to his solicitor, which showed just how steadfastly Ball had planned his departure:

> If the coroner allows it, please have the things put into the trunks and corded, and wait a reply to you or Mr Wilson from Devon, and act accordingly . . . I would wish, if the coroner will allow it, that my body may be dissected by any, or all, of the surgeons here. Firstly, it will furnish practice. Secondly it will, I presume, be to them desirable; and thirdly, it will be advantageous to the public and profitable to me.

Nobody knows precisely what happened in the hours after he was last seen, but one thing is clear: once his letters were written and neatly addressed, William Wheaton Ball took all three phials of laudanum from the shelf, and swallowed the contents with his glass of rum.

At 10 a.m. on 6 April, theatre manager William Mills came to the inn, looking for Ball. He was directed to his room, where he tried unsuccessfully to gain entry. Concerned because he could hear a strange, throat-gurgling sound coming from inside, he ran to the bar and gained the help of the landlord and landlady. They all went inside to find out what was going on, and were met by a gruesome sight. There was Ball in bed; the gurgling sound growing more profound as time went on. He was obviously not dead, but his life hung by a thread. A doctor was called for, and on seeing the empty phials of poison, he sent for a stomach pump. It was too late to save the man's life, however, and around twenty minutes after the procedure, he passed away.

On the dressing table were the letters William Ball had been so busy working on the night before. Wilson picked up the one addressed to him, and read it aloud:

Sir, this will inform you, when you find me dead, the cause thereof. You will find by the contents of the accompanying letters I am poisoned, and by the phials remaining. I have placed on the table a sovereign and a few shillings, with which you will be paid, and any other expenses incurred can be defrayed from Devon or the produce of the effects left.

The letter then went on to instruct Wilson to package up his possessions immediately, and send them in accordance with his solicitor's wishes.

Despite the fact that Ball had gone into great detail as to what should happen to his belongings and his body after death, the man did not reveal any information as to why he had poisoned himself. The only clue came when police officers looked through the huge number of documents on his dressing table, and found a contract of separation between him and a woman called Kate, who turned out to be his estranged wife. There were also other items related to their unsuccessful marriage, and a letter he had written on the evening of his death. This revealed that despite his successful career, the man had not yet recovered from the breakdown of his marriage.

When you receive this, my darling Kate, I shall be free of all the troubles of the world, and I hope in peace . . . I feel I love you still most dearly; may you be ever blessed, and bless those about you . . . Tis now past eight and I think and hope I shall not be alive at twelve. Perhaps I will write a line underneath when I have taken the poison. Use your best endeavours to console my poor mother. May God ever bless you! I have now swallowed the poison . . . Tis now midnight so I shall not be dead until the sixth of April.

An inquest was called to try to discover exactly what had happened to William Wheaton Ball, but despite contacting various friends and relatives to appear as witnesses, the coroner received no response. This strange occurrence forced him to release a statement, saying that perhaps the mail just hadn't been received by them in time. Either way, the case went ahead, but with only the word of strangers and those who had known the man for a matter of days, there was very little to say. The coroner finished off proceedings and asked the jury not to decide what the cause of death was, but rather what his state of mind had been on the night he took his own life. They retired to ponder the question, before finally coming back into the room.

'The deceased died from the effects of the Laudanum he had taken,' they said. 'But whether he was in a sound state of mind or not at the time of taking it, there was no evidence before the jury to show.' The inquest then came to an end, and William Wheaton Ball's death became another Victorian mystery, with no rhyme or reason as to exactly why he had chosen that time and place to take his own life.

The Death of a Faithless Wife

Actress Lillian Rivers was the wife of actor and playwright James Reynolds. Together they had two children and lived a somewhat colourful life in Philadelphia, USA. However, while each partner had their eccentricities, the main point of concern as far as Reynolds was concerned was his wife's lack of morality. This character trait led newspapers to describe the woman as 'a faithless wife'.

In April 1887, Reynolds discovered that Lillian had been having a passionate affair with another actor, Robert G. Hall, who was married and had a family living in St Louis. Despite their circumstances, the two actors showed no signs of remorse and so Reynolds decided to take revenge. During a heated exchange about the affair, the disgruntled husband took out his pistol and shot at his wife. He then turned the gun on himself and was shot in the head and chest.

Despite the close range, it seems that Reynolds's aim was absolutely dreadful because Lillian only received a slight wound to the upper leg. While he ended up in hospital with his injuries, he was deemed well enough to be released several weeks later. The incident did not have the impact Reynolds had hoped it would, but it did present Lillian with the opportunity she had been waiting for. Telling her husband she could no longer live with his violence, she packed her bags and left him – and her children – behind. Her lover did the same, and the two moved in together.

For a time, the new couple lived in a rented room in a Philadelphia boarding house, registering as Mr and Mrs Burton, and presenting their landlady with a certificate which pledged themselves in marriage, 'the same as though such had been consummated by ceremony'. It certainly wasn't a legal document since Lillian was still married to Reynolds at the time, but it was enough to convince the landlady (and themselves) that they were man and wife.

In the months ahead, they lived a fairly quiet life, until suddenly the tables turned and Hall suspected that his common-law wife was having an affair with a man called Alfred. She denied the accusation, but it was a big turning point in the relationship and they spent their days quarrelling furiously. Having left his wife and children for someone he now believed was cheating on him, Hall soon found himself in a depressing spiral. On 18 May 1887, he wrote a distressing note to his father. 'By the time this letter reaches you,' he said, 'my life will have been ended by my own hand.'

Eleven days later, on 29 May, he wrote another; this time addressed to the local coroner. In the note, he begged the man to tell his father about the death, and to instruct him to do what he wanted with the body. He also wrote that his passing and that of his 'wife' was because of her unfaithfulness with the aforementioned Alfred. Whether or not Lillian knew of the existence of the letters is not known, but the unmailed notes were certainly not hidden, since police found them easily in the days and weeks ahead.

On the evening of 2 June 1887, the couple fought so much that Lillian stormed out of the house, ran to the local sheriff and asked him to arrest Hall for assault and battery. She then went to a friend's house and stayed the night, before returning to the boarding house early the next morning. Unfortunately for her, the sheriff had not yet arrested Hall, and he was waiting for her to return. Incensed that she had spent the entire night away from him, it gave him further reason to doubt her faithfulness. At approximately 7 a.m., the man took out his pistol and shot his lover twice. As she lay gasping on the ground, he then took out a razor and slit her throat from ear to ear.

Hearing the commotion, the landlady ran for the sheriff, as Hall turned the razor on himself and cut his own throat too. By the time police arrived, Lillian was dead and Hall was barely breathing. As the man was rushed to hospital, the news of the woman's death was broken to her first husband. Instead of staying around to find out what happened next, he sensibly packed his bags, took his children and left the town – and unwanted attention – behind.

Doctors were concerned that Hall's injuries would result in his own death, but miraculously he survived and regained consciousness. When he realised that he was still alive and would now be charged with murder, the killer ripped at the bandages on his throat, and literally tore apart the already wounded flesh. As blood flowed from the newly opened wound, doctors announced that there was almost no chance of survival. The loss of blood and trauma had been just too much, they said.

However, much to his chagrin, once again Hall rallied, and as soon as he left hospital, he was taken to a cell in order to await trial. Newspapers were intrigued by the events that had taken place, particularly because Lillian's husband had tried and failed to shoot her just months before. 'What a remarkable coincidence,' wrote one journalist.

The trial took place in October 1887 before Judge Arnold, and surprisingly, Hall showed up in a rather sunny disposition. He spent his time watching the jury, playing with his watch chain and messing around with pieces of paper on his desk. It had been decided by the actor and his defence that he should plead insanity, so as to gain a lighter sentence. It was up to the prosecution, therefore, to convince the jury otherwise. They called upon Dr David P. Richardson, who told the court that he'd visited the prisoner four times in his cell, and had made copious notes about his behaviour.

'I consider that Hall was a very bright man; a man who could talk well on almost any subject that you would suggest. He was very courteous to me and on one occasion I said, "I would to God you were insane, then there would be some excuse for your crime." He replied, "Yes, that when the case came up for trial I would like to be violently insane for forty-eight hours." He talked well on all subjects and I was satisfied from my examination that his mind was not affected from any disease.'

Not so, claimed the defence, and called up Hall's friend and colleague, John C. Ingham. He told the court that between acting jobs, the two had worked as house painters together. According to him, during that time he noticed several things about Hall that led him to think his mind was certainly affected, though he was not forthcoming about what those things were. When pressed, he admitted, 'I was always of the impression that Hall was insane.'

It became apparent that the man was desperately trying to defend his friend, but their boss, Charles C. Smith, poured water over the theory of insanity. He told the court that he had never seen any kind of strange behaviour from Hall. 'I thought he was a man of excitable disposition, quick witted and sharp,' he said.

After the defence gave their closing statements, Hall had one last attempt at playing the insane card. Leaning forward in his chair, he boomed, 'That was beautiful! It was the finest argument I ever heard.' His odd behaviour was not enough to convince the jury, however. They only took minutes to decide that the man had no mental issues and was definitely guilty of murder.

A motion was made by the defence for a new trial, but there could be no get-out clause for Hall. He was sent to prison, and then in May 1888, almost a year since the murder took place, the actor was hanged. He had tried desperately to convince everyone that he was insane, but in the end the belief of all involved was that his motivation had been jealousy. 'His plans for the murder were laid out with the utmost coolness,' wrote one reporter.

The Terrible Shooting of Minnie Allen

Minnie Allen (real name Millie Lighthawk) was an American actress and singer. In the days after her death, newspapers would describe her as a third-rate performer who appeared in second-rate establishments. Actually, this was not true. Minnie was in her early twenties and by 1900 had already toured around the United States with various companies, appearing in burlesque, melodrama and farce. She had a huge amount of support from the public and critics alike and was praised wherever she appeared.

In October 1900, the woman was in *The Bifurcated Girl* with actor Will H. Murphy. In the show, Minnie played a stage-struck young woman who was more than prepared to squander $20,000 on her dreams of becoming a star. When the company reached Boston, a reporter from the *Sunday Post* went to see the show and made a special point of praising the two actors: 'They are spoken of as two very clever young entertainers. Miss Allen is said to possess much beauty and magnetism; and to be an accomplished musician and vocalist. Mr Murphy is an eccentric comedian and dancer of the higher grade. Success for them is confidently predicted.'

The reporter was correct. The show was very popular with audiences, and went on the road for some months. In early 1901 they reached Syracuse, where a journalist noted: 'Miss Allen is a clever helpmate in the dual performance, which closes with a neatly contrived and somewhat startling illusion.'

In July 1901, Minnie travelled to Atlanta, where she performed in a play called *An Uptown Flat*. There, a journalist was exceptionally kind with his comments, describing her as: 'A clever comedienne who for several seasons past has been prominently featured in several of the leading farce comedy productions. [She] will be on hand and will try and sing and dance herself into the good graces of all present.' During the show, Minnie received heaps of support from the audience, and was forced to add another song to her act to quell their enthusiasm. She was praised considerably for her 'clever work', according to one reporter from the *Atlanta Constitution*.

As soon as she had finished work on *An Uptown Flat*, Minnie travelled to Omaha, Nebraska. A talented scriptwriter, Minnie had penned a play – *The Arizona Female Bandit* – which was said to have included 'all the colour of western life she could find'. Her intention was to train a cast of amateur actors and then take the performance on the road, playing in small theatres and other establishments.

The audition process was undertaken with great care, and finally Minnie felt she had chosen the correct actors for the job. Rehearsals began in earnest, but it was soon discovered that there was a problem. Thad Brookie, a former painter who had spent the past twenty years in and out of prison for burglary, had been hired to play the character of detective, William Desmond. He had recently turned his attentions to acting, and was described locally as a rather odd, eccentric fellow. Why Minnie thought he was the right person for her play is unclear, but she would go on to regret her decision. As rehearsals continued over the next few days, Brookie became utterly obsessed with her, to the point of insanity.

The actress was married (and her eight-year-old stepson was on tour with her), and any advances from Brookie were turned down. Still, he would not give up, and during rehearsals his attentions grew more and more intense. He even complained that his role gave him no chance to be close to Minnie at all, and at one point the man even threatened to kill her if she did not succumb to him. Instead of firing Brookie there and then, the actress simply ignored his bizarre comments and continued with her work.

The disinterest in both the advances and the threats had a significant effect on Brookie, and led to even more anger. When he discovered that the main lead actor – Bert Adams – was required to run into Minnie's arms during one of the last scenes, he protested. The lines to accompany the scene were highly emotional, and Adams delivered them with great flair. 'Thank God I have found you at last,' he exclaimed. 'Never again shall you leave my sight.' He then kissed Minnie passionately.

The jealous Brookie decided that the scene was totally uncalled for and inappropriate. During a rehearsal on 4 August 1901, he created such a stir that the scene was interrupted.

'Oh cut that out!' he cried. 'That don't go in rehearsals!'

Despite his protests, Bert Adams and Minnie both agreed that it was a pivotal part of the storyline and needed to stay in.

'Cut out this kissing business!' shouted Brookie, but he was told to be quiet.

Bert Adams, who was described locally as a rather dashing young man, seemed to enjoy Brookie's antics. He stirred the pot even more by suggesting that the kissing scene was such an important part that perhaps the two should rehearse it a second time. Not surprisingly, Brookie objected strongly to this suggestion and lashed out at the two actors. Bystanders told the man that he was making a fool of himself and eventually threw him out of the boarding house where rehearsals were taking place. They did not use the door though; they apparently hurled him straight out of the ground-floor window.

Adams and Minnie brushed themselves off from the outburst and began rehearsing again, enrolling the help of another actor to play the part of detective William Desmond. Brookie was considered to be fired, and the acting company did not expect to see him again. However, the man's obsession with Minnie was not going to dissipate so easily. After being thrown from the building, the disgruntled man disappeared for a time, but then secretly returned with a pistol in his pocket.

Unknown to the cast, Brookie managed to gain access to the building and waited in the shadows for the fateful scene to play out in front of him. When it did, he quietly stepped into the room, pointed the gun at Minnie and fired two shots into her chest. As the other actors scrambled to restrain him, the actor silently turned the pistol on himself, took a shot to the head and died instantaneously.

As Brookie's body lay on the ground, various cast members and other guests at the boarding house raced to Minnie's assistance. She was still alive but barely, and was carried into an adjoining room before being rushed to nearby Clarkson Hospital. The next day newspapers told readers that she clung onto life but family had been told there was no hope. They were correct, and the actress passed away just hours later. Outside the boarding house, crowds of people exchanged views and stories of the events. Some, who knew the rehearsals were going on, believed the gunshots to be part of the play. Others discussed Brookie and his unsavoury character, while shaking their heads in disbelief.

Newspapers were ablaze with the story, describing every part in gruesome detail. 'A third rate actor kills the leading woman and then blows out his own brains,' wrote a journalist for the *Burlington Evening Gazette*, while the *Democrat* described it in rather more flowery terms. 'Love turns to tragedy,' it declared.

Given that Minnie Allen was only in her mid-twenties when she was murdered, her talents as an actress, singer and playwright would never be fully recognised. However, the *Burlington*

Evening Gazette gave her a fairly fitting tribute when they announced that the actress 'had given considerable of her time to dramatic composition, an art in which she displayed great perseverance and some skill'.

The Attempted Assassination of the Queen

The attempted assassination of Queen Victoria comes under the category of a 'stage' murder, not because she was an actress, but rather because she was (and still is) one of the most famous women in the world. However, just because she was beloved by many thousands did not mean she was immune from criticism from that ever-so-modern phenomenon, 'haters'. During her lifetime, Victoria was said to have had at least seven attempts on her life, but perhaps the most shocking was on 10 June 1840, when she was pregnant with her first child.

The scandal happened when Queen Victoria and her husband, Prince Albert, were riding in their carriage around 6.20 p.m., having just left Buckingham Palace. Unknown to them, a young man by the name of Edward Oxford was currently standing in Green Park, anticipating their arrival. One woman who saw him was Sarah Brown, a tourist who happened to be waiting for the entourage to pass. As she walked through the park, she was whistled at by Oxford, but this did not impress her. She did, however, turn around, but not until she was at a safe distance. When she did so, Brown was shocked by what she saw.

'He was stooping and in the act of loading a pistol,' she said, 'the handle of which he concealed under the tail of his frock coat. I distinctly saw him put something into the muzzle of the pistol, after which he stuffed in some paper and then rammed the whole down.'

Brown went about her business, and watched as the royal couple's procession moved along Constitution Hill. She, like various others, had a great interest in waving to the Queen as she passed, but as she did so, Oxford stepped out from the small crowd, raised the pistol and fired towards the carriage. The onlookers screamed, dogs barked and the Queen's horses rose up into the air with shock. From inside the carriage, Prince Albert turned to see what the noise was. As he did so, Oxford drew out a second pistol from the back of his coat, and fired that too. By this time the carriage was a little past the would-be murderer, and neither the first nor second shot went near their intended target.

A holidaymaker by the name of Perks was quite a fan of the Queen, but had never seen her in person. On hearing that she was to be making an appearance, he had gone out of his way to find a good spot where he would be able to get a clear view. What he didn't know, of course, was that he was to get much more than just a glimpse of the Queen. He later gave a statement to officers. 'The prisoner was standing near me,' he said. 'He had his hands folded across his coat. As the carriage came within a few yards of him I saw him take his right arm from the left side of his coat, and pulling out a pistol he fired it. He held it as if he was fighting a duel at point-blank. I thought it was an act of rejoicing, but instantly afterwards he drew a second pistol from his breast. He then crossed his arms and stooped as he took aim, and then fired.'

While Perks recalled Prince Albert being very red in the face, the Queen seemed somewhat calmer and apparently stood up slightly, before being pushed back down by her husband.

Witnesses said she then leaned forward to speak to Albert, though the official line was that she had stooped forward to avoid being hit. The couple then moved on quickly towards Hyde Park. 'I felt stunned and stupefied,' recalled Perks. 'I could not believe that Her Majesty's life was attempted.' He then ran towards Covent Garden, where he told a local policeman what had happened.

Another man, by the name of Woodstock, also saw the debacle, and described how the Queen's carriage was so low that the bullets must have passed straight over the heads of the royal couple. He recalled that there were no screams, that the cortège did not slacken its pace, and that Edward Oxford very calmly stayed where he was after he had fired the two pistols.

Whether the man was waiting to be seized or merely too shocked by his own actions to run away could not be deciphered right away, but he gave his opinion to police, just a day later. When asked if he had made any kind of attempt to leave the scene, Oxford answered, 'Oh, no, to be sure – that would have been of no use. I should have stood just as much chance as a fly in a treacle bottle.'

So the shooter stood stock-still and was wrestled very quickly by various members of the public, one of them being a man called Joshua Lowe, who had been standing away from Oxford at the time of the shooting. On seeing the events unfold, however, he rushed forward and seized him. At the same time his nephew, Albert, took the pistols from Oxford's hand.

Across the road, cabinet-maker William Clayton had heard the gunshots and was so incensed that he made it his mission to find the culprit. 'Where are they who did it?' he cried, 'Where are they who did it?' Sarah Brown, the young woman who had seen Oxford in the park, pointed him out without delay and Clayton ran over towards the man, who was still being handled by Albert and Joshua Lowe. As other members of the public came up to detain Oxford too, things became confused and Clayton saw the gun and actually believed the younger Lowe to be the guilty party.

'You confounded rascal, it was you! How dare you shoot at the Queen?' Clayton shouted. He then snatched one of the weapons and collared the lad. Before Lowe could argue, however, Oxford himself spoke out. 'It was I, it was me that did it,' he said. Clayton let Albert Lowe go but the damage was already done. After being pointed out as the culprit, Albert found himself the object of the crowd's disdain. He later told the court that the mob knocked the pistol out of his hand, and as he stooped to pick it up, various men seized him from all angles, tearing at his clothes and kicking him repeatedly.

The elder Lowe was now so worked up that he decided he would not unhand Edward Oxford until he was well and truly locked up at the police station. Even though officers were now leading him away, the man continued to hold onto his collar, while Albert Lowe trotted alongside, holding the pistol he had been able to retrieve from the ground. During the journey to the station, Joshua Lowe turned to his nephew. 'Look out, Albert. I dare say he has some friends.'

'You are right, I have!' Oxford cried, as Lowe and the police continued to haul him away.

As the group marched down the road, the attempted murderer was jeered at by various members of the public. One brazen young lad shouted that the pistols probably didn't have any bullets in them anyway, to which Oxford replied, 'If your head had been between the carriage and the pistols, you would have known whether they had or not.'

Once at the station, Oxford was searched. On his person was found a knife, a small amount of money, a key and a piece of wadding. The wadding had the mark of the pistol's hammer on one side and the cap on the other. When asked why this was on his person, Oxford replied that it was to stop the gun going off in his pocket. 'If you go to the park, you will find the other piece of wadding,' he said.

'Were there balls in the pistols?' a policeman asked.

'There were balls in the pistols,' Oxford replied.

The man was then charged with 'maliciously and with intent to destroy life, firing two pistols at Her Majesty the Queen and His Royal Highness Prince Albert'.

In a bizarre twist, William Clayton, the cabinet-maker who had mistakenly thought Albert Lowe was the shooter, was thought to be an accomplice and led away to the station as well. He was placed in a cell, searched, discovered to still have one of Oxford's pistols in his possession, and then – according to him – left alone with it. Apparently Clayton wasted no time in investigating it. He stuck his finger down the barrel and left a mark so that he could later decipher which gun he had actually seized. The policeman who arrested him gave a different story, and said that the man was never left alone with the gun. He did admit, however, that Clayton left a mark in the barrel, which could still be seen when the case went to court.

Meanwhile, instead of going home, the royal couple went to visit the Queen's mother to assure her that everything was okay. After the short visit, they once again climbed into the carriage and past throngs of people who had heard the news. The crowd cheered and cried as they saw them heading past, and then proceeded to walk with the carriage as it headed back to Buckingham Palace.

While the Queen smiled and waved to everyone, it was widely reported that the moment she entered her private rooms at the palace, reality hit and Victoria broke down and wept for a long time. That done, she regained her stoic attitude, went downstairs for dinner and greeted a variety of friends and family who had come to wish her well and see for themselves that she was okay. 'The Queen appeared perfectly recovered from the effects of her recent alarm,' said one reporter.

Back at the station, the investigation was in full swing, Officers found that the guns used by Oxford were duelling pistols, and while no powder was found on his person, the guns had recently been discharged. During the first round of questioning, the prisoner's main concern was whether the Queen and Prince Albert had survived the attack, and several witnesses heard him ask over and over again if they had been hurt.

'Neither appeared at all alarmed,' an officer told him.

'Oh, I know to the contrary,' snapped Oxford. 'For when I fired the first pistol, Albert was about to jump from the carriage and put his foot out, but when he saw me present the second pistol, he immediately drew back.' The man then seemed to revel in the knowledge that he had caused such a fuss on an otherwise mundane evening.

'None of them knew it was I that did it', he said, 'until I declared that I was the man, upon which, two of them seized me by the collar, two more kept pulling at the skirts of my coat, and one of them grabbed me behind, which was quite unnecessary, as I had no intention to run away ... There is plenty determined to be in the investigation. I suppose they all speculated upon being called as witnesses.'

Once the dramatics had calmed down slightly, Oxford gave his address as 6 West Street, West Square, Surrey, and reeled off the names of his family and associates. He then told police that he had never been ill a day in his life, 'except when I was blown up by gunpowder'. His mother later confirmed and explained this story. Apparently the boy had been playing with a cannon in the garden, and it went off, singeing his hair, eyelashes and eyebrows, and burning his face to such a degree that his mother had to sit up with him every night, bathing it with a special lotion.

Oxford was asked by officials what object he had used in his attempted assassination of Queen Victoria. 'These gentlemen will tell you my object,' he replied, pointing to police officers. 'There are thousands by this time know my object; the act shows it.' The attention brought to him seemed to make Oxford extremely excited. Indeed, when the police began interviewing witnesses just yards from his cell, the man was seen sauntering up and down, listening intently and looking remarkably pleased with himself.

When it was time for cabinet-maker William Clayton to be interviewed, he asked for a cup of water first. Oxford – who by this time was seated in the inspector's office – heard the conversation and demanded he have some too. As Clayton passed him, the prisoner unexpectedly asked if he believed the Queen was injured.

'What did you put in the barrels?' Clayton said. Oxford wasn't about to discuss his case with a fellow accused, however.

'I have answered a dozen questions,' he said. 'I shall answer no more.'

Luckily for Clayton, during his subsequent interview it was discovered that he was an innocent man who had merely tried to restrain the real shooter. He was instantly unhanded and allowed on his way.

Police Sergeant Howie then offered Oxford a cup of coffee, which the prisoner held up in a toast. 'Well, old fellow, here's to your good health.'

The surprised sergeant replied, 'I'm glad you like it,' and Oxford burst into peals of laughter.

'Yes, but I've tasted a good deal better before,' he replied.

Oxford was exceptionally glad to talk about his crime to the authorities; in fact, he relished every question and piece of information he could give. When the questions stopped, however, he became agitated and disturbed, filling any and all silence with intense whistles or random observations.

'I consider the Queen unfit to reign over English people!' he boomed.

'Why?' asked an officer, but the prisoner just gave him silence and a vague look.

All of the information gathered in the station was relayed to journalists and printed far and wide. While reporters told the public that the man had the appearance of a mechanic aged between eighteen and twenty years old, Oxford actually told police that he was seventeen and 'had been brought up to the bar'.

'What, as a barrister?' asked an astonished officer.

'No!' snapped Oxford. 'To the bar of a public house!' He then played something of a cat-and-mouse game with the police, as they tried to decipher what it was he actually did for a living. When asked if he was a pot boy, he screwed up his face and declared himself above such duties. A publican, perhaps? No, he had not been quite that high up. After much prodding, it was discovered that the young man was a barman; first in Birmingham and then in London. His last place of employment was the Hog and Pound, located in a lane opposite Oxford Street.

Scandal-loving members of the press rushed to the pub to interview the landlord. 'He left my services on 1st May,' the man told reporters. 'He had lived here for three months and the only eccentricity he was possessed of was a habit of continual laughing. It was as a consequence of this, that the man was discharged.' One example of his cackling was when the landlady fell down the stairs and was left relatively unhurt but very much shaken. Instead of rushing to help, Oxford merely stood and chuckled hysterically at her misfortune.

Questions continued at the station, where Oxford informed officers that money was no trouble in his life, and he could quite easily have as much as he pleased. He also told them that he had been shooting for quite some time, but was a much better aim with a rifle than he was with a pistol. He did, however, declare himself to be 'a very good shot' with both.

'You have now fulfilled your engagement,' an officer told him.

'No I have not!' Oxford replied, to which the policeman shouted that as far as the attempt on the Queen's life was concerned, he had gone as far as he would ever go. The prisoner stared at him in silence.

While a stern watch was kept over Edward Oxford, officers were sent to his lodgings to find out more about him. Searching the premises, they found a locked box containing a sword, some gunpowder and balls suitable for the pistols used in the assassination attempt. They also found a strange black cap, alongside which was a list of fictitious names of a secret society. Later the prisoner was dismayed to be presented with the items, claiming that he had meant to destroy them before his encounter with the Queen but had completely forgotten to do so.

Oxford did not deny that he belonged to a secret society, though refused to give any further information about it. However, the discovery of some 'letters of a serious nature' on his person confirmed that he was in correspondence with an organisation called Young England. The rules of the society included that each member be supplied with pistols, a sword, a rifle and a dagger; should use a fictitious name at all times; be willing to take the oath of allegiance; be armed every time the society is ordered to meet; be prepared to wear disguises if ever travelling around the country or going abroad; to never speak during debates; and to obtain full permission if ever absent for more than a month.

The documents found were intriguing and exceptionally detailed. They included minutes of meetings and a peculiar note detailing one particular get-together. According to the author, the debate was taking place when there was a loud knock at the door. Convinced that the enemy had arrived, the society members covered their faces and drew their swords. One member even rushed to the fireplace with an armful of secret papers, while another readied himself to set the whole house ablaze. Finally, an old woman – presumably the landlady of the establishment – was sent to the front door, only to discover a group of young boys, cheekily playing 'chap door, run'.

Because all names on the documents were fictitious, there was no way of finding out who the real members were. Oxford remained tight-lipped, as per the society guidelines, which left the police to wonder if the organisation really did exist. They wondered aloud if the prisoner had somehow dreamt the whole thing up himself, but this seemed too far-fetched even for him. However, officers were proved correct when Oxford's mother recognised his writing in every one of the documents, and the society was confirmed as just a figment of his imagination.

Reporters were intrigued by what appeared to be a crazy fantasist, and made it their duty to find out everything they could about his former employment. They discovered that in one job, Oxford was known as being a very forward boy, while in another he fought consistently with a fellow barman and was dismissed as a result. Yet another described the man as having a 'sullen temper and very reserved in his actions'.

However, the best piece of news for reporters and police alike was when they returned to the Hog and Pound to interview customers. There they discovered that instead of leaving quietly after being fired, Oxford frequently told people he was still working at the establishment. He would then constantly turn up there and engage in conversation with regulars.

One customer – a perfumer called Thomas Lawrence – disclosed that he had known Edward Oxford quite well, and on Easter Sunday had gone with him to Hyde Park. There was quite a crowd gathering there, and Lawrence surmised that they were probably looking for the Queen.

'They will be disappointed,' replied Oxford. 'She is at Windsor.'

This knowledge of the Queen's whereabouts took Lawrence by surprise, but he did not say anything more about it. Shortly after, as they were in the parlour at the Hog and Pound, Oxford told Lawrence that he had just lost some money in a bet made at a local shooting gallery. When his acquaintance showed surprise that he frequented such a place, Oxford pulled out a flattened ball to prove it.

'You would be more fit to shoot at a haystack than at a target,' quipped a customer who had overheard the conversation. This did not please Oxford one bit.

When police heard the comments about the man visiting the shooting gallery, they investigated further. They found that he had been a regular for some time, and had behaved in rather a strange manner while there. One example of this peculiar behaviour was when Oxford told the proprietor that he had been locked in a house for a considerable amount of time, and then an attempt had been made on his life. Despite his strange demeanour, shooting galleries around London still allowed him onto their premises. An associate later came forward to confirm that the man had been to various arcades in the past few months, and had frequently bragged about having owned pistols.

Around the time he was hanging around the shooting arcades, Oxford was also tracking down places to buy new revolvers. To that end, he appeared at several establishments, and eventually bought two distinct pistols and a powder flask. However, before he did so, Oxford asked all manner of questions, such as how far the guns would fire, and whether or not he could obtain a discount. Shop assistant Frederick Garrett later said that the man spent ten minutes bargaining on the price before they finally reached a deal that both were happy with.

Shortly after, he visited another shop in order to enquire about the sale of bullets. Strangely, shop assistant John Gray was someone Oxford had gone to school with. However, Gray pretended not to recognise him until forced to do so by Oxford. Later in court, he was asked why he had done this, and replied that he had no wish to take up an acquaintance with him again. The two exchanged small talk for a while, and Oxford tried a few caps for his pistols and enquired about small canisters of gunpowder. However, when it became clear that nothing in the store was of any interest, Gray directed him to a gunsmith and did not hear from him again.

The attempted assassination of Queen Victoria was deemed as treason and taken extremely seriously by the palace and the government. Ministers were sent to investigate the matter completely, which included interviewing the prisoner. He assured them that he always slept extremely soundly, 'and so I shall do here', pointing to the bed in his cell. He remained eerily calm and together, and the next morning his greatest concern seemed to be that he could get washed and dressed, so that he 'can be conveyed in a clean slate before the parties who are to judge of my conduct'. Later he had a question: 'Are the cells in all station houses as good as the one to which I've been confined?' he asked.

'Yes,' replied the officer in charge.

'From what I have heard and read in the newspapers, your account is very incorrect,' Oxford said.

While Oxford was being interviewed, Her Majesty was visited by various members of her family, friends and cabinet. Indeed, on the day after the shooting, it looked as though there was a never-ending stream of people going in and out of the palace. Finally, however, it was time for her daily carriage ride, and while some courtiers imagined she would decline to go that day, Victoria brushed their opinions aside.

The Queen sat with Prince Albert and they rode through the park together, while all around them crowds whistled and cheered her bravery. 'The cheers of a vast assemblage of British subjects instantly burst forth, with an animation and sincerity we have seldom witnessed,' wrote a journalist for the *Examiner*. 'Every hat was waved, and every heart seemed gladly to beat on seeing their Sovereign apparently in good health and spirits still among them.' The journalist went on to describe how the cheers of the public were a great punishment for the man who was not successful in cutting the Queen's life short.

In the days following the shooting, a great number of people walked to Buckingham Palace in order to try to gleam some kind of knowledge as to Victoria's health. Pregnancy in Victorian times was a complicated and often deadly experience, and no one was more aware of this than the Queen. She had heard many stories of family members dying in childbirth, and was continually reminded of the dangers by her advisors and ministers. Great discussions were held over what would happen if she did pass away, and who would take over the responsibilities of her position. Newspapers printed whole articles on the subject, and every mention of the baby's imminent birth was often concluded with the words, 'if preserved amid the dangers from which the highest rank is not exempt'.

But it wasn't just the Queen's health that interested the people. Curious members of the public – along with amateur sleuths – wanted to see the spot where Oxford had tried to take her life. There they discussed what had happened; gave their opinions on why it had taken place; dispelled rumours and created many more. One of the Queen's guards was the first to examine the wall close to where the shots had been fired, and found a white mark, the size of his hand. According to him, it looked as though the brick had been knocked out in that area, and thoroughly believed that it was made by Oxford's bullet. However, he later had to admit that while he was confident on the cause of the hole, he had not seen any remnants of fallen brick nearby, and furthermore, absolutely no trace of any bullets.

During the hours that passed after the shooting, police had combed the area, first with their hands, then with a broom. While they did not find any immediate trace of balls from the guns, a lot of interest was found in the original mark on the wall, and a second found fourteen yards away. Still, it could not be confirmed that these were made by a bullet, and the search for the offending items continued. Finally, a great deal of dirt was taken back to the palace to be sifted. Even that extensive job proved to be in vain when no bullets were found, and everyone scratched their heads in bewilderment.

In the end, it was two young boys who found what they believed to be one of the bullets, flattened under some gravel. They handed the item over to the police and enjoyed being of great interest to reporters the next day. The excitement was short-lived, however, as when police examined the ball, they discovered it was much too big to fit either of Oxford's pistols and had absolutely no relation to the murder attempt at all. Officers concluded that the evidence must have been planted there, and the search for the actual bullets continued.

Rumours circulated widely that the pistols were not loaded with any balls at all, and the whole thing was a farce. However, things looked up when 'a very intelligent gentleman' decided to investigate the crime scene and found another indentation on the wall. He deciphered that it had been made by a bullet, but rather strangely it was his own son who contradicted that theory. The man was connected with the gun manufacturing industry and when summoned to appear before the Privy Council was unable to say one way or the other as to whether the pistols were loaded at the time of the shooting. The police remained confused, and the search for any evidence continued.

While hundreds of people milled around Buckingham Palace in the hope of finding a bullet, many more trekked to the Home Office in Whitehall. There they tried to catch a glimpse of Edward Oxford arriving for interview, and asked attending officers if there was any hope of being allowed inside. 'No persons but those engaged in the investigation will be permitted to be present,' came the reply.

While reporters were disappointed, they were happy when whispers came from the court, claiming 'traitorous conspiracies' had occurred. There was talk of an accomplice who gave a signal to Oxford shortly before he began shooting at the royal party. Journalists were intrigued but soon disappointed. Further reports came out that the whispers were wrong; the only guilty party was Oxford, who planned 'the insane and wicked project' himself. The prisoner was then sent to Newgate Prison to await trial. His crime was high treason and a commitment was written by the Home Secretary of State:

To the Keeper of Her Majesty's Gaol in Newgate . . . These are, in Her Majesty's name, to authorize and require you to receive the body of Edward Oxford, sent you for high treason, and you are to keep him safe and close until he shall be delivered by due course of law, and for so doing this shall be your warrant.

As is the case with most scandals, journalists took great delight in delving into the life and family of Edward Oxford. They discovered that his father had died twelve years before, and his mother – Hannah Oxford – had formerly owned a coffee shop. In the months before the assassination attempt, she had lived with her daughter in London lodgings, and Oxford frequently moved in and out with them.

His mother later told the story of how she came to lose the coffee shop. Apparently Oxford would disturb and intimidate the customers to such a degree that they complained bitterly about him. One day, she locked him in the cellar as punishment, but on his return he still acted up and caused a scene. Eventually people stopped frequenting her establishment altogether and the business went under.

During one particular violent exchange between Oxford and his mother, he punched her in the face and bloodied her nose. Hannah left London shortly afterwards and, in an attempt to escape her son for good, went back to Birmingham, where she had once lived. Just days later, the attempted shooting took place and the police travelled to the city in order to interview her. When they knocked on the door of the place Hannah was currently residing, they were met by a severely shocked woman.

Oxford's mother had no knowledge of what her son had been up to and, on being told the circumstances, responded with great emotion. The woman took the first train back to London, but not before police interviewed her and discovered a great deal of stories about Oxford's distant and more recent past.

One particularly insightful tale revolved around the man's interest in pistols. Hannah Oxford told officers that her son was known to have had one for several months, but he told her it belonged to a friend. Initially she did not think anything of it, since she believed he would never use it. However, when Oxford began playing with gunpowder in his bedroom, Hannah became concerned, but only because she felt the hobby was a waste of money. One day, the housekeeper of the lodging house noticed a pistol sticking out of his pocket and confronted his mother about it. The woman did not know quite what to say, but assured the housekeeper that she was not to worry; that she was sure her son was hoping to gain a job, but he needed shooting experience to qualify.

The housekeeper made no further enquiry, though she and the other residents of the house became very concerned when the man was seen and heard taking part in shooting practice from his open bedroom window. It was also revealed that Oxford had a creepy habit of locking himself in the room like a hermit, only emerging when his mother called him for dinner. Later, a friend came forward to reveal that the very night before the attempted shooting, Oxford had taken great pleasure in showing him one of the pistols.

'Is it loaded?' asked the friend.

'It is loaded,' he replied.

When the police asked Hannah Oxford if her son had given any indication of acquiring pistols for an unseemly purpose, she shook her head. 'My boy was always a quiet, good boy, of steady, sober habits, and of mild disposition,' she said. However, when police interviewed Oxford's sister, she gave a very different view. According to her, he was frequently given to rages, and would often throw items at her as she innocently walked past. On at least one occasion, he had held a gun to her head while she was in bed.

Poor Hannah Oxford was in a terrible position. On the one hand, she wanted to protect her son, but on the other, she knew he was a temperamental person who had done more than one bad thing in his life. In the end, her conscience got the better of her, and instead of cementing the notion that Edward Oxford wouldn't hurt a fly, Hannah knew she had to tell the truth.

A breakthrough came when Mrs Oxford admitted that her son had been destructive in the past. She also, very sorrowfully, said that in spite of what she had stated previously, she really had been worried about his love of pistols. Taking the lead from her daughter's admission that Edward held a gun to her head, Hannah told police that he had done that to her, too. This, she said, had terrified her greatly. Another time her son had been locked out of the house, and became overcome with anger when he was finally let back in, taking a knife and slicing up his bedclothes.

These revelations were extraordinary, but there were more. Hannah declared that her now deceased husband had shown signs of insanity, and that she too had 'laboured under nervous delusions'. She disclosed her belief that her son's mind had been affected by his parents' mental problems, and added, 'I believe that no balls were in the pistols. The whole thing was a mere boyish frolic.' While many people agreed that the prisoner showed moments of madness, the subject of insanity was later declared ridiculous by the prisoner's brother-in-law. He told investigators that he had never shown any signs that his mind was impaired.

In Newgate Prison, Edward Oxford had suddenly become depressed, presumably as the seriousness of his actions finally sank in. The man was found to be in tears on various occasions and sought comfort from the prison chaplain. According to reports, during the meeting Oxford cried and told the chaplain that his own life was over, and he now feared for what he had brought onto his mother. He also wrote letters, predominantly to his solicitor, Mr Pelham:

My Dear Sir – Have the goodness to write to Lord
Normandy and ask him to let me have some books to read

– such as *Jack the Giant Killer*, *Jack and the Beanstalk*, *Jack and his Eleven Wives*, *My Little Tom Thumb*, *The Arabian Nights' Entertainments*, and all such books from such celebrated authors. And ask him, as a prisoner of war, whether I may not be allowed on a parole of honour, and on what grounds ask him, does he detain one of Her Majesty's subjects. I remain, respectfully, Edward Oxford.

The letter was leaked to the newspapers, where it was dubbed a silly attempt by 'this young ruffian' to claim insanity and therefore escape jail. Not so, said a note written by a reader. He had heard that Oxford had not asked for such childish material after all. Instead, his request was actually for more 'grown-up' titles such as *Mary Magdalen* and *The Premier and His Eleven Wives*. According to the writer, the letter was apparently handed to Lord Normandy, and 'tears came into the eyes of his Lordship as he read this letter. He slapped his forehead and cried, "What a clever boy – what a knowledge of our literature – what a discrimination in the choice of books. And must he die?" '

By this time, the opinion of Edward Oxford in some quarters was beginning to change. Whereas the would-be assassin had previously been deemed a complete villain for daring to take aim at the Queen, now some members of the public and press were willing to forgive and forget. A reporter for the *Age* observed:

The more the circumstances connected with the alleged attempt to assassinate Her Majesty are calmly considered, the more clear becomes the conviction that the whole thing was nothing but the mischievous action of a most foolish youth, for whom the fitting punishment would be a good flogging at the cart's tail from Newgate to Constitution Hill, and back again. There is now little doubt that the pistols were not loaded with ball; and, therefore, people may spare themselves the trouble of firing against their own garden walls, and taking the flattened bullet to pick it up in Green Park . . .

In risking these remarks, we do not for a moment desire that the young vagabond Oxford should escape punishment. The heart of the empire has received a shock, and he who caused it must not escape with impunity. Viewing his conduct in the mildest light it was that of a cowardly ruffian, impregnated with those liberal principles which Ministers so delight to patronise. The scholar is worthy of them.

The charge of treason against Edward Oxford finally went to court in July 1840. While Queen Victoria was not in attendance, her representatives most certainly were, and so too were various members of the public who had obtained tickets from the Sheriff. When Oxford came into court, all eyes were on him. He once again seemed to play up to the attention, smiling smugly and scouring the public gallery to make sure people were being entertained. Once on the dock, he leaned on his elbows and played absent-mindedly with some flowers that were in front of him. The people in court were intrigued.

Once the jury had been sworn in, the Attorney General Sir John Campbell, on behalf of the prosecution, stood up and addressed them. 'May it please your Lordships – Gentlemen of the jury – you are now called upon to discharge a most solemn and important duty. Such is the entire confidence on both sides in the jury, which has now been summoned here today, that there has not been a single challenge either on the part of the

Crown or the part of the prisoner. Gentlemen, the prisoner at the bar stands charged before you with high treason, the greatest crime known to the law, and he stands charged with that offence in its most aggravated form, via that he has made a direct attempt upon the life of the Sovereign . . .'

When the initial introductions were over, the witnesses were called. These included those at the scene; people who knew and worked with Oxford; police officers and many more. The evidence included huge amounts of detail on the mental health of his father and grandfather, both of whom had been known to have episodes of madness. In his granddad's case, these scenes included attacking a family member with a spit, declaring himself 'the Pope of Rome', and smashing up his entire house.

His father's episodes were even more brutal. When Hannah initially refused to marry the man, he took out a knife and threatened to kill himself with it. When this violent plea did not work, he then presented a pistol and said he would blow his head off. The woman eventually agreed to marry him, since by this point she was too scared to turn him down. However, this still didn't stop the emotional blackmail.

On various occasions before the wedding, Mr Oxford became inebriated and abusive. Then when he received a bad character reference just hours before their marriage, he set fire to the couple's savings, right in front of his fiancée. Once the couple began having children, Oxford Sr became extremely violent and threw items at Hannah's head and body. He would then starve his pregnant wife and make fun of her appearance by imitating a baboon.

On one particularly horrific occasion, the man held a gun to her head, and then stabbed her breast with a file. As milk and blood poured from the wound, he showed no emotion whatsoever. Then during another episode, he led a fully grown horse into the living room of their home, in an apparent attempt to get a reaction out of his wife. Despite leaving the family on many occasions, Oxford Sr continued to return and victimise them. Finally, however, it all ended in 1829 when he passed away.

The trial of Edward Oxford was intense, and questions covered every detail, from his bizarre habit of crying and hysterically laughing at the same time, to bullying his friends by beating them with stingy nettles. A story was even shared by his mother that showed Oxford terrifying a pregnant woman as she travelled in a carriage. Apparently he had somehow got behind the vehicle and put his head through the window, making an almighty noise in the process. This bizarre event resulted in him being arrested and escorted home. The next day, his browbeaten mother visited the woman to make sure she was okay, but according to her, Oxford remained indifferent to her welfare.

When everything had been presented to the court over a couple of days, the presiding judge, Lord Denham, summed up the whole case to the jury. Putting a great deal of emphasis on whether the man actually intended to kill the Queen, Denham told them that they must 'determine whether Oxford fired the pistols, and whether they were loaded with bullets, and then to consider whether the prisoner was insane'.

The jury listened carefully and then retired to consider their verdict. Despite the fact that the case had gone on for days, it took the gentlemen only forty-five minutes to discuss the matter and come back to court with a decision. On their return, the spokesman stood up.

'We find the prisoner, Edward Oxford, guilty of discharging the contents of two pistols, but whether or not they were loaded with ball has not been satisfactorily proved to us, he being of unsound state of mind at the time.'

As soon as the verdict was read out, a long discussion erupted between the Attorney General and the rest of the courtroom. The main bone of contention seemed to be the fact that the jury had been unable to come to a conclusion as to whether or not the guns were loaded. If this – coupled with his insanity – was the case, then the man would be acquitted.

'I refer their lordships to an Act of Parliament,' said the Attorney General, 'the 40th of George III, which provides that persons acquitted on the ground of insanity shall be imprisoned during Her Majesty's pleasure. I presume that the jury intend to acquit the prisoner on the ground of insanity by the verdict they gave, and therefore I apply to their lordships under the Act of Parliament.'

The conversation raged on, with one barrister scolding the Attorney General for seemingly trying to change the wording of the Act of Parliament, 'in order to suit the purposes of the Crown'. It was then requested that the jury be sent back to their room to discuss whether or not the gun had actually fired any bullets. 'They have not applied their minds to this point,' said the Attorney General, sarcastically.

'We could not decide the point, because there was no satisfactory evidence produced before us to show that the pistols were loaded with bullets,' replied the foreman. That said, they were still instructed to retire and reconsider their overall verdict. While they were away, the Attorney General once again stood his ground.

'It would be monstrous,' he said, 'to suppose that a person like the prisoner should be again let loose upon society to endanger the life of Her Majesty or her subjects.' After an hour the jury returned and gave the verdict of not guilty on the grounds of insanity. 'That being the case,' said the Attorney General, 'I have now humbly to move your Lordships, on behalf of the Crown, that the prisoner at the bar, Edward Oxford, be confined in strict custody during Her Majesty's pleasure.'

'That is a matter of course,' replied the judge, before discharging the jury and declaring the court closed until next session.

While Edward Oxford was carted off to begin his new life in an asylum (which would eventually end with him being shipped to Australia to reinvent himself), the Queen was told of the developments and was absolutely furious. For her, it was purely unacceptable to think of the man living in an asylum when he should have received much worse for the attempt on her life. She told ministers that if only Oxford had been hanged, it would possibly deter others from trying the same thing. She was ultimately proved correct on this point, as she suffered many attempts on her life in the years to come.

The newspapers did not spend much time lamenting Oxford's lack of punishment, and claimed that it was inevitable that he be found insane, since mental illness seemed to run in his family. The *Evening Standard* decided on the more poetic route, telling readers that 'the whole country has reason to rejoice at the demonstration that no sane man in her dominions could be found to offer violence to a being as formed to be moved and reverenced as our young and lovely Sovereign'.

Other newspapers praised God that the object of Oxford's deluded attention was safe and well. One daily rag – the *Morning Chronicle* – went so far as to wonder what would have happened if the ghastly deed had been successful:

In the event that one shudders to imagine, the lamentation of the people might, indeed have been – 'Then you, and I, and all of us fell down, while bloody treason flourished over us.' And what would have followed, who can realise? We mean not merely the private anguish of a princely heart, nor the blighted hope of a royal succession, nor the sorrows of a generous national sympathy, but the dark cloud that would forthwith have lowered over all the prospects of the people.

We should have been at this moment the vassals of a now foreign potentate. We should have been breathing in the dominions of King Ernest of Hanover! Orangeism would have been rampant. Over Great Britain and Ireland there would have been a letting loose of the bitterest, foulest, and darkest hands. The oppressor would soon have been abroad, and close on his track the insurgent whom the oppressor makes and infuriates. It would have been as if the wheels of time were turned back to a period of dismay, disorder, and fierce collision. Thank heaven! Every day, for weeks to come, will be a day of national thanksgiving. The public heart waits not for formularies.

The Sensational Affair in Warsaw

Marie Wisnowska was a successful Polish actress in the late nineteenth century, known for her dramatic characters and stunning beauty. Unfortunately, her onstage roles didn't provide her with enough excitement, and Wisnowska was always in search of the one scandalous event that would make her an enigma. She wanted to be spoken about around the world, and in June 1890, she got just that.

Prince Bartinieff (aka Bartenjeff) was a Hussar officer, and also a member of one of the wealthiest aristocratic families in Russia. He and Wisnowska had been involved with each other for a time, but his relatives were not thrilled with the idea of having an actress join their family. During one discussion, Bartinieff got into such a row with his father that it soon became physical and an attempt was made on the older man's life.

While the relationship was already shrouded with drama, Wisnowska suddenly announced that she intended to study English and move to America. Her hope was that she would find fame even greater than she had in Warsaw, and she went headlong into her plans. Not surprisingly, Bartinieff was not supportive of the idea of his sweetheart moving to the United States, and by all accounts he became jealous at the very idea of her leaving his side.

On the evening of 30 June 1890, Bartinieff invited the actress to his room, where they had dinner together. Nothing more was seen or heard from the couple after that, until at 1.30 a.m. a shopkeeper was woken up with a loud knocking on the front door. When he finally answered, there stood Bartinieff, demanding some notepaper.

What happened in the next few hours was partly explained when Bartinieff turned up at the home of his colonel, at 4 a.m. Shocked to see the officer at his door, the colonel was even more flabbergasted after he asked what he wanted. Bartinieff wasted no time and told the long, convoluted tale of having murdered Marie Wisnowska. As he came to the end of the story, he placed a gun on the table. The colonel digested the confession for a moment, looked at the pistol and then at his officer.

'I suppose you do not need any advice from me,' he said, and then left the room. While the colonel never told the man directly to shoot himself, by leaving him alone in the room with the firearm, it was most certainly implied. However, when the colonel eventually came back, the officer was still very much alive and sitting at the table.

'I do not have the courage,' he said. This scene was then repeated with another superior, and then the police were called. Officers rushed to Bartinieff's digs, and searched the scene. The remains of dinner were still present, and several bottles of champagne and a vast supply of narcotics lay nearby. While it looked for a moment as though the man had tried to poison his lover, it was soon noted that this was not the case at all. Strangely, even though Bartinieff had presented his gun to the colonel, he hadn't shot Wisnowska either.

Instead, the officer had stabbed his lover several times, and her body now lay on the floor with a pool of blood oozing all around. It was a terrible sight and one that prompted the swift arrest of Bartinieff. However, this wasn't done until after his superiors had punished him in their own way: by cutting off his epaulets. 'You are no longer a member of the military,' the colonel told the former officer, before finally handing him over to the police.

Straightaway, the accused found himself in the middle of a huge problem. Because the crime was so gruesome, he could not find anyone in Warsaw who was prepared to defend him. He was forced to contact a lawyer in Moscow, who only arrived shortly before the trial began. Newspapers took joy in telling readers that the attorney seemed to be the only person brave enough to try to defend such a guilt-laden criminal.

When the case came to trial, it gripped Warsaw and made numerous column inches around the world, except in Russia where all reporting of the matter had been banned. Seventy witnesses were called to the dock, and it all became so riveting that questioning would often stretch well into the late evening, ending only when the clock struck midnight.

While Bartinieff had privately admitted to killing the woman, he had no wish to go to prison, so tried to gain sympathy by saying that the actress had actually wished to die. To that end he produced letters that appeared to be in Wisnowska's hand, begging the soldier to murder her. While these were shocking enough, what came next almost sent the courtroom into a frenzy.

The prosecution pulled out fragments of some letters that had been found in Bartinieff's room on the night his lover died. They had been ripped up and thrown away, but once pieced together, the eerie notes told quite a story. Each one was in Wisnowska's hand, and addressed to her mother. 'Bartinieff will not allow me to depart alive,' one of them said. Another added, 'This is my last hour. Come, Mother! I die involuntarily.' The third note was the most revealing of all: 'There is a conspiracy. I must die. Bartinieff is my executioner. God help me! He dragged me into this lonesome place!'

Of course, these letters totally contradicted the first set, and it didn't take long for the jury to work out what must have happened. On obtaining the notepaper from his neighbour, Bartinieff somehow tried to force his lover to write a letter that would clear him of any blame for her death. However, instead of doing this, Wisnowska actually wrote a letter of despair, which was then destroyed. Whether or not the man eventually persuaded her to write the other letters, or went onto forge her handwriting, was never revealed.

The whole case had taken an even more sinister turn, and whispers and gasps could be heard echoing around the court-room. Any hope of gaining sympathy was long gone with the discovery of the fragments, and it was no surprise when the jury brought back a guilty verdict. Prince Bartinieff was then sentenced to eight years in prison, with hard labour, for the murder of Marie Wisnowska. Jealousy was said to be the reason why he had killed the actress, and the letters were the main evidence against him.

'He will probably be condemned to Siberia,' wrote one journalist. 'He probably will never go there, but he will not be able to show his face in society again.'

The Gory Glasgow Tragedy

Grace Hamilton (or Janet Russell as she was known before entering the acting profession) was the daughter of a particularly well-off, Liverpool-based printer. While the family lived for the most part in England, they would often visit the Scottish town of Millport. There she met a boy called Galbraith Macpherson, who was eight years her senior. The two became friends, but since both lived miles away from each other, the only time they ever really had any contact was when the family went on their frequent trips to Millport.

As Grace and Galbraith grew up, each went in very separate career directions. For a time, Macpherson worked in the family business, but he had a real passion for travel and frequently went abroad. His biggest trip was to Demerara, where he helped run a sugar plantation. Before he left home, however, his friends presented him with a leaving present – a shiny new revolver. After working at the plant for a few years, Macpherson returned home to Glasgow, where he lived with his mother and enjoyed a comfortable life thanks to money inherited from his father.

Grace Hamilton, meanwhile, grew up and married a man of whom nobody approved. Her family seemed loath to say exactly what was wrong with the man, but they were not in the least bit upset when the relationship soured and Grace walked out. Leaving the disastrous marriage behind, she became an actress and worked considerably in the theatre; a decision that pleased her family about as much as the doomed marriage did.

During these years, Macpherson and Hamilton kept in touch by letter, and on his return to Britain, the man went to visit her in London. It was very much a holiday-romance situation, but by November 1883, it was about to take a different turn. As luck would have it, Grace Hamilton was cast as the fairy godmother in *Cinderella*, which was going to be performed at the Grand Theatre in Macpherson's hometown.

This unexpected news excited him, and he set about trying to find his friend a place to stay. After talking to staff at the theatre, Macpherson found Mr and Mrs Deans, who ran a boarding house primarily for actors. He then turned up at their establishment, and told them he was looking for a room for visiting actress, Grace Hamilton.

While this seemed like a normal, everyday request for the couple, behind the scenes Macpherson's behaviour was somewhat questionable. The man decided to introduce himself as Mr Hamilton, implying that he was either the husband or a relative of Grace. Macpherson then toured the building, and on seeing all the rooms on offer, proceeded to rent the parlour and best bedroom for the actress's use.

Grace Hamilton arrived in Glasgow on 28 November 1883 and moved into the Deans' house. The couple took to her immediately and described her as 'one of the most beautiful creatures we have ever seen and a lady in every sense of the word'. The feeling was mutual and the actress spent a lot of time with the couple, revealing pieces of her past and family history.

Over the course of the coming week, Hamilton rehearsed *Cinderella* and worked at the theatre until the early hours of the morning. This did not stop Macpherson's desire to spend many hours with her, however, and he was seen at the guesthouse almost every day. Whenever she was free, the couple would go for walks or drives around town, and on one occasion he turned up at the local pub, wearing a rather beautiful ring.

'Gracie gave it to me,' he bragged to the other customers.

While things looked rather rosy, it was all an illusion. One day when Mrs Deans commented on the status of the relationship, Grace Hamilton confessed to something rather shocking. According to her, while once she had been on friendly terms with Macpherson, he was now showing a rather undesirable aspect of his personality, which frightened her.

The woman said no more about it, and certainly his friends at the time saw nothing they thought was out of the ordinary. To them, Macpherson was a very steady, sensible person who did not have a mean bone in his body. He gave time to his family, loved his mother and frequently travelled to visit his aunt. To all intents and purposes, he was a model citizen; so much so that when friends later discovered he had committed a ghastly crime, they assumed he must have succumbed to a bout of insanity.

By early December 1883, Grace was trying desperately to cool the friendship, but Macpherson did not wish to accept it. When he visited her on the afternoon of the sixth, he was shocked to see a bunch of flowers in her room and flew into a jealous rage. The two rowed violently, which only ended when Macpherson picked up a large stick and smashed it against Grace Hamilton's back. He struck her so hard that it broke in half.

'Don't ever come near me again!' shouted the actress, and Macpherson eventually left.

Despite being in a great deal of pain, that evening the actress left for rehearsals as usual and told her landlady she would not be home until the early hours of the morning. Unfortunately, Macpherson had no wish to go quietly and he followed her to the theatre. There he begged the stage-door employees to let him see Miss Hamilton, and when she sent word that this would not be possible, he tried again . . . and again . . . and again . . .

At 12.30 a.m., Macpherson turned up at the door of the boarding house and began ringing the bell for attention. When he was told that the actress was not yet home, he paced up and down the steps, knocking constantly and refusing all attempts to convince him to leave. When Hamilton arrived home, she was shocked and scared to see the agitated man waiting for her at the front door.

'Won't you let me in?' he asked. 'Can't you give me a bottle of stout?'

'Oh no, I can't do that!' she replied. 'What would Mrs Deans say if I took you up at this time of night?'

'If you don't let me in, I'll poison myself!' Macpherson threatened. He was insistent but Grace stood firm. Bidding him goodnight, she eventually let herself into the house and went to bed. Macpherson was finally forced to give up and go home.

The next morning Mrs Deans received a letter for the actress, and took it up to her bedroom. There she made a point of commenting on the commotion caused by Macpherson just hours before.

'I think he is going insane,' Hamilton told the landlady. 'He'll probably poison himself like he threatened to do last night.'

By 2 p.m., Macpherson arrived at the property again, where he was told by Mrs Deans that Grace was still in bed. He told the landlady that he would wait, and before she could do anything to stop him, the jilted lover sat down in the parlour. Minutes later, he appeared by her side in the kitchen.

'I am sorry about my behaviour last night,' he said. 'It was very foolish to conduct myself that way but I have been very ill for some time. I feel very bad now and my head's all in a muddle.'

The landlady accepted the apology but made it clear it must never happen again. The man promised it would not and left the room. Mrs Deans then told Grace Hamilton that Macpherson was waiting for her, and the actress agreed to see him in her bedroom. The landlady showed him in and then got on with her business of helping the charlady with the house-work. At that point, there was nothing to concern herself with; she could hear voices coming from Miss Hamilton's bedroom but – for the moment – they appeared to be friendly and cordial in nature.

Then disaster struck. A dull bump came echoing through the walls and both the charwoman and Mrs Deans could not make out what had caused it. Sensing that something was not quite right, the landlady rushed to the actress's room on the pretext of delivering some coal. The woman opened the door as calmly as she could, and peered inside. Macpherson greeted her while Grace seemed to be asleep on the bed.

'Don't be alarmed,' he said. 'It is only me trying to frighten Miss Hamilton.'

The woman had no idea what he was talking about, but when the man leaned over the bed in order to place some clothes over the actress's face, Mrs Deans got a cold chill. She attempted to speak to her boarder.

'Has he been doing anything to you?' she asked.

There was no answer.

As Macpherson stood perfectly calm, Mrs Deans stepped towards the bed and lifted back the clothes and blankets from Grace's face. She took a sharp intake of breath. Blood was running from the woman's ear and pooling into the pillow, turning it crimson in the process. One side of her face was blackened and the other was as white as a sheet. Mrs Deans was frantic.

'What have you done?! What have you done?!' the landlady screamed.

She begged Macpherson to explain himself but he remained quiet, a small but peaceful smile on his face. The woman ran out into the hall in order to get assistance, shouting to the charwoman that her boarder was now dead. Macpherson watched her go, quietly closed the door, took up the revolver and shot himself in the head.

When the police arrived at the house, they found twenty-year-old Grace Hamilton dead in bed and Macpherson slumped on the floor. His brain was protruding through his skull and a pool of blood was all over the carpet. Next to him was a letter that proved the murder–suicide was most certainly a planned event.

'Dear Mother,' it said. 'Please forgive what I am about to do. You will find £35 in my suit at home . . . It is enough to pay for my funeral . . .'

The Ghastly Lives of Arthur Dacre and Amy Roselle

Arthur Dacre was better known as Dr Arthur Culver James when he met clergyman's daughter, Florence Emily Octavia Owen. They married in England during 1877, though from the very beginning it was a volatile relationship. While Arthur was a hardworking doctor, Florence enjoyed lying in bed until at least midday. Then when he returned in the evening, the couple would argue about money and how to pay their bills. It was later claimed that in order to create drama, Florence would argue just loud enough so that the servants could hear what she said.

Eventually Arthur had enough and he left his wife and moved as far away as he could, to New York. There he attempted to create a whole new life for himself. In that regard, he took up acting full-time and changed his last name to Dacre. In no time at all, the man was earning rather a lot of money and sending some home to support Florence. However, despite making sure she was taken care of, the actor had absolutely no intention of ever resurrecting his marriage, and rarely gave his wife a second thought.

Dacre returned to England with an acting company, though it wasn't long before Florence heard of his arrival and discovered which theatre he was appearing in. One evening, the scorned woman travelled to his place of work and stood outside, waiting for the evening performance to end. When Dacre eventually appeared at the stage door, Florence grabbed him by the arm and threatened to ruin his career. The shocked actor shrugged the woman off so, as an act of revenge, she went straight to the police to report him for assault. When the case went to court, however, she did not bother to show up and it was dropped.

By 1883, the very successful Arthur Dacre was ready to divorce his wife and carry on with his new life. The couple went to court in December and a whole host of dirty laundry was aired in front of the public and media alike. Dacre accused his estranged wife of having affairs with three other men; something which she vehemently denied. Then the actor was on the receiving end of accusations when Florence told the court that, during their marriage, he would often be visited by the widow of a doctor friend. The woman even slept in their house, she said, and the two had been caught cuddling in the family library.

Dacre denied the affair and other claims that he drank very heavily, but admitted that he did take opium to induce sleep. Affairs weren't the most shocking thing to emerge, however. Further scandalous behaviour included a time when the actor pretended to cut his own throat and actually ended up drawing blood. A doctor had to be called to the residence in order to control the bleeding and fix the wound.

The divorce was granted and Dacre continued with his acting career. Meanwhile, another woman was in his sights; this time an actress called Amy Roselle, whom he married in January 1885. From the very beginning of their union, the couple created headlines, often for the wrong reasons. Roselle was extremely successful and many people judged her as the more popular entertainer of the two. However, her career was severely hampered in the years after the marriage, with many suggesting that her problems came as a result of Dacre's attitude.

For some time, theatres had been complaining of the actor's 'cantankerous performances', and this was very much apparent during the first year of his marriage to Roselle. In November 1885, the actress was employed at the Olympic Theatre, London, playing the character of Annie Meadows in *Alone in London*. Her engagement was supposed to be for six weeks, but towards the middle of her run, it was suspected by theatre manager Anna Conover that Roselle was pregnant.

'It was evident that Miss Roselle would not be able to sustain the fatigue of the part of Annie Meadows for many weeks longer,' she wrote. 'There surely can be no rudeness or want of refinement in recognising the fact that a married lady is in such a condition that married ladies must expect to be in. Whatever precedents there may be for "matrons" on the stage continuing to perform their duties as long as possible under such circumstances, there are parts, and Annie Meadows is one of them, in which for the lady's sake, it is desirable that she should not continue to act when in such a delicate condition.'

When Roselle discovered her employment was to be terminated, she was understandably upset. However, the person who took the news hardest was Dacre, who launched into an attack not only on the theatre manager, but also playwright Robert Buchanan. He began bombarding both with letters full of hate and vitriol and even went so far as to spread rumours about the pair around the London theatre district. He made frequent visits to clubs and other establishments, telling anyone and everyone that *Alone in London* was a dismal failure and that his wife had been asked to take a pay cut as a result. The stories travelled so fast that it didn't take long for them to get back to Conover and Buchanan, who wrote:

> If *Alone in London* is unsuccessful as he says, how does it happen that the average weekly returns of The Olympic have exceeded the average monthly returns of another theatre, where Miss Roselle, assisted on that occasion by her husband, fulfilled her last engagement? In point of fact, Mr Dacre knows nothing whatever of the theatre's returns . . .

Despite threats of legal action, Dacre continued his onslaught of abuse against the Olympic Theatre, and at one point made abusive comments to Harriett Jay, actress and co-author of *Alone in London*. She subsequently complained and for a time he was banned from setting foot in the building. Roselle denied ever knowing about her husband's outbursts and after hearing he had been banned from the theatre, threatened to stop acting unless he was allowed back. Management relented but only by allowing Dacre access to his wife's dressing room and nowhere else in the vicinity.

In the week leading up to what should have been her last night on stage, the actress omitted some important lines and exited the stage too early. Harriett Jay complained about the mistake, though the other actors insisted it did not hamper the play at all. By this time, however, the management had endured enough of both Dacre and Roselle. They believed that she messed up as an act of revenge and told cast members that she was now a liability in their show. The actress was given one week's salary and asked to leave her job without delay.

In the days ahead, various letters were written to the *Era* by Dacre, Conover and Buchanan, all arguing over who was in the wrong. Theatre manager Anna Conover had so much to say that it took up an entire column in the newspaper. In it she lamented that her biggest crime seemed to be that she was an outspoken woman, and put the blame on Dacre when it came to the bad feeling the theatre now had towards his wife. She also took the opportunity to advise the actor to stay behind the scenes in future, if his wife was ever going to work successfully again.

The exchange of letters went on for months and various other actors got in on the act by complaining about their own treatment at the theatre. Meanwhile, Roselle wrote to newspapers that had called her a 'resting actress', and demanded a retraction. Buchanan made good his promise of taking legal action against Dacre, so then Roselle announced she would be suing both Buchanan and Conover for unfair dismissal and slander. The most significant issue in court documents was that Roselle objected to claims she had missed her lines on purpose. The build-up to the case was spectacularly covered once again in the letters section of the *Era*.

On 26 March 1886, the actress gave birth to a baby boy, and then the court case loomed large, creating much interest among the media and public alike. Every detail was published, and one columnist added further fuel to the fire by suggesting that the case was far more entertaining than any recent plays shown at the Olympic.

The Conover portion of the trial finished in early 1887 and Roselle was awarded £190, though this was eaten up by having to pay the court costs. The *Pall Mall Gazette* took the opportunity of interviewing both Roselle and Dacre to get their views on the case. However, it was the actor who did most of the talking, and complained bitterly that his wife would have to pay the court costs from the money awarded to her. There then followed a host of newspaper letters from everyone concerned in the trial, including Roselle herself.

In April 1887, the couple were devastated by the sudden loss of their son, who had only just turned a year old. Roselle took to her bed, while Dacre commissioned photos of the dead child with both parents' hands around the body. This was a strange but common practice in Victorian times, since being photographed was a much rarer occurrence than now. A death photo was often the first picture taken of the person – particularly a baby – and photographers would prop up the body to look as though he or she were still living. In keeping with tradition, once Dacre and Roselle had the photograph of their lost toddler, they then distributed it to friends and family.

After the death of the child, the slander case held no significance for Roselle any more. Perhaps prompted by the tragedy, Robert Buchanan apologised profusely for his role in the slander and dismissal, and the actress dropped the case. There then followed a benefit performance of the play *Money* at the Lyceum, where many of the actress's friends gave their time and talents to raise money in her honour.

After a period of healing, Roselle returned to work. Unfortunately for her, Dacre now insisted on acting with his wife on an almost full-time basis. Theatres often couldn't afford to hire both, particularly when they really only wanted Roselle, so the couple declined work and fell into debt. In 1890, Dacre was offered a part in New York, but the trip wasn't a great success so they returned to England. However, even the voyage home was dramatic, as the ship suddenly caught fire. The boat was escorted to port with the help of three steamers, and Dacre bragged to journalists that he had calmed fellow passengers while still wearing his pyjamas.

Safely returned to England, Amy Roselle acquired work for a time as a music-hall star, but Dacre struggled so she returned to acting with him. On her own, the actress was successful and a crowd-pleaser, but most of what they did as a team was depressing. The public hated these melancholy plays and stayed away in droves. It didn't matter what part of the country the couple travelled to; ticket sales were always disappointing. Nothing went smoothly and the marriage became one long, heartbreaking scandal.

By 1895, the acting parts had dried up quite considerably – precisely what Olympic Theatre manager Anna Conover had predicted when she said Dacre should stay out of his wife's career. The couple had attempted theatre management, which proved to be a dismal failure, and with nothing left to lose they decided to give up their life in England and travel to Australia in search of work.

Although initially greeted warmly by theatres and fans alike, from the beginning their trip did not go as expected. At first houses were packed, but then some audiences – just like the ones at home – became critical and complained that the plays were too sombre and depressing. In Melbourne, Amy became unwell and had to step down temporarily from her part. Meanwhile, Mabel Hardy, a young actress they had brought with them to Australia, was anxious to return home. She told the couple that she was concerned about the financial situation and desperately homesick. Dacre listened to what she had to say, and then told his wife he was worried about Mabel's welfare and blamed himself for her despair.

By summer 1895, the couple's shows had been terminated in Melbourne and they had moved to Adelaide, but once again their plays were not well attended by the public. The tour threatened to become something of a personal and financial disaster and, towards the end of the year, both Dacre and Roselle were despondent. A lifeline of sorts was offered, however, when some of their plays garnered good reviews and fairly healthy ticket sales. They were given the opportunity of touring South Africa in the New Year, and a Sydney theatre was anxious to have them on the bill. This promised to be a great opportunity, but no amount of good news could bring them out of the depression into which they had fallen.

Very shortly after their arrival in Sydney, it was discovered that their play, *The Land of the Moa*, was to be withdrawn and replaced with a different show altogether. The curtain was to rise on this project in several days, which put tremendous strain on the couple to learn new lines and attend urgent rehearsals. Dacre especially was unsure about the quality of the play and his ability to learn it in such a short space of time. He complained bitterly to the management, but was told the new play would go ahead with or without him.

On 16 November 1895, the couple attended rehearsals in Sydney, and then dined with residents of the boarding house where they were lodging. Those who saw them said that they seemed to be in a good mood, and were jovial to all they encountered. However, the very next day, things took a terrifying and heartbreaking turn. In the privacy of the Sydney boarding house, Dacre sat down and wrote a variety of goodbye letters to friends, informing them that he and his wife could no longer go on with their lives.

To the manager of the theatre where the couple worked, Dacre wrote a heartfelt plea about young actress Mabel Hardy. In the letter, he explained that she was in a very bad way. 'Her distress,' he wrote, 'is largely down to me, since I brought her to Australia.' He instructed the manager to give all remaining pay cheques owed to himself and his wife to Hardy.

Two other letters were written to a friend called Herbert Leighton and both emphasised how hard it had been for the couple to survive, and how Mabel Hardy and the other actors in their troupe should be helped as soon as possible.

He wrote:

We have really struggled against this. My sweet wife has lived a noble heroine's life, but talent and honest hard work are the last things they want now . . . We have never failed in our duty to the public before. I have never missed a night. Do as much as you can for poor Alice Watson out of what there is and do try to get poor Miss Hardy home.

In the second letter to Leighton, Dacre could not help but vent his heartbreak about life in the theatre. He wrote:

We have really no absurd sentiment, but with my sweet wife's kiss on my lips, with her full permission, I ask you to sell our clothes and the trinkets we have. Bury us as cheaply, unostentatiously and quietly as possible and with-out any name on our headstone or if you put anything, you might simply put – A. A. They loved each other and in their death they were undivided.

He ended by giving his friend some simple advice:

Be anything – butcher, baker or candlestick maker – but get work at anything else than an actor. I have told you over a pleasant pipe or two my wife's life, her plucky, noble career. You see the end. We are broken-hearted . . .

Letters written, he then dropped trinkets and other souvenirs into the envelopes before finally sealing them closed. Later friends would say that at least one of the letters appeared to be signed from Roselle herself, and that the tragedy about to happen seemed very much a joint decision. This wasn't the first time the couple had implied that they might take their own lives. Several friends came forward to say they had shared conversations in the past, where both expressed that the only way out of their bad luck was a joint suicide pact. They recalled Amy Roselle as being perfectly at peace with the idea of dying with her husband. 'When the time came, she would meet her end bravely, as a British woman should,' said one friend.

Dacre's valet arrived to help the actor learn his lines for the new play. He later told police that although he visited late in the afternoon, the couple were still in their nightclothes and Roselle was in bed with a handkerchief over her face. She had taken a soporific to aid her sleep and, as a result, did not say a word to him the entire time he was there.

Rehearsal over, the valet took his leave, and Dacre handed him the pile of letters to be mailed.

'Make sure you post these,' he said, and then insisted that the man place his hand on a nearby Bible. 'If you're ever questioned, please swear that you'll say I was never unkind to you.'

The shocked valet swore he would, then went on his way. As he descended the stairs, he was sure he heard the sound of smashing glass, but then decided he must be mistaken and carried on his way. A short while later, the people in the next room complained of hearing a scuffle, as though crockery was being broken, then a bell was heard ringing incessantly. This brought a maid running, and while listening outside, she was shocked to hear some awful moans.

'Is everything all right?' she shouted.

'I can't open the door,' replied Dacre. 'Burst the door open!'

The woman could not gain entry to the room, and fearing that something was terribly wrong, she asked two boarders for help. They could not get the door open either, so they climbed up to the balcony and got inside that way. The sight that greeted them was simply horrifying.

There in the bed was Amy Roselle, dead as a result of gunshot wounds to her chest. Dacre was still alive, but staggering around with his throat cut from ear to ear. There was blood all over the floor and a revolver nearby.

'Oh what agony! Oh what agony!' muttered the actor. He then buckled onto the floor and signalled towards the bed. 'Put me beside her, there's a good fellow,' he said, before finally passing away. While it was very apparent that the man had shot his wife and then cut his own throat, a bloodstained note on the dressing table implied that he had wanted to die by bullet too. 'God, let us die together,' it said. 'I thought there was a last shot.'

After their deaths, the couple were buried together as requested and many of the couple's detractors saw fit to attend the memorial or send photographs. Media interest was at an all-time high, with many of the articles geared towards the letters Dacre had written about Mabel Hardy. Several months later, the young woman did indeed make it back to England and managed to find work. 'Amy Roselle,' she said in an interview, 'was a sincere artist, a devoted wife, a noble, unselfish woman.' Mabel also wrote to the *Era*, to give her side of the suicide letters:

> Sir – Will you do me the kindness to relieve some misapprehension which, on my return to England, I find existing in reference to my financial position in Australia? I had been in receipt of remittances from home, ever since the sudden termination of the Dacres' season in Melbourne. Poor Mr Dacre laboured under a painful illusion in imagining that he was responsible for, or, indeed, that I was in any pecuniary embarrassment. I am, dear Sir, Yours truly, Mabel Hardy.

The reporting of the couple's deaths went on for several months, and while sympathy was rife for Amy Roselle, few people felt it for Arthur Dacre. One journalist summed up what several others were thinking when he described the actor as an 'impulsive, impressionable fellow, who, to tell the honest truth, was never quite sane . . . He shot his wife's brains out with a revolver and then cut his throat with a razor. Could there be better evidence of insanity?'

Love, Murder and Suicide in Paris

Gabrielle Morales was a Parisian actress, active during the late 1800s. She wasn't particularly successful and, in fact, newspapers at the time described that she 'confined her histrionic displays to parts in which there was little speaking and less clothing'. Still, she was fairly popular when it came to photographs, with one picture – that of her paying tribute to Cupid – prominently displayed throughout Paris.

While her career was not in the same league as many of the London theatre actresses, that in no way meant she did not crave the finer things in life. In 1877 she became acquainted with a young playboy called Eugene Riandel, who was wealthy thanks to a generous allowance from his mother. At that point in time, Morales was in debt and bad health, so meeting someone who could give her the lifestyle she craved was greatly welcomed. The two began seriously dating and travelled to Nice and Monaco, where Morales apparently developed a particular fondness for the gambling establishments.

Word soon got back to Riandel's mother that he was spending a huge amount of money on his new love. The woman did not appreciate her estate being squandered in such a way, so she cut off the generous allowance and replaced it with pocket money for clothing only. Riandel was upset, but not as much as Morales, who had come to rely on the lavish lifestyle he provided her. She broke off their romance and turned her attentions to an older gentleman who was apparently not short of money.

While Morales may have moved on, Riandel was at a standstill. He had lost his love and his money at the same time, and hearing that Morales had found someone else sent him into a jealous rage. He wrote her letter after letter, but in spite of his passionate words, the actress refused to see him and returned all the notes to sender. This only served to enrage Riandel even more and he became a regular sight outside her front door, pacing up and down as though waiting for an answer that never came.

Early one morning the man travelled to the actress's apartment once again, but this time did not wait outside. Instead, he banged on the door and was let in by the actress's servant. Once inside the building, Riandel found Morales in the living room and demanded an explanation for her lack of concern. She was too busy to entertain him, however, as she was writing a letter to her new lover, begging him for money.

It will never be known exactly what happened in the next few minutes, but it is believed that Riandel looked over her shoulder and read what she was writing. Perhaps he finally realised that their relationship was over, or possibly he saw that she was asking for money and realised that had been her only interest in him, too. Whatever it was, at that moment Riandel reached into his pocket, took out a revolver and shot his former lover at point-blank range. On hearing the commotion, the servant ran from the apartment to find help, while Riandel went to Morales' bedroom, locked the door and sat down in an armchair, facing a mirror. He then took out his revolver once again, and shot himself through the mouth.

For the next few days, Morales' home became a scene of morbid curiosity, as fans of her photographs travelled to see not only where she met her death, but also where she now lay, ready for her funeral. For a time, her death enabled her to achieve the fame she had sought in life, though the media's angle was firmly to show others that money cannot bring happiness. 'This tragedy points a moral which is as old as the proverbs of Solomon,' said one.

Harold Russell: The Scoundrel Actor

During Victorian times, actresses were often thought of as drama queens and looked down on by members of the higher classes. Actors fared better, though anyone thinking they were all upstanding members of society need only look at the newspapers to discover a good share of scoundrels and rogues. Take Harold Russell, for instance. He is unheard of now, but in the late nineteenth century he was a fairly well-known, eminent actor who often toured with the D'Oyly Carte Opera Company, a troupe of actors that worked up and down Britain.

In 1883, Russell was married with a young child, but that did not stop him from pursuing a life of freedom and excess. His wife, described as 'a very respectable young lady', had come to the marriage with a selection of jewellery and beautiful clothes. Whether this was the reason Russell had taken a shine to the girl is not known, but they were precisely the items he went looking for when he was in need of spare cash. It wasn't long into the marriage before Russell started selling off his wife's possessions and using the proceeds to entertain other young women. Not only that, witnesses said he often treated his wife in a brutal and disgraceful manner.

Understandably, Mrs Russell's brother, William, was not pleased with the developments and tried to support her and the child when Harold was out of town. Whenever he returned, William would insist that the rogue treat Mrs Russell with the respect she deserved, though the actor rarely – if ever – did as he was told.

Things came to a head in early 1883, when Harold took off on an acting tour and sent no money to support his wife or son for an entire six months. The woman was destitute and had to apply for poor relief, since she was now without money, clothes or jewellery. When her brother discovered what was going on, he was furious.

Spurred on by this and a need to do what was right by his sister, William did some investigating and discovered that Harold Russell was carrying on with other women while on the road. There was nothing new about that, except that in this instance, he was currently involved with a married actress called Ethel Strathmore, the wife of an Army captain. The two were going by the name of Mr and Mrs Russell and living together under the same roof.

An infuriated William took his findings to the police, and an officer visited the home in the middle of the night. There he found Harold and Ethel in bed together, and they both admitted adultery. Not only that, but the actor quite blatantly told police that he was now relying on Ethel to support him whenever he was out of work. He also said that he had been sending money to his real wife on a regular basis, which of course was a lie.

When the matter went to court, the judge was disgusted by the man standing before him. 'You are a worthless fellow,' he said, and sentenced him to one month's hard labour. He was also required to send his wife 15s a week. However, this wasn't the end of his roguish ways. Many years later he was back in court on similar charges.

Instead of providing his ridiculously patient wife with the court-appointed amount of 15s a week, the actor decided that two guineas would be more than adequate. This time the magistrate ordered the actor to pay £9 or risk going to prison for another two months. It was never reported what he chose to do because, by this point, his career had hit a slippery slope.

Karma had finally caught up with the scoundrel; he fell out of the public eye very quickly, and his acting career was over.

The Mysterious Disappearance of Mabel Love

Mabel Love was a legendary Victorian and Edwardian actress, who had a huge following as a stage star. One only needs to visit an antique or collector's fair to see the vast number of postcards that featured the girl. Indeed, it is said that Winston Churchill once wrote to request an autographed card, and her signature is still a popular find to this day. However, while she eventually went on to have a long and distinguished career, in 1889 (when she was still in her early teens) it looked as though it would be over before it had truly begun.

On Friday 15 March, Mabel appeared at the Gaiety Theatre, London, where she had a small part in a musical called *Faust Up to Date*. That evening she went home to her parents' house, accompanied by a servant, but her mother complained that she was late returning from the theatre and reprimanded her. The next day – with the scolding still on her mind – Mabel followed the same routine she did every weekend and walked to the Gaiety in order to receive her salary. This time, however, she did not return to her home and promptly disappeared.

On discovering her absence, Mabel's parents were frantic, but hoped it was a simple case of her going sightseeing or shopping without informing them first. After all, she had left with no change of clothes or overnight bag, which gave the indication that she wasn't far away. Unfortunately, when the actress failed to turn up at the Gaiety that afternoon, alarm bells rang and it was quite clear that something must have happened. The police were called and investigations began.

For days after the disappearance, officers examined the case and the media reported on the scandalous story. All kinds of people stepped forward to claim they had seen her. Someone was convinced she had been seen in the company of an old lady – possibly a fellow actress – while another said she had been at Charing Cross station, where she caught a mail train and ultimately fled to the Continent. Rumours swirled that Mabel had received a mysterious letter shortly before her disappearance, but had kept it secret from her mother.

Meanwhile, her parents made desperate pleas for their daughter to come home, but no contact was made. The police were intrigued, but from the very beginning silenced reports that she could have been abducted, citing the fact that there were 'no good grounds' for thinking such a thing.

George Edwardes, Mabel's boss at the Gaiety Theatre, agreed with officers and told reporters that he did not believe there was anything suspicious about her disappearance. She worked hard, he said, and her behaviour had always been professional and exemplary. Behind the scenes, however, the manager was aggravated that the upcoming star had fled and he hired a private detective called Mr Moser to investigate the case.

Moser was glad to take on the inquiry and soon received a tip that Mabel had been seen at the Great Northern booking office on the Strand, looking at an ABC travel directory. Onlookers told the detective that the young woman was seen studying the D section, before leaving and being observed walking on Piccadilly. She was last seen waiting for a train on her own, at Euston station.

Armed with this information and determined that the letter D was important to the story, Moser went to Euston. There he discovered that a train to Holyhead had left on the day of Mabel's disappearance. From there the actress could quite easily have taken a ferry to Dublin, although why she would do such a thing was quite a mystery. Further inquiry revealed that a young woman answering to Mabel's description had been seen at a hotel and boarding house in that city.

'I followed up the clues already mentioned,' he told reporters, 'and wired to my own agent in Dublin, from whom I received a reply stating that the young lady was there and advising me to go over.'

Not knowing whether the actress was on her own or in great danger from an abductor, Moser instructed Dublin police to speak to Mabel and decipher what was going on. They did and it soon transpired that the dramatic teenager had travelled to Dublin alone to take revenge for the argument with her mother the night before.

The police persuaded Mabel to return to England, which she did almost a week after her mysterious disappearance. Suffering greatly from seasickness, the actress was met at Holyhead by Moser, and proceeded to tell him all about her adventure. The facts all matched up with what the police had reported earlier, but gave one extra titbit: during her time in Dublin, she had tried and failed to gain work in a variety of local theatres, including the Theatre Royal and several other comedy establishments. Her work intentions were of no interest to Moser, however, and after avoiding the crowds of fans waiting at Euston station, he finally managed to get the runaway home.

While Moser may not have been concerned about Mabel's career, boss George Edwardes most certainly was. In the past few days, he had been contacted by the manager of the Gaiety Theatre in Dublin. The man told him that Mabel had appeared in his office asking for work. He had told her that there were no vacancies and sent her on her way. Edwardes was furious. In the past week, he had comforted her parents, published statements about her fabulous work ethic and even hired a detective to find her. But in all that time, his young employee was actively seeking work in rival companies. There was only one thing he could do to save face: fire the actress immediately.

'Miss Love will not reappear at the Gaiety,' Edwardes told reporters. 'Miss Kate Barry has been engaged in her place.' All posters mentioning her name were taken down from outside the theatre, and her name removed from all the bills. As far as he was concerned, Mabel Love was old news and would never return to his theatre.

Having been fired from her job, Mabel was now most apologetic. Moser told reporters that she 'was sorry she had left home; that she had been most kindly treated during her stay in Dublin and that no harm of any kind had come to her'. While this may have been true, it was of no comfort to her mother, who was in a state of high anxiety and had taken to her bed. The newspapers took great delight in telling readers about every aspect of her breakdown, while Mabel's father was reported to have contacted friends in Dublin to make sure that everything the young woman had told him was true. Having satisfied himself that it was, the family tried to get back to their normal lives and the story finally fell from the pages of the newspapers.

Behind the scenes, however, things were not quite what they seemed. While no public mention was made, Mabel was absolutely devastated that she had lost her job at the Gaiety Theatre.

Together with her parents, she travelled to see Mr Edwardes and begged to be reinstated. He declined the offer, but still the teenager pleaded.

'It was only after urgent entreaties from her parents and herself that I consented to take her back,' he said, 'and then after an absence of six weeks and on her repeated assurance that her happiness depended on my re-engaging her and that my refusal would seriously damage her future professional prospects.'

The browbeaten manager had finally relented, but he stood firm on exactly how much interaction Mabel would have at the theatre. From now on she would appear there for just five minutes per night, and with only two lines to speak. 'Her part at the Gaiety was an entirely subsidiary one,' he said. When she finally reappeared on stage, it was to rapturous applause. 'Chorus girls would give their eyes for the advertisement that the little vivandière obtained by her flight to Dublin,' wrote one sarcastic journalist.

Ironically, while her part was small, it was also rather biting. 'I am the only one who didn't run away, I stuck to my post,' she recited. Fans couldn't help but wonder if the line had been picked by Edwardes deliberately for the disappearing actress.

Things were quiet for a few months, until July 1889 arrived and Mabel made headlines once again. This time she sneaked out of her home in the middle of the night and headed straight for the Thames. Once there she dramatically threw herself into the water from steps located close to Whitehall. At 4.30 a.m. she was spotted floating in the river by a fire crew, who hoisted her out of the water and took her to shore. There the freezing actress was attended to by a doctor, before being taken to hospital.

Once in the care of a medical team, Love disclosed that her life was miserable and she was determined to end it all that evening by killing herself in the river. This may have brought sympathy from her frantic parents, but not so from the police, who promptly took the actress to Bow Street Police Court, where she was charged with attempting suicide.

Prosecutor Mr Vaughan questioned the young woman about her age (she was fourteen) and the reason she had thrown herself into the river.

'I can't understand how I did it. I did not know what I was doing,' she replied.

Mabel's mother was beside herself and gave an impassioned speech. 'My daughter has been studying very hard lately,' she said, 'and she has had some sleepless nights. She is studying for the stage.' The woman then added that Mabel had recently suffered from typhoid fever and was under the care of doctors. 'She has also complained of pains in her head,' she explained.

When asked about Love's movements, her mother said that she had been working at the Gaiety and had been there on the night of her suicide attempt. Something about this statement aggravated Mr Vaughan and he launched into a lecture on what he believed should be the next step.

'You ought to communicate with the manager of the theatre and say that she cannot continue her engagement there. She must cease study altogether and unless some such arrangement is made, I cannot let her go.' Love's mother assured Vaughan that she would take her away from the city straightaway. That said, the prosecutor told Mabel Love to rest completely, breathe the air of the country and cease even reading. He then agreed to let the teenager go.

This should have been the end of the matter, if not for the fact that people began to whisper about the exact circumstances of the suicide attempt. Based on her mysterious disappearance, some felt that the whole thing was a publicity stunt, designed to create even more attention. Things were not helped when George Edwardes heard the comments made in court about her career. He was incensed at what he believed was a finger pointing firmly in his direction, and took the opportunity to write to the editor of showbiz newspaper, the *Era*.

> Sir, I shall be glad if you will give publicity to a few remarks of mine regarding the eccentric conduct of the Gaiety actress who attempted to commit suicide a few days ago. From the remarks of Mr Vaughan at the police court, one would be led to imagine that the strain of professional work had driven Miss Mabel Love to the rash course of attempting self-destruction . . .

The aggravated man then went on to explain that Love only had the smallest of roles and even that was only given to her after she and her family had begged him to.

When the *Era* tipped off Mabel's mother about the letter, she took the opportunity to answer it in the pages of the newspaper. Explaining that Mr Edwardes and everyone at the Gaiety had always treated her daughter with the greatest of kindness, she also alluded to some underlying bitterness. His note, she decided, 'is calculated to give a wrong impression as to the nature of my evidence before Mr Vaughan'. She went on to say that the parts for which her daughter had been studying were not linked to the Gaiety at all, but rather to several different roles coming up in the next few weeks.

While the publicity surrounding her disappearance and suicide attempt may have soured relations somewhat between Mabel Love and George Edwardes, the publicity ensured her name was on everyone's lips for many years to come. She later travelled with Edwardes' company to New York and became extremely well known in Paris too. However, the actress tired of appearing in burlesque and pantomime and sought out other parts.

'I do not intend to go upon the music-hall stage,' she said in 1905. 'My ambition has always been to go in for more serious work, such as modern comedy.' Eventually all kinds of acting work became too tiresome and she retired in 1918. Love later owned a dance studio before eventually passing away in 1953.

In true Mabel Love style, she caused a scandal even after death, when the BBC *Heir Hunters* programme discovered she had given birth to an illegitimate daughter called Mary Loraine in 1913. She had left £2,600 worth of bonds to the woman, but Mary knew nothing about them. By the time they came to light, the woman was long dead and so too was her son. The money was eventually shared out between various cousins of Mabel's grandson, who had no idea they were in for such a windfall.

Ilda Orme – A Paranoid Actress?

Ilda (aka Ida or Hilda) Orme was an American actress and singer who made her living in plays and musicals in the United States and England. She also wrote songs and was considered to be a fairly successful woman in her time. However, while her onstage antics were entertaining, they were nothing compared to the dramatics she encountered – and often encouraged – during her lifetime.

While she often worked in her home country, Ilda was appearing with the Wedding Eve Company in London by the start of 1892. So in-demand were her services that by the end of the year she had sailed back to America with comedian John F. Sheridan, who had personally hired her for a five-week appearance in New York.

A short time later, Ilda was appearing at London's Trafalgar Theatre when she was suddenly fired. The actress blamed the sacking on theatrical manager Marcus Mayer, and accused him of spreading rumours about her. The reason for these claims became apparent some time later, but for now Ilda Orme was involved in a lawsuit, in which she was suing an ex-colleague for taking a song she had written, along with various letters. When the notes were read aloud in court, it was revealed that Orme had described 'stabbing and murdering a prominent man'. The judge told her she should not be writing such things, but returned the letters anyway.

Orme travelled to many cities in search of work but was turned away from all of them. Once again, she blamed Mayer and returned to the United States, but by April 1897 the woman planned to travel once more to England. Before she set sail, she gave a frank and somewhat disturbing statement about what she intended to do there.

'I will make disclosures against some theatrical managers, which will startle people,' she claimed. 'For the past four years I have been pursued by relentless villains. My engagements were mysteriously cancelled. A wicked dentist ruined my teeth so that I could not sing and others conspired to ruin my reputation not only as a singer but as a song-writer . . . I am going to England to make trouble for my enemies.' When the comments appeared in newspapers, one journalist noted that while she was not promoting good diplomacy, her intentions seemed to be 'sledge-hammer vengeance'.

Just two months later, Ilda Orme sued the dentist she had mentioned during the bizarre press conference, and the case appeared in many newspapers around the United Kingdom. According to the actress, the surgeon had clipped and capped three of her front teeth, but within a few months, one of the enamels had fallen off. When she returned to the dentist's Strand offices, he tried to reattach the tooth but on doing so, broke the stump of the existing one and it ended up being removed. As indicated in the press conference, Orme was livid with this turn of events and her singing career was put into peril. When she brought the issue to court, the defendant countersued her with a bill for the dental work.

While the dentist had proper legal representation, Orme decided to forego her right to a solicitor and take on the case herself. Her reason for doing so, she said, was because her choice of counsel had tried to dissuade her from taking the case any further. Standing in the dock, she gave a long, impassioned speech, worthy of the actress she was. During the disclosure, she tearfully told the judge that her mental state had been compromised by the terrible ordeal and her professional life stalled.

The judge listened with great interest but when it was discovered that she had actually written a letter about how wonderful her teeth were, and had congratulated the dentist on his skills, he decided to rule in the latter's favour. He then threw out the countersuit and told everyone to go on their way. However, there was one question left unanswered.

'The lady's tooth is still in the possession of the defendant,' said a lawyer. 'We do not know whether she wishes to have it, because we do not wish to have another suit about that.'

As everyone looked on, Orme shook her head.

'No, I do not wish to have it,' she said and then left the court.

Newspapers christened the story 'An Amusing Action', but there was a much bigger, more painful and scandalous event to come, just three months later. Orme believed that this particular episode was as a result of something that had happened a good ten years prior.

As a young woman living in the States, the actress had married a lawyer, the son of a powerful millionaire. His parents massively disapproved of the union and convinced him to break up with the actress and marry someone more 'respectable'. He did, but Ilda Orme refused to go quietly. She sued the family and eventually settled out of court for $1000. According to her, they then subjected her to a torrent of abuse over a ten-year period, which included recruiting theatrical manager Marcus Mayer to make her life a misery. 'I have been the victim of a series of attempts to drive me into the gutter or the grave,' she told reporters.

On 18 September 1897 a disturbing event occurred, which made her even more determined that her former fiancé's family were out to get her. By this time, the actress was living in lodgings on Keppel Street, London, and was returning home in the early hours of the morning when she was approached by a strange man. Due to the dark night, she was unable to gain a good look at her assailant, though later described him as a beggar who spoke with an American accent.

He began a fairly ordinary conversation with Orme, but before she could bid him farewell, he suddenly reached into his pocket, took out a pistol and shot her straight through her right breast. Mercifully the actress survived, but with a great deal of pain and scarring to her chest. 'The attack made upon me at Keppel Street was the sixth attempt that had been made upon my life, and as that failed, my persecutors desired to shut me up,' she said. It was clear through her comments that she still believed her fiancé's family and manager Marcus Mayer were out to get her.

In the week after the attack, Ilda Orme lay in bed recovering from the ordeal. After a few days of rest, she was then visited by a policeman, who asked if she could accompany him to Bow Street station.

'We would like you to identify the man who shot you,' he told her.

Orme was still in a great deal of pain, but knowing this could be the beginning of gaining justice, she agreed to accompany the officer to the station. However, according to her, the invitation was actually a gigantic trick and she was taken to the insane ward at St Giles's workhouse. 'I soon realised that I had been trapped,' she said. 'But I kept calm and demanded to know why I had been brought there.'

While nurses refused to tell her at first, the shocked woman eventually discovered that she had been committed because officers believed the gunshot wound was self-inflicted. The charge brought against her was of attempting suicide; something she vehemently denied. Ilda's doctors then put her into a padded room, where her roommate was a tormented soul who was tied to her bed every night.

Several weeks into her stay at the asylum, Orme received a visit from her landlady. The woman told her she had no choice but to rent her room to another lodger and this information sent the actress totally over the edge. Magistrates decided that her reaction to the news was so desperate that they had no choice but to send her to Colney Hatch, a hospital better equipped to deal with the breakdown she was in the midst of having. Ilda was totally against the move, but it actually turned out to be something of a breakthrough for her. Doctors at the new facility examined Orme and decided that there was simply nothing wrong with her mind all. They also investigated the gunshot wound and realised there was no way she could have inflicted it upon herself. The hospital contacted police and insisted the suicide accusation be dropped. It was, but still Orme was not released. When she complained, the woman was sent to another asylum; this time in Salisbury. Thankfully, from there she was able to get word to her sister, who arrived in England and contacted the American Ambassador. He was appalled at the treatment of Ilda Orme and ordered her release as soon as possible.

After seven months of confinement, the woman was now free to resume her life. Reporters flocked to her door for a statement and she did not disappoint. Pounding her fists on the table, Ilda told them that her representatives had arrived from America and 'An attempt is now being made to get me out of the country, but I won't go until this matter has been cleared up. I have been treated shamefully.'

Despite the actress's determination to gain justice, she found out that the relevant papers detailing her committal had apparently been destroyed. Ilda Orme was forced to admit that she would not be able to take things further through the courts and eventually went back to the States in an effort to find work. Her reputation as a lunatic had followed her, however, and she was unable to gain any acting jobs; a problem she blamed – once again – on her ex-fiancé's family.

Ilda Orme's unrelenting desire to seek revenge on all those she felt had done her wrong continued. In 1899, just a year after leaving England, she was able to do just that on theatre manager Marcus Mayer, the man she blamed for the sudden termination of her contract at the Trafalgar Theatre, and many more wrongdoings. Now, however, she added another crime to the story. Suddenly she no longer blamed her former fiancé's family for her admittance to the asylum. Now the blame for that was given to Mayer.

'He has spread the report that I am insane,' she said. 'It was through his machinations that the English police kidnapped me and took me to an insane asylum . . .'

The bizarre revenge took place on the American liner, *St Paul*, which was just about to depart for England with Mr Mayer on board. Orme had no intention of travelling herself but knew Mayer would be sailing with his latest protégé, actress Olga Nethersole (whom we encountered in 'An Actress is Arrested'). Armed with that knowledge, Orme somehow managed to get onto the ship and the two came face-to-face on a flight of stairs leading to the ship's saloon.

After some heated words, Ilda reached into the folds of her heavy dress, brought out a horsewhip and proceeded to slash the manager across the face with it. As if that wasn't enough, she then whipped his hat clear off his head, and then worked her way to his shoulders, cracking the whip again and again, while she made her way down the stairs.

Newspaper reports said that the shocking episode was witnessed by two thousand people. While this seems grossly overexaggerated, it was certainly seen by the people in the saloon, as well as Mayer's friend and business partner, George Lederer. As Ilda Orme headed towards the ship's gangway, she was stopped by a policeman and Lederer, who demanded her arrest. Quite bizarrely, Marcus Mayer did not wish to press charges and, even though his friend was eager to press them on his behalf, Orme was allowed to go free. As she sauntered down the gangway, the actress turned and snapped at Mayer.

'It was calumnies that I promised to thrash you for and I have done it. If you ever repeat them I will whip you again.'

One would think that after encountering such a steady stream of scandals in the past, Ilda Orme would grow tired of the attention. However, in 1901 she was back in the press again, this time for suing several theatres who – she claimed – had unfairly dismissed her. The first she accused of moving her from principal to chorus line within a week for no apparent reason. The second she said fired her because she refused to spend time with male theatregoers, sitting in a 'wine room' and tricking them into buying fake liquor after the show.

The newspapers took a great deal of interest in the cases, especially when she lost one suit and refused to pay the damages. It was only when officials visited her home and the theatre where she was currently working that she relented. Faced with having to hand over her worldly goods or paying the court, Orme took out a huge wad of notes and handed the money over.

In 1902, as she was leaving home to head to Klondike, a reporter asked what she intended to do there. She replied, 'I'm going to buy horse whips to whip all of my enemies with!' In reality, however, she was going to spend the summer entertaining miners.

'She is a woman with a history, and has woven enough romance, adventure, conspiracy and persecution into her life to fill a three-volume novel,' wrote one reporter in response to her quip. Yet another described her colourful life: 'A fate appears to pursue her, which makes managers break their contracts and forces her to have frequent recourse to the courts in order to secure what she claims are her rights.'

The last firm mention of the dramatic actress appears in the personal ads of the *Era* newspaper in 1903. 'Wanted, Dates for Ilda Orme, that Saucy Yankee Soubrette, who refuses to be suppressed.' Whether or not the advert gained her any jobs is debatable, but the passage is surely a fitting epitaph for a woman who spent her entire life seeking vengeance for those she believed had done her wrong.

Scandals to Amuse, Bemuse or Perplex

WHEN ONE THINKS about our Victorian ancestors, we are often prone to finding them rather stiff-upper-lipped, unsmiling and 'not amused'. However, this could not be further from the truth. The public and press as a whole were often titillated – obsessed even – by stories that kept them wondering, guessing and scratching their heads.

For instance, in 1900, a young girl was walking past the Market House Tavern in London when she was stopped by two boys. They pointed in the direction of a scruffy-looking man with a sack in his arms. Nothing too unusual in that, perhaps, but on further examination, there was a small, naked foot sticking out of the sack and a pile of clothes on the floor. On seeing the girl's shocked reaction, the man threw the sack over his shoulder and ran away. When police arrived at the scene, the girl's story was confirmed by various other members of the public and the bundle of clothes was taken away. Despite giving the story coverage for the next few days, no one ever did find out who was in the sack, nor why the man had them in there in the first place.

While some Victorian scandals could be gruesome, disturbing and even eye-watering, there were many others that raised more than a titter or two. Take a story that happened in Berlin during 1890. A woman's multimillionaire husband passed away very suddenly and just two days later she was seen in the company of two men who had been performing at a local circus. They were all dressed 'to the nines' and took great joy in parading around town together, showing off their newly inherited wealth and scandalising the neighbourhood at the same time.

Everyone who witnessed her flamboyant attitude came to the conclusion that the woman was no ordinary, grieving widow. It wasn't long, therefore, before a stop was put on her husband's dwindling bank account by police who had grown suspicious of her actions. While no evidence could ever be found that she had anything to do with her husband's sudden death, her attitude did eventually lead to trouble.

When her new companions told the circus manager that they enjoyed the widow's company and would not return to the circus, the man blamed her for taking away his two most popular performers. She was then taken to court and sued for the loss of earnings caused by her 'theft' of the men. The story created headlines around the world, under the title, 'A Strange Scandal in Berlin'.

Then there was the story of Henry Barrett, a young Chicago man who was engaged to be married to his sweetheart, Susie Washington. However, just a day before their wedding, the woman had a change of heart and dramatically dumped her fiancé, claiming she preferred the much richer Joseph Wingfield.

Barrett was then left to explain what had happened to friends and family, and suffered an additional blow of having the entire matter splashed across the pages of local newspapers.

Despite what the woman had done, Barrett still loved her, but when he heard she planned to marry his rival, he decided to do something about it. One afternoon the man watched Washington leave her house, and then snuck into her bedroom. He knew there was no way she would ever marry anyone in her everyday wear, so he bundled up her fancy wedding dress and spirited it away. When Susie returned, she did exactly what Barrett expected her to do – she declared herself unwilling to marry and called the entire thing off.

Some weeks later, Barrett decided that it would be safe to contact his former fiancée again. They began writing back and forth for some time, and then miraculously her wedding outfit reappeared. Instead of berating Barrett for the theft, Susie just put the outfit on and then the two ran off to get married. Friends whispered that she had never stopped loving Barrett, but the thought of marrying the much richer Wingfield had 'tempted her vanity' for a while. The new husband did not care, however. He had won his former love back and taken revenge on his love rival all in one fell swoop.

Just like a good detective novel, mysterious disappearances often kept Victorians entertained, and if they came with a twist in the tale, that was even better. One such story involved an innkeeper from Kidderminster, who went missing in October 1879. For a month, his friends and family searched fruitlessly for him, until stories came from the United States that he had slipped out of England and sailed for New York. His family were perplexed, and wondered why he had done such a thing.

A month later, the man walked back into his home, and greeted his family as though nothing had happened at all. Understandably, they were all ecstatic to have him home again. However, after giving no explanation as to where he had been or what he had been doing, it wasn't long before the innkeeper decided to go for a walk. He bid his family goodbye once again, then headed straight for the canal, threw himself in and drowned . . .

Jilted lovers, mysterious disappearances, sweethearts airing their dirty laundry in public and grooms who have no idea they're attending their own weddings . . . the Victorians had it all. The following are just some of the tragic, strange or perplexing stories that bemused the public, well over one hundred years ago.

The Actress on the Train

Twenty-year-old Lillie Bamford was an actress; at least that's what she told everyone, anyway. The reality was that the Durham-born woman had only achieved a tiny amount of success in that area, and was more well known for her dressmaking skills, making clothes for locals from her father's home. Eager for more success in the acting business, however, Lillie joined a travelling troupe, but her dreams of stardom were thwarted when she became involved with the wrong man and fell pregnant. She returned to her parents' house, gave birth to a son, then moved to Derby in order to stay with an aunt. Her son was left in the care of her parents, though Lillie kept in touch with them; the last message being that she was settling down and intended to find work as a barmaid.

Belgian-born Robert Feron was – by all accounts – a respectable young man who had come to England to study. After his classes had ended, he had somehow migrated to Derby, where he acquired jobs as a silk merchant and foreign correspondent. Always well dressed and from a fairly rich family, Feron impressed people wherever he went, and it wasn't long before he was seen out and about with Lillie Bamford.

Relatives and friends later told police that there was nothing particularly outrageous or strange about their friendship. Lillie had only been in Derby for a few weeks, so the relationship with her new beau was light-hearted and fun. Together they seemed to enjoy some good times and nothing aroused any suspicion or concern from Bamford's relatives. However, on the evening of 13 April 1889, as the young woman was getting ready for a date with her boyfriend, she said something that attracted a definite raising of the eyebrows.

'I must put on some clean clothes,' she said. 'I'm going to die before the evening is over.'

While the comment was strange – creepy, in fact – it was said in such a calm way that the relative thought she was just making a bizarre joke, and said no more about it. A short time later, Feron came to pick up his sweetheart in a cab, presenting her with a bunch of lilies as he did so. The couple bid the family goodbye and went on their way.

They arrived at Derby station at 6.20 p.m., where they were seen laughing and being affectionate on the platform and in the first-class lounge. The couple then boarded a train to Nottingham where they headed to a local hotel for refreshments. While there, nobody reported any suspicious or agitated behaviour. However, when they made their return journey to Derby at 9.20 p.m., things were about to take a sinister turn.

Feron and Bamford were the only couple in the carriage and, as the train pulled into Trent station just six miles away, the conductor opened the door to check their tickets. Instead of a standard conversation, however, he was shocked to discover the young couple completely covered in blood. Closer inspection revealed that Lillie had been shot in the right temple and Feron in the left. He was quite dead, but she still showed signs of life.

The panicked conductor called for assistance and it was decided that the couple should remain on the train to Derby. The hope was that they could be transferred to the main hospital, where Bamford might possibly be saved. During the journey, the train staff had time to investigate the surroundings. The scene was grizzly, bloody and mysterious. Who had shot the couple and where had they gone?

All became clear when a revolver was found in the carriage and six spare bullets were discovered in Feron's breast pocket. It was obvious the man had shot his girlfriend and then himself at point-blank range. When the train pulled into Derby station, the couple were transferred to the hospital, where Feron was pronounced dead on arrival. Bamford hung on but passed away just fifteen minutes after arriving.

Nobody could understand why the tragedy had happened, since no quarrel or fight had been heard either before or during the train journey. Passengers in the next carriage – who were reported to be in a great deal of excitement after hearing the news – told reporters that there had been no signs of violence coming from their carriage at all. Furthermore, they swore they hadn't even heard any gunshots echoing through the walls.

An answer to the mystery seemed in sight when detectives searched Feron's pockets and found an abundance of notes and letters to his parents and various friends. 'I intend to take my own life,' said one. 'You will know the reason later on.' Unfortunately he never left any other clues as to why the tragedy occurred, and friends surmised he may have been jealous because Bamford was considered a great beauty with many admirers.

Lillie Bamford's family were left to forever ponder the strange comments she had made earlier that evening. Had the woman known she would be murdered because her jealous boyfriend had threatened it? Was it an agreed double-suicide, based on her disappointing acting aspirations? Or was her remark about dying just a strange but coincidental comment? They never found out and the mystery of the railway deaths was never solved.

Jack the Ripper and Emily Edith Smith

Nowadays – with the evolution of DNA testing and other techniques – it is relatively easy to discover the perpetrator of a crime. Sometimes the guilty parties are even found many years after they committed the deed. However, in Victorian times it was much harder to find the true culprit of a crime, leaving some serial killers – such as London's Jack the Ripper – nameless even more than a century later.

Many books and countless articles have been written about Jack. Was he a prince? The husband of one of the victims? A conman? A thief? A barrister? Or someone else entirely? The simple truth is that we will never know. The conspiracy theories and new stories are entertaining and enthralling, but Jack continues to be an enigma. He was one of the most famous people in the world, and yet we don't actually know him at all.

What we do know for sure is that there were five clear victims of Jack's crimes: Mary Ann Nichols, Annie Chapman, Elizabeth Stride, Catherine Eddowes and Mary Jane Kelly. However, there may have been more than the official victims. At the time of his reign of terror (*c.* 1888–91), there were other murders and attempted murders that looked very much like Jack's work. One woman swore that she had not only been attacked by Jack, but was able to gain a good look at the man too.

On 22 November 1892, newspapers carried the story of eighteen-year-old Emily Edith Smith. She had been a dressmaker and an artist's model in days gone by, but now some journalists described her as 'a young girl of the unfortunate class'. Others, however, did not believe this to be true and said she was a woman with 'a good education, quietly dressed and respectably connected'.

Smith claimed that on 5 November she was walking towards St Paul's Cathedral at about 5 p.m. As she did so, she was approached by a gentleman who called out, 'Goodnight, Nellie.' She had no idea why he had called to her in such a way, so kept on walking. The man, however, was not far behind. As he caught up he tried to make conversation again.

'Would you like a cup of tea?' he asked.

Smith ignored him.

'Would you like to go to my office?' he continued.

This time the woman acknowledged his presence and ended up accompanying him to a pub in Sutton Street. There the man ordered a small soda.

'I never drink anything stronger than soda,' he told her.

As they sat together in the public house, the woman was able to get a good look at her companion, and later remembered remarkable detail. According to Smith he was a pale man, approximately five foot nine, with dark hair and a bowler hat. His moustache was curled and did not match his hair colour; his teeth were somewhat rotten; and his eyebrows were described as 'very peculiar'. When later asked what she meant by that, Smith said that the ends turned up towards the temples and met in the bridge above his nose. His eyes were piercing, with one light brown in colour and the other blue/grey. His blinking motion seemed exaggerated, strange even, and he squinted very regularly. The man's clothes consisted of pinstriped trousers and a single-breasted coat; and he spoke as though educated, but with a slight foreign accent.

After finishing the drink, the man asked Smith to accompany him to his Whitechapel office. She agreed, but when she found herself being led down a dark, long, narrow passageway, she refused to go beyond.

'Let us go on a bit further,' the man said. 'My office is at the end of the passage.'

'I will not,' replied Smith.

'Then I'll settle you now,' he said and dragged her by the collar into a dark corner of the passageway. The terrified Smith told police that they were face-to-face, but then the man tried to turn her around. It was at that moment she saw a knife – described as the kind used by gardeners – and realised that he planned to slit her throat.

If this was indeed Jack the Ripper, he was about to get a huge surprise. Whereas his other victims had been fairly easy to control, Smith was not about to let the man murder her without a fight. She let out a huge scream and then kicked him between the legs as fast as she could. The man buckled over but still made an attempt to stab her as he did so. She dodged the knife and ran into the night, bumping into two women walking down Sutton Street. The witnesses managed to comfort and aid the victim while she told them her story, though by this time the would-be murderer had managed to escape. Smith was covered in bruises, but it was a small price to pay in comparison to what could have happened.

When the girl went to police, they agreed that it sounded very much like the circumstances surrounding Jack's other crimes. Even her description of the man was uncanny and matched almost exactly what they previously had on record. Despite the fact that Jack had been very quiet of late, officers seemed to take the story and description very seriously.

The girl's interview lasted three hours and her statement ran to ten large pages. In daylight hours, she visited the scene of the attack once again, and went over every detail of where, when and how it had happened. Reporters were intrigued and hailed the incident as the 'Return of Jack'. They gave readers a long and detailed description of what he looked like and one journalist even went to the passageway himself, just to make sure everything tallied up. It did.

However, despite reports saying that the police were taking the matter seriously, when the reporter visited the station closest to the scene of the crime, he was told they had not been informed of any event taking place. The reporter then called into Scotland Yard to hear for himself what they intended to do with the information Smith had provided. Unfortunately, it became apparent that while the story and description were intriguing, the police were not keen to do any follow-ups at all.

When questioned further, they said that the authorities had received literally hundreds of similar statements from so-called victims, and that they were unable to take Smith's story any more seriously than the others they had received over the years.

As a result, nothing ever came of the sighting, and the mystery of Jack the Ripper and his would-be victim remained unsolved.

The Strange Tale of the Tomato Girl

Mr and Mrs Savage from Boston, USA, had been excited to discover they were expecting a child. As with many pregnant women, it wasn't long before Mrs Savage began having cravings, and her food of choice was tomatoes.

When baby Grace Savage was born in 1890, on the back of her neck she displayed a bright red birthmark. This in itself was not unusual, since many babies are born each year with marks on their body. What made this remarkable, however, was that the mark looked exactly like a tomato, the object of her mother's cravings. As she grew, the marking took on a whole new meaning, when the little girl's favourite food became – you guessed it – tomatoes. She loved them so much, in fact, that they were the only thing she ever wanted to eat, and was frequently seen around her home with a tomato in her hand.

Sadly, the little girl did not live to see adulthood, and passed away in 1888 at the age of eight. She was buried in Holy Cross cemetery, and her parents planted several flowers on her grave to remember her. During the summer of 1900, Grace's father visited the plot and was stunned to discover that, among the wild flowers, there were several tomato plants growing there. This remarkable discovery was mysterious because the man claimed to have never planted them.

The plants became a positive symbol to the Savages and they believed that their daughter was still watching over them. In the weeks ahead, the couple took care of the plants as though they were the most beautiful of flowers. When they started to bear fruit, Mr and Mrs Savage became even more impressed, and shared the story with various friends and family members.

One day during a visit to the cemetery, Mr Savage was shocked and saddened to discover that the plants and flowers had all been stolen from his daughter's grave. So angry was the man that he went home and wrote an advert for his local newspaper, telling the story of the tomatoes and offering a reward of $10 for the capture of the fruit thieves.

In the days ahead, the story was reported in various newspapers, but the thief was never found. There were, of course, various people willing to share their thoughts on the matter. Some put forward the claim that perhaps a homeless person had seen the fruit and taken it to eat. Others, however, said that it was only fitting for the tomatoes to disappear under such mysterious circumstances, given the part they had played in the life – and afterlife – of little Grace Savage.

The Weymouth Outrage

Weymouth is known as a beautiful British seaside resort, which in the past has played host to kings, dukes and many other people of importance. However, in 1889 it was a working-class man who made the headlines in the most foul and stomach-churning way.

Frederick Burt was a cab owner who was frequently seen driving round the streets in his horse-drawn cart. Sarah Guy was a young woman who – in the words of the newspapers – 'lived at a wretched home at Weymouth and supported herself by her shame'.

In reality she lived with her father, John Guy, though their house could very well be described as wretched. Mr Guy drank heavily, and was abusive and brutal. Her mother had passed and her stepmother was currently living in the poor house. Sarah Guy had two illegitimate children – one of whom died and the other had been made a ward of the parish. She did not have regular employment, though the description of her supporting herself by her shame would imply that she was a known prostitute.

While Mr Guy claimed to be getting his house back in order, the police kept a watchful eye and regularly called in to see if everything was all right. On one occasion, they reported seeing Sarah Guy lying on sacks because her father had pawned her bed. On another they stated that she owned no shoes because her father had sold them for drink. John Guy denied the latter accusation, but fully admitted to pawning his daughter's bed in order to pay the rent. He did not think this was a terrible thing to do, however, and had no idea why the police had such an interest in his house.

In 1888, Sarah Guy began spending time with Frederick Burt, who had once rented a room in the family home. Her father did not particularly like the cab driver and later recalled marching to Burt's stables and finding her there with him. On that occasion, Mr Guy forced his daughter to return home, but a short time later – in July 1888 – Sarah Guy disappeared altogether.

Her father later told the coroner that he had been worried about his daughter's whereabouts and had asked literally hundreds of people if they had seen her. He had also taken his queries to the police but they were unable to help him. However, one day he was walking along the Weymouth Esplanade when he saw Frederick Burt in his cab.

'Burt, have you seen or heard anything of my daughter?' he asked.

'No, but she said she was moving to London,' replied the cab driver.

In reality, however, Frederick Burt knew exactly where the girl was, and it most certainly wasn't London. At the end of July 1888, Sarah Guy had gone with Burt to his house as she had done several times before. However, on this occasion she was prevented from leaving by the cab driver, who proceeded to lock her in the shed at the bottom of his garden. This outhouse also happened to be within easy reach of the stable where she had been caught by her father a short time before. Strangely, however, at no point did John Guy ever think to look for her there. His excuse was that he had believed Burt when he told him she had moved to London and saw no reason for him to lie.

Inside the shed was an old box and some rugs and sacks, and these things were to become Sarah's sole belongings in the months ahead. According to reports, Frederick Burt's intention for having the woman in his shed was for 'immoral purposes' and, in that regard, he would visit only to assault her and provide meagre rations of stale bread and mouldy cheese. If she ever asked to leave, Sarah Guy was met by an avalanche of abuse and threats, before the door was firmly locked once again.

For the next nine months, the woman lived a life of absolute torture. The shed was only four feet high, so at no time was she able to stand up straight. Added to that, Burt refused to give her any change of clothes but expected her to keep things clean. This often meant she was in a severe state of undress while she tried desperately to wash and dry her things in a bucket. The only time Sarah Guy was allowed to leave the shed was at the beginning of winter when things took a sudden cold turn. Then Burt transferred her to the stable and locked her in his cab, before taking her back to the shed when he had installed a small stove.

Officers who later saw the building noted that it was pitch-black when the door was shut, and wasn't fit for a dog to live in, never mind a human. The situation was horrifying. Guy found it impossible to tell between night and day and her mental and physical health both suffered. On most days, she remained silent in the outhouse, despite children playing in the gardens around her and servants hanging out washing just yards away. However, on one particular afternoon, the cook of a nearby doctor was in the garden and heard a woman's voice coming from the shed. She leaned over and saw Frederick Burt doing something outside.

'Is that your wife in the shed?' she asked.

The man scowled and replied, 'Mind your own business.'

The woman got back to her work and thought no more about it.

Another servant had been sleeping with her window open during the summer months and was woken with a scream.

'Murder! Murder! Murder!' the voice echoed through the night air.

'I looked out the window and saw a light in Burt's stable,' she said. 'I continued to look out for about ten minutes and saw that the light was continually blown out and relit. The stable door was open. After the third scream everything went quiet and I went back to bed, but the light in the stable was still on. The next morning I told my employer about it. Several others had heard the screams too.'

Meanwhile, Burt continued his cab-driving business, and bumped into John Guy on a variety of occasions. Each time the girl's father would ask if he had heard anything from her.

'Burt, haven't you had a letter from her?' he asked.

'No,' he replied. 'I should think Jack the Ripper got hold of her.'

One day in mid-March 1889, John Guy bumped into Burt again and asked one more time if he had heard from his daughter.

'No, there's something very strange about it,' he said, before pretending he was on a call and driving away.

In the same week as Frederick Burt told Sarah's father that something odd was going on, the girl herself finally managed to escape from the shed. It all came about because the cab driver left the door open while he was entertaining some male friends in the stable. The girl sneaked up to the stable door and listened intently.

'I have got her in the shed,' Burt told his friends. 'I must get rid of her.'

The girl went back to her place of captivity and was eventually locked back in while Burt left the back garden. Then, taking a piece of iron – the top half of a poker – the woman was able to prise the hinges off the door and crash straight into the back garden of a man called Dr Brown. It was ten o'clock at night, and Sarah Guy was terrified.

In the kitchen, Dr Brown's cook was attending to her duties when she heard a knock at the door. From the window, she could not see whether or not the visitor was a man or woman, so rushed upstairs to find Mrs Brown. By the time the two women came back into the kitchen, Sarah Guy had let herself in and was curled up on a chair.

Wearing a sweater, a man's jacket, an old skirt and no shoes, Guy was shaking and in a clearly agitated state. She looked like a homeless woman and her hair was covered in small papers, the kind used to try to create curls. She later admitted that these papers had been in her hair for months and it was almost impossible to get them out in one piece. Despite the obvious despair, however, Sarah Guy managed to tell Mrs Brown the story of her captivity and how she had managed to escape.

'Burty will kill me! Burty will kill me!' she shouted over and over again.

As Guy rocked back and forth with the iron still in her hand, Mrs Brown made up her mind that the woman was clearly not well.

'I thought she was a lunatic,' she said. 'Her eyes were starting out of her head and she looked wild.'

After asking some initial questions – which the shaken woman was able to answer – Mrs Brown sent for the colonel who lived next door. He surmised that she was either a lunatic or had escaped something terribly traumatic. He phoned the police then took Guy into his home. Servant Isabella Cruikshank was put in charge of her until help arrived. She wasted no time in asking the woman exactly what was going on, and Sarah Guy told the story of Frederick Burt planning to murder her. This time, however, she said he had accomplices who were going to help with the crime.

Cruikshank listened in wonder and then asked if the woman had been drinking. She hadn't, and insisted that for the past four days she had been starved of all food. The servant made Guy something to eat, but she was so weak it couldn't be eaten. She then sipped on some tea before Cruikshank helped her to bathe and put her to bed.

Back at Dr Brown's house, the cook returned to her work in the kitchen, and decided to pull down the blinds at the back window. From where she stood, the cause of Sarah Guy's fears was soon revealed. There in the moonlit garden was Frederick Burt on his hands and knees, crawling around the flower beds.

'Is that you, Burt?' she shouted from the window.

'Yes, miss,' he replied.

The woman rushed next door to alert a police officer who had arrived at the colonel's house. After listening to her story, he found Burt just outside the garden, in a sheepish state. At first, the man denied all knowledge of being in the doctor's garden and tried to make a run for it. He was handcuffed and taken away under a charge of trespassing.

The next morning, Sarah Guy was given fresh clothes and managed to eat an orange. She could not keep it down, however, and was soon taken to hospital to be examined and treated for her injuries. Once there she managed to give investigators snippets of what had happened in the past nine months, but it was clear to everyone that she was in terrible health.

'Her mind is so weak as to necessitate her being sent to the local lunatic asylum,' prosecutors said. 'It is considered doubtful whether she will survive, her physical and mental condition being terrible.'

As she was suffering not only from mental problems but consumption, too, it was impossible to officially question Guy about her ordeal. The result of this was that when Burt appeared in court, Guy had to be supported by friends and could only mumble incoherently. This gave rise to the notion that the woman was either suffering from insanity or on the brink of it. As a result, prosecutors could only deal with the trespass issue, since they had no concrete evidence that Frederick Burt had imprisoned Sarah Guy for almost a year. The case was adjourned and the poor woman taken to an asylum to face an uncertain future.

When Burt went back to court in April, a letter was read out from the asylum doctor. 'April 6th 1889 – I have to certify that Sarah Guy is the subject of mental disease of an open and pronounced nature; that she is also suffering from acute disease of the lungs, and is wholly unfit to appear or give evidence as a witness. – P. W. MacDonald, M. D.'

The solicitor for the defence jumped on this disclosure and begged the magistrate not to adjourn the case once again. According to him, his client had been through enough already and the woman was quite simply 'insane through her own misdeeds . . . It is simply torture for Frederick Burt to be remanded time after time, while he all the time knows he has a clear answer to it. Let the case be struck out; and then if the girl recovers and is in a fit state to be brought up, he should be happy to offer any encouragement or assistance for the hearing of the charge to be proceeded with.'

Despite the prosecution's appeal against the notion, the case was dropped due to lack of evidence. Unbelievably, Frederick Burt was then allowed to walk free. Local people were absolutely aghast and disgusted at the events that had taken place right under their noses. When Burt left the Dorchester court, he was attacked and hit by the baying mob, which then followed him to the police station and repeated the events there. So indignant were the crowds that the man was unable to leave the station by the front door in order to make his way home. In the end, frustrated police officers opened the back door and helped the man over a wall. From there he ran several miles over various fields, until he finally arrived at his house.

While Frederick Burt was able to get on with his life, the same cannot be said for poor Sarah Guy. As the prosecutors predicted, the frail woman did not recover, and just a month later she was found dead at the asylum.

A variety of witnesses were called to the inquest, including Frederick Burt, policemen, neighbours and servants from a nearby house. The latter told the court they had heard a woman screaming on several occasions. The colonel who had met Sarah Guy on the evening of her escape said that once he had heard a terrible fight coming from the garden. He assumed that it was going on between Burt and a woman, though he did not enquire further: 'It was my place I suppose, to go and tell Burt to put a stop to the disgraceful brawl, but I did not do so, and it never occurred again.'

Dr Brown's cook repeated the story of how Guy believed Burt and several other men were trying to murder her and that had prompted her to escape once and for all. The colonel confirmed this by explaining that Guy had mentioned the names Baker, Hinton and Miller to him on the night of her escape. Apparently, these men were fellow cab drivers and associated with Burt.

Despite all evidence to the contrary, the coroner told the court that there could not be any assumption that Sarah Guy had ever been confined to the shed. 'People should not pay attention to all they saw in the newspapers,' he said. 'The difficulty is how can we prove there had ever been a confinement?'

The policeman who arrested Burt for trespassing on Dr Brown's property thought he had the answer. When questioned, he told the coroner that the following conversation had transpired between himself and the arrested man:

'You are charged with being on Dr Brown's premises for an unlawful purpose and you will now be charged further with detaining this girl, Sarah Guy, against her will for the last twelve months.'

Apparently Frederick Burt shook his head and replied: 'No, 'tis not so long as that. Not more than six months . . .'

Another policeman told the court that on inspecting the shed, he'd found it in a terrible condition and it was apparent that someone had been living there. There were a variety of belongings scattered around, and an old sack showed vomit and bloodstains.

'I didn't know she was living here,' said Burt. 'But Hinton knew.'

One of the nurses from the asylum got up and said she had never heard Sarah Guy talk about being imprisoned but she had exclaimed how 'wicked' her life had been in the past. A doctor then spoke of the terrible condition the woman had been in on her admittance to the asylum. According to him she was barely coherent for the whole time she was there, and had to sleep with the light burning in her room. Her condition grew weaker each day until finally the poor woman passed away. After a post-mortem examination, he came to the conclusion that the immediate cause of death was consumption. When questioned as to whether or not confinement in a shed could cause such an illness, the doctor was fairly positive in his response.

'Confinement in an unsanitary place would produce disease,' he said. 'But I am not prepared to state that the condition of the deceased woman was produced by such a cause.'

When it was time for Frederick Burt to take the stand, he did so with a huge speech prepared. According to him, Guy was an immoral woman whom he had known for several years.

'I used to go with her from time to time at her father's house and have been there when other men have come for a similar purpose. Have been there, stopping in the house for three weeks or a month together and her father was aware of the relations between us, and had been in the same room. I would give the father money for beer and food sometimes, after I'd been with the deceased.'

According to Burt, Sarah Guy had left her father's house because he was a hopeless drunk who threatened to beat her up when she could not give him money for alcohol. She went with him voluntarily and would sleep in his cab through the night and then live in the shed through the day. To his mind, she could have left any time she wanted, as he only locked the building at night and left her with the keys during the day. Nevertheless, according to Burt the woman much preferred the time alone in the shed to living with her abusive father, so chose to stay where she was.

It was apparent to many that the time Guy spent in the shed had been a significant factor in the state of her health. However, because there was no evidence that she was not there against her will, no criminal charges were ever brought. 'The women died of natural courses,' the coroner said. The case was then finished and Burt and the rumoured co-conspirators walked away as 'innocent' men.

The Many Instances of Terrible 'Trigamy'

While bigamy was a big enough crime in Victorian times, a new word was invented by the media for when one or even two wives were just not enough. Trigamy was the name given to

those men and women who were accused of having three part-
ners, and while taken very seriously by authorities, the stories
were often baffling, bizarre or downright amusing.

Peter Giles was brought to trial in New Albany, Indiana,
during 1857 after he had been charged with trigamy by three
women – Mary, Bridget and Nancy. Described by journalists as
'Three large and healthy-looking, but not very refined women',
it seemed that they had all been involved with the man at the
same time and, once this was discovered, had set about taking
revenge.

Their reprisal took the form of telling authorities that Peter
had married each of them separately, and since he had never
divorced any of them, he was committing trigamy. The judge
poured great scorn over Peter's attitude towards women,
describing him as someone who 'erred most grossly against the
seventh article of the Decalogue, and was withal a reckless
trifler with female affections'. However, he could find absolutely no evidence whatsoever that he had actually gone through
with even one wedding, never mind three.

The characters of the women were gone over in great detail
during the short trial, and their countless transgressions were
listed, one by one. At no time did any of the women show
shock or even concern that their lives were on show for all to
see, and a journalist noted that 'none of the would-be wives
were of a kind to beget a great degree of sympathy'.

The judge realised that the three women had come together
in order to plot against Peter Giles, so the case was dismissed.
The scorned lovers were furious that their plans for revenge had
not worked out and, as they left court, were overheard plotting
what they could do next to him. Peter, meanwhile, fled from
the building a wounded man; scared no doubt of the women,

but also – it was claimed – because he did not want the judge to bring up any other offence that could be proven in court.

Fifteen years later, another trigamy case was revealed, when Georgetown man J. H. McCurdy was said to be married to three different women at once. His dilemma arose after he had wed his first wife only because she paid him. Her motivation was never determined, but McCurdy apparently didn't think the marriage was legal, and after their separation he wed again. When that too did not work out, the woman reluctantly agreed to divorce him, but only if he promised never to marry again in her lifetime. McCurdy agreed and the declaration was written into their divorce papers. Should he go against this rule, the divorce would become null and void.

A few years after that particular separation, he fell in love yet again; this time to a wealthy heiress from Pennsylvania. They wasted no time in getting married, with McCurdy's father officiating at the ceremony. However, while the groom's father might have been perfectly happy with the union, the bride's was not. He did some investigation into his new son-in-law's life, and discovered that his first marriage was not dissolved. Not only that, he also uncovered the divorce agreement with the second wife that McCurdy had conveniently forgotten.

The groom found out about the discoveries when he received a letter from his father-in-law, which sent him straight to his lawyer's office. However, McCurdy's visit was not to sort out affairs with the first or even second wife. Instead, it was so that he could draw up a will. In the document, he promised $300,000 to wife number three and then conveniently skipped town – or as one newspaper put it, 'he left by coach for some other field of usefulness'.

In 1899, an interesting but sad case appeared when an elderly American man by the name of Charles E. Leslie was arrested and sentenced to prison, on the charge of having three wives. His sorry story began when he married wife number one, some years earlier. Shortly after the wedding, Leslie realised that he had absolutely nothing in common with the woman, and later claimed she made his life an absolute misery. He moved out of their shared home and went straight to a lawyer to file for divorce.

Leslie paid the man a substantial amount of money, and sometime later the attorney brought him a receipt and claimed the divorce was now final. Being somewhat inept at the legalities of this kind of thing, and being 'an ignorant person' as the newspapers called him, Leslie trusted that the lawyer had kept the divorce papers on file, and went on with his life. Of course, the law man had done no such thing, since he had never actually filed the divorce and had merely kept Leslie's money.

Not knowing about any of this, and thinking he was a free man, Leslie married again. However, wife number one was aware there was no divorce between them, and had been tracking Leslie's whereabouts ever since. When she found that he was now with another woman, she wasted no time in having him arrested and locked up for bigamy. Leslie then served a year in prison, and on his release told friends that he would not return to either of his wives. According to him, wife number one was a virago whom he was well rid of, while wife number two would – quite understandably – have nothing more to do with him.

Unbelievably, Leslie now thought that his year in prison had voided both his first and second marriages. Why he thought that, and why no one told him otherwise, is a mystery, but the man happily told friends he was now a free man and was ready to find love for a third and final time.

Leslie moved to the country and met a widow called Mrs Mary Holzworth. Her children were violently opposed to her having anything to do with the man, but she did not agree with their evaluation. The couple married and settled into what they hoped would be a peaceful life. Unknown to them, however, wife number one was on the warpath and once more managed to track down her yet-to-be-divorced husband. Armed with documents proving the two were still married, she arrived in Leslie's new town, gave her story to the authorities and he was arrested once again.

The man pleaded his innocence and told the sheriff that he couldn't possibly be married to three women at once. As far as he was concerned, the year in prison had voided all other marriages and he was now only betrothed to the former Mrs Holzworth. It was explained to him that all his prison sentence had done was give wife number one the grounds to divorce him should she wish. His disapproving stepchildren looked on as he was led away and ultimately sentenced to two years in prison.

'The world has been using me very badly of late,' he wrote to friends. 'My pension is being paid to my first wife and in my old age, I am a convict without money or home.'

There was never any word as to whether or not wife one ever decided to divorce the man, but third wife Mary certainly did. On hearing that he would be released from prison a few months early, the woman went straight to an attorney, who filed separation papers in August 1900. Charles was then released a month later, when he was spotted in New Philadelphia, 'attending to business matters'. He then finally retired to his old home in

Wood County, to live out the rest of his days in peace and without romantic entanglements.

The Startling Confession of Priscilla Guppy

In November 1857, ninety-year-old Priscilla Guppy was living out her last days at home in Weymouth, England. Her body was frail but, even so, she was about to make headlines all over the country.

As she struggled to draw a breath, Priscilla gathered her family around her in order to share her last words. However, there were to be no declarations of love, and no last wishes or final goodbyes. Instead, she had a confession to make . . . Sixty-five years previously, when she was a young woman of just twenty-five, Guppy had been involved in a terrible crime – the murder of a local man.

Her family were shocked. For over half a century, the woman had lived quietly, had never made headlines or caused any particular scandal, and yet here she was, admitting to something utterly disturbing.

It soon transpired that the woman had worked in a house of ill-repute, which was frequented by a gentleman by the name of Tillroyd Morgan. On one particular evening, he got into a fight with a farmer called Hardy, and ended up being hit over the head to such an extent that he died straightaway. How it had happened was always a mystery to police, and it wasn't until his body was found wrapped in a sheet that they knew anyone had been killed at all.

Blood had been discovered at the bridge where the man was found, and led all the way from there to the brothel where he had last been seen. With this information, police gathered up the three most likely candidates for the crime – Guppy, Hardy and his friend Tiddins. All were taken to court but there was virtually no evidence to charge them. Hardy in particular had an airtight alibi – he had been home at the time of the murder and his servant had seen him there. How could he have possibly committed the crime if he was miles away at the time? The three were acquitted due to lack of evidence and the case was eventually all but forgotten.

It wasn't until 1857 that Priscilla Guppy felt it time to explain exactly what had happened on the night of the murder, and what her involvement had been. According to the woman, although Hardy had argued with the murdered man, it wasn't he who had served the fatal blow. Instead she had done it, crashing an iron rod into his head with enough force to shatter the skull. Hardy and Tiddins wrapped up the victim and placed him on Hardy's horse, ready to be thrown into the harbour. However, they were disturbed at the last moment and ended up dumping the body under the bridge.

'I beat him in the head with an iron!' the old woman shouted. 'May God have mercy on my soul!'

Priscilla Guppy's family were totally shocked at the confession, but it didn't end there. According to the woman, when she appeared in court, she had brazenly hidden Morgan's gold watch and chain in her hair. Guppy's confession was shocking, but it also meant that there was another mystery to unravel. If Hardy had been on the scene when the murder occurred, and had also been the one who dumped the body under the bridge, how could he have been seen at home by his servant? Had the employee lied to protect her employer? Guppy shook her head; she knew exactly how Hardy had acquired an airtight alibi.

After committing the crime and returning home that evening, Hardy had turned the house clock back by two hours. Shortly afterwards he woke up his servant and asked her to go downstairs to check the clock. She then told him the time, not knowing that the piece had been deliberately tampered with. This meant that while Hardy had been dumping Morgan's body, his servant would always believe he was at home with her. She had no reason to believe he would lie.

Shortly after her confession. Priscilla Guppy passed away. Her family then took the story to the police and press, but because she had been the last remaining suspect, nothing more could be done. Instead, several reporters interviewed old Weymouth residents, who confirmed that Guppy was whispered to have been at the house when Morgan was murdered. They then directed the journalists to the graveyard of St Mary's Church, where they found the victim's gravestone, complete with a chilling message:

This stone was erected by Public Subscription in remembrance of the cruel murder committed on the body of Tillroyd Morgan, who lies here, on the 27th April, 1792, aged 22 . . . Here mingling with my fellow clay, I await the awful judgment day, and there my murderer shall appear, although escaped from justice here.

Miss Bailey's Bizarre Bournemouth Nightmare

Louisa Bailey was a colourful woman from South Wales, who made a stir in the newspapers in 1885 by taking out a breach-of-promise suit against a mining engineer called David Morgan

Llewellyn. The man had courted her, kissed her passionately and – according to Bailey – promised to marry her. During their time together, she undertook several college courses in an attempt to better herself, but even so, Llewellyn never thought she was quite good enough for him.

The man's family apparently did not approve of the relationship and so Llewellyn used this as an excuse to break up with her on a variety of occasions. Finally, after his admittance that he preferred a bachelor life with lots of different women, Louisa realised that the entire relationship had been a farce and brought a breach-of-promise suit against him.

Evidence lodged with the court included 105 letters between the pair, as well as diaries and other testimony. By this time, Llewellyn was adamant he had never asked Bailey to marry him; he had merely promised that he may ask in the future. Eventually the woman won the huge sum of £1200, which was later amended to £950 on appeal. However, this was not the end of the matter; not by a long shot.

For the next ten years, Louisa Bailey's name was linked to Llewellyn's in a variety of bizarre episodes. Three years after the initial court case, they were back in court again; only this time it was because Llewellyn had accused Bailey of starting a fight with him while he was in the company of his new sweetheart. According to witnesses, the woman threatened to murder her former love and drown herself in the river. Llewellyn was then accused of taking Bailey by the throat and kicking her knee.

After airing their laundry once again, the couple got on with their lives, which for Miss Bailey included sending threatening notes to Llewellyn. According to the woman, she had been hospitalised due to the injuries inflicted by him on her knee, and did not intend to let him get away with it. The letters and threats ended with her being taken to court in 1895, where she was fined and sent on her way.

In spring 1896, Bailey seemed to have finally exorcised Llewellyn from her life and was trying to turn her fortunes around. In an attempt to change direction, she wrote to a prominent Bournemouth businessman, Mr King, to see if she could gain employment in his fancy store. The answer was positive, so she moved to the English coast and began working for the remainder of the year. Quite strangely, however, no sooner had the woman set up home in Bournemouth than a gentleman began making enquiries about her, predominantly in the King's store. One employee later recalled a conversation between the man and herself:

'Does Louisa Bailey work here?' he asked.

'She does, sir,' replied the assistant.

'That is all I wished to know,' the man said and promptly left the building.

The encounter was creepy and could very well have been related to the Llewellyn scandals, but nothing more came of the enquiries and the man disappeared. Miss Bailey continued her work at Mr King's store, and when her contract came to an end, she hosted a small party for six of her colleagues in a room she had rented above a restaurant. There the women all said goodbye by toasting Bailey with a half-bottle of brandy and having some 'jollification', as she later described it.

While one job had ended, another was due to begin in Margate just two weeks later, so Miss Bailey decided to stay in Bournemouth until then. However, the day after the party, she was unexpectedly visited by Mrs Digby, a customer from King's shop. Bailey was surprised to see her, since she had never had anything to do with her at all, but she invited her into the room anyway. Once there, Mrs Digby apparently saw the open bottle of brandy on the bedside table and drew some rather strange and negative conclusions from it. As a result, Digby then rather unexpectedly invited Bailey to her home, and she accepted.

What happened next is sketchy and mysterious, but by all accounts she was taken to a nursing home-type establishment, which was presided over by Mrs Digby. There she was visited by a doctor who forced her to be examined and assigned a nurse to her case. The terrified woman tried to leave the house but was prevented from doing so. Things became worse when some of her clothes were taken away during the night and she had no idea where they had gone.

For the next two weeks Bailey was essentially a prisoner in the house and only allowed to go into the garden under supervision. Unbelievably, during that time she was asked to sign a document declaring she was an inebriate, the idea being that she could then be locked in a secure facility for at least six months. Miss Bailey refused to sign anything at all, declaring that at no time was she ever addicted to alcohol.

'If you do not sign, something worse will happen to you,' said the doctor, but still Bailey refused to leave her mark. This left Mrs Digby and her fellow captor with a dilemma – either they let the woman go or they take her against her will.

In the end, they did a mixture of both. The couple allowed Miss Bailey to escape and then phoned the police to report that a 'wandering lunatic' was on the loose. Bailey was found, taken to Bournemouth police station and spent the evening in a cell. When the woman asked what exactly she had done wrong, the sergeant refused to tell her. The next morning she was taken to court, where four magistrates were waiting for her.

'What have I done?' asked Bailey, to which she was told to be quiet. The men then studied some documents handed to them by the doctor who had kept her prisoner in the first place. When asked if she could see the documents herself, Bailey was refused, and then one of the men spoke.

'Miss Bailey, if you had a friend here to take you out of court, I would let you go,' he said. 'Instead, we are going to send you to an asylum.'

The woman was understandably incensed, and totally confused at what had happened to her in the past few weeks. She protested bitterly, but this only made the magistrates even more confident that they had made the correct decision. At that moment, Bailey knew that there was nothing she could do but quietly face her fate.

'In my defenceless condition,' she told an interviewer, 'what could I do? But I must say that one of the four magistrates shook his head and declined to sign the committal order. Nevertheless, amid frantic protestations I was wheeled away into captivity.'

The woman was taken to the train station, where she boarded a train to Knowle asylum, a red-bricked building which housed almost one thousand patients. After her ordeal, Miss Bailey described the experience of reaching the 'jail-like' institution to reporters at *Lloyd's Weekly Newspaper*:

'My heart sank within me. A bell clanged, the gates swung open and we passed into a broad yard where an attendant came to the carriage. He wanted to assist me to alight, but I refused saying, "I can get out by myself. They are bringing a sane person here, not an insane one." "So much the better for that," was his reply.'

Bailey was taken into the office, where the policeman in charge of her handed over paperwork to a waiting doctor.

'I am perfectly sane,' she told him, 'and protest against being brought here. There has never been anything the matter with me.'

'Oh very well,' he replied. 'We must see. Many tell us that and you will have to stay here until we see.'

The woman was then bathed, weighed and measured, before being taken to an infirmary where she was to stay with seven other women. The nurse in charge – a stern woman called Julia – then demanded she hand over everything she had been wearing. This disturbed Bailey, who asked if she could at least keep her house keys.

'No,' the nurse replied with a grin. 'You can keep nothing. We keep the keys here.'

Her first night was horrifying. Describing some of the women as 'absolutely raving mad', Bailey had to contend with screams, shouts and groans, some of which were aimed at her.

'In all my life I never had such a terrible experience,' she said. 'The smell of the room was awful. Not a wink of sleep could I get for the noise which the mad women made all night. One woman in particular, with a broken leg, kept pointing her finger at me and crying "Whoo-o-o" in most unearthly tones, and this lasted for hours.'

The next morning Miss Bailey was examined by a doctor, who declared her perfectly well. Sensing a sympathetic man, she then explained her situation in the hope that he would fight her corner. Unfortunately, this was not to be the case, and the man told a nurse to take the woman into the day room in order to mingle with the other patients. Bailey was greatly displeased at this new development and pleaded with the doctor to let her stay in the infirmary.

'They will not hurt you, Miss Bailey,' he replied. 'And you must comply with the rules.'

Things took another bad turn when Nurse Julia was asked to help her get dressed. The asylum uniform was made of very coarse cotton and thick, uncomfortable corsets. The nurse seemed to take great delight in hurting Miss Bailey while 'helping' her into the garments. When she asked Julia to be gentler and to please stop calling her by her Christian name, the woman laughed.

'Pooh!' she said. 'I'll do as I like. You'll have to behave yourself here or I'll put you into a padded room.'

Life in the asylum was grim, dangerous and downright disgraceful. Curious visitors – including a variety of doctors and a priest – all came and went. But in spite of the fact that Miss Bailey told each and every one that she was there against her will, nobody did anything at all to help. This seems to have been a problem with the asylum staff more than anything and the woman later complained that no matter how much the visitors seemed to believe her story, someone would always whisper, 'She's just deluded,' and that would be the end of the matter.

After her time in the infirmary, Miss Bailey was placed in a ward of forty deranged patients. Food was scarce and when it did come it was barely edible, being made up primarily of a tiny piece of meat, one potato and thick, hard bread. If a patient refused to eat what was put in front of them, they were wrestled to the ground and force-fed with instruments.

On one particular day, Miss Bailey was told by doctors that she really shouldn't be in the institution, and that if a friend or relative came for her, she would be free to leave. This was quite positive news until the doctor dropped a bombshell: 'I wrote to them,' he said, 'but your friends do not want you in Bournemouth and your brother wants nothing to do with you. Therefore you must remain.'

This was all rather sceptical and Bailey took it upon herself to try to get letters out to her friends. She wrote several and hid them in her clothes while she went walking in the grounds. At last an opportunity presented itself when a wagon went past and she was able to throw the letters onto the back. Unfortunately a warden saw what she had done, stopped the driver and retrieved the notes. The spirited woman then refused to return to the asylum until the letters were returned to her. This resulted in her being wrestled to the ground and literally pulled along the gravel path towards the building.

'Run away! Run away!' she shouted to her fellow patients, and several took the opportunity to try.

The punishment for trying to get letters out into the world was a transfer to H Ward, where the most deranged women were kept. One day when out walking in the courtyard, Bailey's life took a turn for the worse:

'I was attacked by a mad woman, who sprang upon me like a savage dog. She not only bit my cheek to the bone, but tore my lips, blacked my eyes, and bruised me from top to toe. The medical superintendent was evidently much alarmed at the occurrence and had me put into another ward where, for a time, I was completely prostrated.'

Her removal from H Ward came as a relief but it was short-lived. Determined to make an escape from the asylum, Bailey managed to steal a chisel from a carpenter, but it was found before she could use it. Then she scaled a wall, only to be hauled back as she got to the top. Her punishment for both incidents was to be transferred back to the ward, where 'the inmates filled me with terror and aversion'.

After eleven months of captivity, a proper chance to escape finally came thanks to an injured passer-by. Miss Bailey and other patients had been allowed beyond the walls of the asylum, in order to exercise in a field nearby. They had been outside for a while when a cyclist came past and fell from his bike. As wardens and other patients ran to try to help, Bailey took the opportunity to slip through a gap in the hedge and sprint across several fields. There she found a bush with a large hole underneath and crept in, out of sight from everyone.

Of course, the superintendents at the asylum were not going to let her get away easily. As soon as they discovered she had gone, the alarms went off and a troop of wardens was sent out to try to catch her. Bailey later described how she could hear gunshots going off all around her, but never did she move from the hole. At one point, she recalled some of the wardens coming quite close to where she was hiding, and one exclaimed, 'Poor thing, I hope she will get clean away this time.'

When the staff eventually gave up and went back to the institution, Bailey remained still. It was not until 11 p.m., when she heard the chimes from the asylum's tower, that she felt confident enough to come out of her hiding place. By this time the woman was drenched with rain and very cold, but managed to shelter under a tree until the clock struck two. Realising she was most likely safe, Bailey then made her way over fences, fields, railway lines and brooks, hiding in the tall wet grass whenever she thought she could hear someone coming her way.

Eventually Miss Bailey found herself at Botley station. She was soaked, with bloody hands and hair that had literally been pulled through a hedge backwards, but she did not give up her quest for freedom. It was 6.45 a.m. and another passenger on the platform took pity on her. 'She noticed that I looked very ill,' she said. 'She gave me some tea, and we travelled together to Southampton.' Once there, Miss Bailey managed to get a message to a friend using a four-shilling coin that she had been hiding in her asylum uniform. 'This coin saved me,' she said.

The events of the eleven months prior to her escape were haunting and depressing, but at no time did Miss Bailey allow herself to be moulded by them. Several months after her ordeal, she took her story to the press in an effort to clear her name. *Lloyd's Weekly Newspaper* was especially sympathetic and offered her ample space to disclose her story.

'Throughout, Miss Bailey protested against the proceedings,' they reported, 'and very naturally, for they appear to have been illegal and informal from beginning to end, and the conduct of all concerned in them, it is urged, calls for close and immediate inquiry.'

When Louisa Bailey was interviewed after her escape, she made comment that she believed her previous altercations with former love David Morgan Llewellyn had something to do with the terrible experience she had just been through. She went no further with her remarks, but perhaps she believed her threats towards the man had resulted in some kind of bizarre revenge plot. It was forever unclear as to whether or not the two situations were related and certainly Llewellyn never made any public comment, one way or the other.

While Bailey was determined to get her story into the public domain, it would seem that no inquiry or action was ever taken against the asylum or those who put her there. Even after the woman's freedom was gained, there came no apology from anyone at all. When reporters knocked at the door of one of the magistrates that had originally sectioned her, he refused to comment, except to declare it 'a lovely case for the newspapers and Miss Bailey'. The asylum doctors then took their own revenge for the escape when the woman asked if she could send a friend to collect her clothes. They laughingly replied, 'Since you were not properly discharged, the clothes will not be given up.' The garments were then sent to Bournemouth and remained in the care of authorities there.

After that, Miss Bailey all but disappeared from the public eye. Her relationship with David Morgan Llewellyn seemed to be forgotten and certainly no mention of altercations ever appeared in the newspapers. After recovering sufficiently from the ordeal, Louisa acquired work in another shop and told her employer all about what had happened while in captivity. He was stunned and in disbelief that anyone would think the woman was mentally ill.

The Knowle asylum – under a variety of different names – continued to operate for the next one hundred years. It eventually closed in the 1990s and is now an apartment building.

Mary Stansbury: The Selfish Housewife

Mary Stansbury was the exceedingly beautiful wife of a baker, residing near Edgware Road, London. To outsiders she seemed to have everything: attractiveness, money, a servant, expensive clothes and a husband who loved her. However, it was all an illusion. In reality, Mary was a bored housewife who longed to go on an adventure and on Monday 1 May, 1837, she decided to do just that.

The baker's wife told her husband that she was going to her brother's house in Haymarket and would be home by 11 p.m. In order to keep up appearances and not to alarm Mr Stansbury, she took her servant, Eliza Colebury, with her, though she never intended to be with her for long. As soon as they reached a suitably busy street, Mary gave the young girl the slip, and fled off into the crowds. For a moment, Eliza did not notice, but that soon changed and she became extremely concerned that her mistress had suddenly disappeared.

The servant walked around London for three hours, desperately trying to find Mary Stansbury. She had absolutely no luck in locating her, however, and returned to the bakery empty-handed. Worried about getting into trouble with Mr Stansbury, Eliza made up a story. She told the man that Mary was still at her brother's house, and had sent her home early.

The servant told the concerned man that his wife intended catching an omnibus home, later that evening. By midnight though, Mary had still not returned, and her husband became more than a little agitated. Trying to calm his fears, and digging a bigger hole for herself, Eliza told Mr Stansbury that she had probably decided to stay overnight at the brother's house, since his children were ill and he needed help looking after them. She then went to bed and prayed her mistress would be home when she awoke the next day.

The next morning Eliza went downstairs, clinging to the hope that Mary would be there. She wasn't. Instead, Mr Stansbury was readying himself to visit his brother-in-law, in order to bring his wife home. All Eliza could do now was wait and hope that somehow Mary had turned up at her brother's house and stayed the night. One can only imagine what went on in her mind as Mr Stansbury made his way to his brother-in-law's house, but by the time he got home, he was frantic.

According to the man, when questioned, her brother knew absolutely nothing about Mary's visit and was as confused as the husband as to where she could be. Mr Stansbury now demanded to know why Eliza had lied, and what was actually going on. The poor girl explained that she had somehow lost Mary on the way to the house, and had spent three hours looking for her.

When she told him that the entire story of the evening before had been made up, Mr Stansbury was furious and inundated her with questions. Why did she fabricate such a story, he demanded, but all Eliza could say was that she just wanted to account for the woman's absence so that he didn't worry.

Mr Stansbury stormed off to the police station, in the hope that someone knew where his wife was. However, despite spending hours trying to track her down, there was no trace, and the man had to give up and return home. On entering the house, he was met by an eerie silence. Not only was Mary still not there, but there was no sign of Eliza either. He presumed she must have gone out, until he entered the kitchen. There was the poor servant woman, hanging from the rafters, quite clearly dead. Fearing that she would be blamed for the mysterious disappearance, Eliza Colebury had taken her own life and would never discover what had actually happened to her boss.

In the days and weeks following the disappearance of Mary and the death of Eliza, Mr Stansbury was beside himself. He enrolled the help of friends and family, and together they determined to find out what had gone on. When no new information could be found, he went to the newspapers and the story was distributed far and wide. One report incorporated a sad development:

So strongly is the impression on the mind of Mr Stansbury that his wife has met her death by unfair means that it has incapacitated him from attending to his business, which he has consequently given up, and it has so operated on his mind that he is constantly wandering about town and the suburbs in the hopes of obtaining some intelligence of her.

The poor man had lost his wife, his servant and his business, but what had really happened to Mary? Well, the lost lady wasn't lost, missing or murdered at all. When she managed to give Eliza the slip in London, she travelled to Bristol, where she arrived on 2 May. Her intention was to sail to the United States to start a life a long way from her husband and the boredom of the bakery. However, when no immediate ships were available for her passage, she had no alternative but to check into a nearby tavern.

The woman had only been there a few days when she became acquainted with a man by the name of Mr Blewer. He was a journeyman tailor who worked for a high-street store, and he and Mary had a great rapport from the moment they met. In fact, so well did they get on that it was only a matter of months before Blewer proposed to the woman. Even though she was already married and on the run from her husband, the brazen Mary Stansbury said yes. They were joined in matrimony in Bristol on 20 August 1837 and set up home as man and wife.

The new bigamist may never have been found out, if not for the fact that Mr Stansbury had circulated her description and story, far and wide. While nobody could shed any light on the disappearance in London, Inspector Stephens of Bristol was about to crack the case. Reading the information given to him, the officer realised that he had seen a woman meeting her description just days before. He made further enquiries and, sure enough, managed to find not only Mary Stansbury but her new husband too.

A very brief mention of the story was printed in various newspapers in the weeks after the reappearance of the woman, during which it was said that the Home Office knew all about the sorry episode. However, no mention was ever made as to the future life of Mr Stansbury, or the sentence given to Mary after her dabble with bigamy. However, when the *Bristol Mercury* wrote about the story in August 1837, they rightly did not want anyone to forget the real victim of the selfish disappearance of Mrs Mary Stansbury: 'There is one melancholy circumstance connected with the affair which all must equally deplore. We allude to the suicide of the servant, Eliza Colebury, who from the dread of being accused as the murderer of her mistress, put a period to her existence by hanging herself.'

Maria Gorman's Lost Years

In 1872, a young woman by the name of Maria Gorman was left devastated when her husband passed away a short time after their marriage. Raised as an orphan in Kingston, New York, the woman had been remarkably popular in her hometown but had left everything behind to marry her love and live in Providence. Now that he was gone, she was alone and in desperate need of friends, all of whom still lived in Kingston. To her advantage, however, her husband had left a large amount of property to her, meaning that she would never want for anything financially again.

While the money would come in useful, it could never replace her husband or her friends. Maria had received many letters in the time since the man's death, and each one encouraged her to go back to her hometown and settle down with people she knew. She thought long and hard about it, then decided to sell everything she owned in order to raise money for her trip to Kingston and a home when she arrived.

In June 1872, the woman finally set off with $20,000 cash on her person. She told friends that she would keep them abreast of her movements, and for the first few days she did. Shortly afterwards, a trunk belonging to Maria arrived at the destination, but with no owner to go with it. Her friends figured she may have been delayed slightly, so held onto the luggage in the hope she would soon turn up. She never did, and after a couple of months passed, they finally decided to investigate her whereabouts.

It was soon found that the woman had bought a train ticket to Kingston, but while she managed to check in her luggage safely, Maria herself ended up taking a train to New York City. Since that was the last anyone had ever seen of her, nobody could decide if the trip was on purpose or a mistake. Regardless, the woman was still missing and police were called to examine the evidence. The fact that Maria had $20,000 on her person gave rise to the belief that somebody had murdered her and run away with the money.

Several years later, the friends who had been looking after Maria's trunk suddenly passed away. During an auction of their property, a neighbour bought the now infamous chest and discovered a wealth of beautiful clothes, lingerie and other items inside. While the purchase was of interest to the women in his family, it was a disappointment to the buyer, as he had desperately wanted to find a diary or address book; something to tell him all about the elusive Mrs Gorman.

An astonishing twenty-seven years later, a woman walked into the Kingston police station and complained that she was unable to find her friends. She had travelled all the way from Providence, she said, and they were supposed to be there to greet her. When she gave their names, the confused woman was told that those people were long-since dead. Then it became even more perplexing when they asked for her name. 'I am Maria Gorman,' she said.

The file on her disappearance had long-since been closed, but her story was still known around the city. The astounded officers asked Maria what year she thought it was, and she replied without hesitation. 'It is 1872,' she said, and was deeply disturbed to hear that actually it was 1899.

'How can that be?' she demanded to know. 'I left home only a few days ago, and that was in 1872.' The officers assured Maria that it was not, and she was taken into the back room for a thorough examination. What the woman told them was astounding. 'I was taken ill,' she said, 'while journeying from Providence to Kingston, and was taken to hospital. I suffered a seizure and was paralysed, so couldn't talk or write to my friends.' The officers listened intently and nodded at appropriate moments, but then came a bombshell. 'A few days after I had been taken ill, I recovered and came straight away to Kingston . . .'

Where Maria had been in the twenty-seven years prior was anyone's guess, and she remained convinced that the year was still 1872. The woman had no clue what hospital she had been in, and her once elaborate clothing was hanging as rags on her body. It was obvious that Maria Gorman had been sleeping rough for quite some time, and was in desperate need of help. Since she had nobody to look after her, it was decided she should move into a care home, where staff promised to make her comfortable for the rest of her life.

While officers originally thought the woman was insane, the staff at her new home realised that it was not the case at all. She was eccentric, and often walked up and down the halls singing to herself, but she was no lunatic. She was, however, often confused and would ask staff where her friends had gone. No amount of explaining could ever allow her to believe that the year was 1899 and her friends were long gone.

While it was hoped that one day the woman would suddenly remember where she had been all those years, it was not to be. Maria Gorman died not long after arriving in Kingston, and the memory of what had happened died along with her. After her death, those who had spent a lot of time with the woman decided that it was fairly likely she had become ill on the initial journey to Kingston in 1872, and her money had been stolen from her. The trauma of such an event could have sent her into a nervous breakdown, from which she never fully recovered. The only thing that burned bright in Maria's mind was the location of her hometown. She had finally arrived, albeit over a quarter of a century later.

The Great Excitement in Normal, Illinois

In late April 1893, articles appeared in the newspapers about a woman called Helen Biggs, who lived with her husband in Emporia, Kansas. He ran a wholesale hide and leather business, while she stayed at home to look after their young son. The story went that Helen and her child had travelled to Normal, Illinois, in order to visit her brother, Edward Wood, on a matter of some importance. To begin with, however, journalists could not fathom exactly what that business was.

The woman and her son arrived in Normal on the night train, but from the very beginning her visit was clouded in strangeness. For someone so intent on seeing her brother, it came as a surprise that Mrs Biggs had no idea where he lived. Since she arrived very late at night, she was unable to do any investigations straightaway, so checked into a local boarding house, where she stayed until morning.

The next day, she asked the landlord if he had ever heard of a woman called Mrs David Valentine. He replied in the positive and gave Mrs Biggs directions to her house. She visited for a short time, with her first priority being to find out where her brother lived. 'I must find him even if it takes a week,' she told the woman. She was in luck; Mrs Valentine did indeed have his address, so Mrs Biggs thanked her and set off with her son. Unfortunately, despite the urgency of finding her brother, newspapers reported that she never arrived at his home.

A few days later, Edward Wood was told that his sister had arrived in town and was trying to find him. His version of events revealed that this had come as a shock considering he wasn't expecting a visit from her. Even odder was the fact that when he asked where she now was, nobody could tell him. According to Wood, he realised that something must be wrong and contacted everyone he could think of, including Mrs Biggs' husband, who was still in Illinois.

From there came an urgent telegram, saying that the woman had not returned home and should be presumed disappeared. The same reply came from her father, who said he had not seen her at all. After searching for days, the brother was urged by friends to contact police, and as a result reporters knocked on

Edward Wood's front door. All were anxious to know if he had heard anything at all from his sister.

'I am greatly mystified to know where she is,' he said. 'I have searched almost every boarding house, restaurant and hotel in the city and found that she has been at none of these.' What did the man think had happened to his sister? reporters asked. 'I do not like to be too hasty in coming to conclusions,' he replied, 'but I am in great fear for her safety and suspicion that foul play has befallen her.'

Edward Wood then explained that his mother had recently passed away and had left a large amount of property. It was his belief that perhaps his sister had papers related to this inheritance on her person. 'Perhaps they have been taken away from her by force,' he said. 'This is the only way I can account for her disappearance, but hope she has not met with any foul play. She is a bright woman and has never been subject to insanity, and it does not run in the family.'

Shortly after the story was made public, a local person came forward with an alleged sighting. According to him, Mrs Biggs had been seen at the local station, checking in her large trunk and buying tickets to Peoria. On hearing the news, Wood announced that he would track her down there if at all possible but, shortly after, told reporters that the sighting proved to be a red herring, and his sister and nephew remained unfound.

Several days after the disappearance of Helen Biggs, newspapers reported yet another lost person in the area; this time a German man by the name of William S. Klaassen. Reporters couldn't contain their excitement that there could possibly be something connected. The *Bloomington Weekly Leader* reported:

Bloomington has been in the throes of great excitement for the past week over the disappearance of Mrs Helen Biggs and son of Kansas who came here to visit and have not been located yet. An excitement equally as great and wonderful comes from our little neighbouring town of Weldon, and on this occasion it is caused by a man.

Klaassen lived with his wife and four children on a local farm. Fairly affluent, he was rumoured to be an heir to a huge German estate. When he had originally moved to the United States, he had done something of a moonlight flit, leaving without even telling his family. They only found out once he had arrived in his new country, and moved out to join him shortly after.

Once the family were all in the States, they had bought a farm but that had recently been sold and they had moved to Weldon on a temporary basis. Their intention was now to move back to Germany, though this apparently angered Mr Klaassen greatly, as the departure was only happening because his wife wished to return home. All he wanted to do was live and work in the country he had now made his own.

Described locally as a man 'subject to freaks and cranky movements', William Klaassen was last seen by his family at 9 p.m. on 29 April, when they left him at the family home while they went to visit Mrs Klaassen's sister. When they returned on Monday morning, the house was shut up and the only way they could gain access was to break down a door. Once inside, the woman was shocked to discover that her husband had disappeared without trace, and her furniture and other belongings were strewn all around the house. It looked as though someone had broken in and ransacked the place and jewellery and cash were missing. Bedclothes were hung at the windows in order to keep the place dark, and the remaining blankets were piled high on the bed, in disarray.

The authorities were perplexed that three people could have gone missing in the area within just a few days. Stories were put out by Mr Klaassen's wife that he must surely have been victim of a break-in and abduction. She told reporters that she was sure he had been murdered elsewhere, since there was no blood or sign of his body on the premises.

Others were not so sure that he had been kidnapped, citing the fact that he had once left his family in order to run away to America. It would not be so hard to imagine that the man had done the same thing this time, only in reverse. Mrs Klaassen would hear none of that, however, as she refused to believe that after leaving her once, he would ever do so again. Besides, she said, it was she who wished to return to Germany, not her husband. Her brother-in-law arrived in town and told reporters that no man could ever convince him Klaassen had left without his wife and family.

On 16 May 1893 the mysterious disappearance was solved when Mrs Klaassen received a telegram from Germany. It was, of course, from her wayward husband, who had done exactly what she and her brother-in-law said he wouldn't – abandoned his family once again. She smiled sweetly, however, and told reporters how relieved she was to finally find her husband alive and well. Mr Klaassen – on hearing the uproar he had managed to create at home – swore he would make it up to his wife by sending money for her and the children to join him in Germany. The woman happily made plans to return, but whether or not he actually did get around to paying her fare remained a mystery.

One missing person had been found, but there was still no trace of the other two. Newspapers stopped mentioning poor Helen Biggs after a few weeks, and people presumed that she and her son must still be missing or possibly even dead. The story was put to bed soon after and the woman was never mentioned in the press again. However, the reason for this was not because of a loss of interest on behalf of reporters; far from it. They stopped mentioning the woman because, in reality, Mrs Helen Biggs did not actually exist. The character had been completely made up . . .

The true story of the mysterious lady was revealed just a few weeks after her disappearance. The talk of her being seen at the railway station was true, but Edward Wood's determination to find her was not. In reality, she was the very last person he ever wanted to see because she was not his sister, but his first wife. Her name was Kittie Wood (formerly Doyle) and the child she had with her did not belong to the fictitious Mr Biggs of Indiana, but to Wood himself. Incidentally, since leaving her, he had bigamously married a woman called Ida and together they had three children. Kittie's arrival in Normal, therefore, had sent the man into total hysteria and when she told towns-folk that she was his sister, he quite happily went along with it, for fear of being arrested.

After leaving town without seeing the man, the first Mrs Wood had travelled to Quincy but returned to investigate his whereabouts once again. This time she would not go quietly, and decided to give police her side of the story. Officers were surprised to see 'Mrs Biggs' reappear, and even more baffled when they heard her tale. As soon as it was all jotted down, they went to Mr Wood's house, arrested him for bigamy and sent him to court.

By this time, the story of the reappearance of the 'sister' had gone all round town and the couple had become legendary. As a result, many people travelled to the courthouse in the hope of seeing Edward Wood. They were left disappointed, however, as the bigamist was unable to pay the $500 bond and was thrown in jail. Both of his wives were there to witness the proceedings; Kittie accompanied by her mother and two little boys, and Ida with her three daughters. Afterwards, the two women met in the city hall and exchanged greetings with each other, though what actually transpired between them forever remained a mystery.

From jail, Edward Wood spoke to a reporter from the *Bloomington Weekly Leader*. However, he still managed to lie about the story, first of all saying he did not know Kittie at all, and then changing his mind ever so slightly:

'Yes, this is the same woman who claimed to be my sister from Kansas City, and now she claims to be my wife, but she is not. You see, we had a little trouble when I knew her in Decatur concerning this child, but I emphatically deny that she is my wife. No, I cannot give bonds today, but have telegraphed my father in Wyandotte, Kansas, and he will be here to give bonds in a few days.'

While Edward Wood was determined not to claim Kittie as his first wife, friends came forward to say that on numerous occasions over the past seven years, he had told them about a wife he had once had, in Decatur. According to them, 'he'd had trouble with her' and had left their home. When news came from Decatur that a marriage licence had been issued to the couple but never returned, it was wondered if Wood had been correct in his plea of never marrying her. This was thwarted slightly when Kittie announced she had all the papers to prove they were legally married, and her mother came forward to say she remembered being at the wedding.

The scandal was intriguing and reporters rubbed their hands with glee, especially when Kittie agreed to tell her side of the story. According to her, the couple had been married in 1881, had two children and lived together for five years, until he had deserted the family. As time went on, Kittie came to believe that Wood must be dead, but when she accidentally discovered he had remarried and was currently living in Normal, she was more than anxious to pay him a visit.

As if that wasn't juicy enough, it was also revealed that Wood's current wife was previously known as Miss Ida Valentine and was from the very family Kittie had gone to visit when she had arrived. 'The case looks like a very strong one against Wood,' one journalist wrote, 'and will be watched with keen interest on both sides.'

Amusingly, newspapers took Kittie Wood into their hearts and described her in nothing but glowing terms. 'She is rather small in stature, has black eyes, black hair and a rather pleasing countenance.' The same could not be said about Edward Wood: 'He appears to be a man of about forty years of age and looks as though he had been subjected to anything but a life of serenity.'

Several times in the months ahead, Edward Wood was brought back to face the court, where he entered more pleas of not guilty, and was then hauled back to jail. Things finally came to a head in October 1893 when it was decided that he and Kittie really had been married, details of which were published in the Illinois marriage index. As a result of his second marriage, Wood was now a bigamist, something he had known for quite some time. He was carted off to Joliet prison to serve a year's sentence.

Directly afterwards, the first Mrs Wood got on with her life as mother to two boys, while the second wife headed to court. Her appearance this time was to petition a divorce against her estranged husband. During the case, the woman said that the pair had separated in July 1893 – shortly after his arrest – and that she now wished to have custody of her three daughters, and the reinstatement of her maiden name. The requests were granted and, together with her children, she made a clean break away from her rogue of a husband.

The Perplexing Tale of Bertha Dennis

Bertha Dennis was a respectable young cook living in Reigate, England. Newspapers at the time described her as being 'well-behaved and neatly dressed', while her parents were 'industrious and respectable people'. She was engaged to a coach painter and due to be married very shortly. To all who knew her, Bertha's life was quietly lived with no sign of scandal or intrigue. However, that all changed in the latter half of 1884 when her parents were away and she was looking after the house on her own.

One day while in the front garden, she was approached by a man who was known both to Bertha and other local people. The two got talking and while it was all rather innocent at first, it wasn't long before the man asked if he could be allowed inside. Bertha said no but he wasn't about to let that prevent him. Ignoring her pleas, the vicious man gained entry to the house and proceeded to rape her.

Bertha was extremely traumatised but kept the crime to herself, fearful that her fiancé would break off the engagement if he found out she'd been 'ruined'. However, a few months later Bertha realised she was pregnant and the only possible father was her attacker. The woman's mother was extremely ill and could not be burdened with such a terrible and tragic secret, so she decided to hide it for as long as she could. In March 1885, she decided to travel to Ladywell to ask advice from her aunt. She imagined the trip could be done in a day, so asked a friend to travel with her on what she pretended was a nice day out. However, the two missed each other at the station, so Bertha ended up on the platform alone.

After minding her own business for a while, the girl was approached by a middle-aged woman (unnamed in the press and referred to here as Mrs X), who was described as being well dressed but very much worried about travelling on her own. She asked where Bertha was going, and the young woman replied, 'Ladywell.'

'Well,' sighed Mrs X, 'I am going that way and as we do hear of such awful things nowadays, perhaps you will not mind me riding in the same carriage as you, as we shall then be a protection to each other.'

Bertha did not mind, so agreed to stay with the woman during the journey. However, by this time she was tired from being on her feet, so told Mrs X she needed to sit down.

'You're not well, are you?' the woman asked.

Bertha shook her head.

'Are you married?'

'No.'

Mrs X took a good look at the young lady sitting beside her and then launched into a seemingly well-intended speech about how Bertha looked as though she needed a friend. The girl nodded, told the story of her mother not being well and promptly started to cry.

'But you have another trouble my dear, besides that . . .' Mrs X gazed towards Bertha's growing stomach, received confirmation that she was indeed in the 'family way' and then took it upon herself to take on the role of confidante. 'Never mind, my dear, you sit there till the train comes in, and I will get your ticket.' She then left Bertha sitting on the platform, while she went to buy two tickets. They were not, however, to Ladywell, but to a town further down the line.

The two women boarded the train and Mrs X continued trying to befriend Bertha. She seemed rather worldly-wise and promised that she could help. When the train pulled into Ladywell station, the young woman gathered together her things but Mrs X stopped her from leaving the carriage.

'Will you come on to my house?' she asked. 'It is not much further. Then we can talk the matter over. I will tell you what to do and then you can go and consult your aunt afterwards.'

Bertha was not keen on the idea but by that time the train was pulling away from Ladywell station and she had no choice but to go with the woman. Several stops later the two departed the train in a city she presumed was London. After a long walk, they arrived at a house filled with women. It was, of course, a brothel, though Bertha knew nothing of this at the time. Instead, Mrs X introduced her new 'friend' to the other women present, and launched into a speech about her terrible condition and how she was looking for help.

'Don't you think Mrs So-and-So would make her very comfortable and see her safely through it all for just a bare recompense?' she asked. The women nodded and one of them assured Mrs X that the woman of whom she was talking was the perfect person to look after Bertha.

'She couldn't go to a better place,' she smiled.

Mrs X assured Bertha that she would be well looked after in the other house, but she must first promise to never tell anyone where she had been or what she had done there. The young woman agreed and was then subjected to a long inquisition, during which time she was required to divulge the details of her family, her friends, her address and the people she had previously worked for. This information was supposedly taken down, 'just in case something should happen'. In reality, however, giving all her personal details was something of an insurance policy, designed to keep the girl quiet.

Questions answered, Bertha told Mrs X that she would like to leave soon, so if she was going to be introduced to another lady, they had better go. The woman agreed and proceeded to take her down various narrow streets and alleyways until she arrived at a grubby, two-storey house. Inside was much the same as the first house – full of women who took great interest in the new arrival. This time, however, Bertha was asked how much money she had in her purse. She answered that there was not much at all.

'How much money do you think you can raise?' one woman asked. 'We must have a deposit so we can make arrangements.' Bertha was confused but after much discussion, parted with one of the three sovereigns she had brought with her. A number of whisky bottles were then brought out, and the women tried – but failed – to ply the young lady with drink. At this point, Bertha still did not know what kind of house she had willingly gone into, but the terrible realisation was to come with the arrival of a number of 'low class men'. The pregnant woman made a dash for the door but was physically restrained.

'You made an agreement,' one of the prostitutes told her. 'You must keep it.'

In the weeks that followed, Bertha was subjected to terrible abuse and forced to sleep with a long line of men. She would then be forced to turn over her earnings to Mrs X, and when that was declared not enough to cover her board and lodgings, she was told to give up her personal belongings too. Over the course of time she handed over her coat, umbrella, silver chains, a gold ring and an engraved locket. Mrs X wanted to take her watch too, but Bertha refused.

'I will not let you take that,' she said and steadfastly held onto it.

The situation was a nightmare and Bertha would regularly beg to be allowed home. Mrs X would always know the perfect way to prevent her from leaving:

'If you attempt to escape, your friends, family and employers will all be written to and a full disclosure made.'

On 11 May 1885, Bertha gave birth to a baby boy. The labour was endured on a cold, bare floor and as soon as the child was delivered, he was immediately taken away.

'Your baby died,' one of the women said, though no evidence of this was ever provided and Bertha did not see the child before he was whisked away. She was then ignored and the proper medical treatment she needed after giving birth was never given. She later told reporters that it was at that precise moment she decided she must fight back and escape the house of horrors. Stripped of her belongings, jewellery and now baby, Bertha had nothing left to lose. She was so broken that even Mrs X's threats did not frighten her any more. She desperately needed to get away.

Slipping out of the house at 11 a.m. one morning, Bertha walked for a full twelve hours before finally arriving at the home of her brother. Having been worried by her disappearance for weeks, he gave her a huge welcome and took her straight into his home. However, Bertha was not the same person she had been before her disappearance, and her brother noticed straightaway that she looked ten years older, was emaciated and dressed like a beggar. He asked what on earth had happened and where she had been.

Bertha was still terrified of Mrs X and her threats of hunting her down if she ever dared say a word about her experiences. So to answer her brother's questions, the young woman made up an elaborate tale of travelling on a train and being attacked by an unknown woman, who held a handkerchief to her face. The only thing Bertha knew, she claimed, was that she had passed out and after regaining consciousness, was led through the streets wearing a blindfold, so she could not see exactly where she was. She was then kept hostage in an attic for the next eleven weeks. Her brother was outraged and called the police.

When interviewed, the young woman stuck fast to her tale of an unknown woman drugging her. However, she opened up slightly about her living conditions and told officers she lived with a group of women who wore wigs and painted their faces. They had told her that she would need to go out at night and do as they did, but she had refused and was beaten for her trouble. She then said that the women had worn her clothes and her coat had even been altered to fit a larger lady.

Friends of Bertha Dennis told reporters that they had never known her to lie before and wholeheartedly believed her story. Her parents said that the motive for the kidnapping was most likely robbery, and never entertained the notion that she could have been forced into prostitution. However, while Bertha was determined to keep her experience and pregnancy secret, holes appeared in the story when she was asked to repeat it several times. Each time she did, different details would be added, distorted or taken away. The police decided to drop the matter completely because they did not believe that the woman could have been rendered unconscious on a train, blindfolded and then led through the streets in broad daylight without anyone noticing.

More and more doubt was poured over Bertha's story and the newspapers labelled the incident as 'bizarre' and 'strange'. As time marched on, it became exceedingly apparent that the young woman would either have to admit she had altered the story, or be branded a liar for the rest of her days. In the end, she withdrew her initial statement and told police the full story, with the name of Mrs X and the location of her houses carefully concealed. However, even then, she was branded a fake in the newspapers and they falsely said that Bertha had admitted to making up the entire incident. This claim was wholeheartedly denied.

No charges were ever brought against Mrs X, thanks mainly to the fact that the specific details of the story were so vague that officers had nothing to go on. Bertha Dennis got on with her life, though the recent events had left her deeply emotionally scarred. She was never able to find out what had happened to her lost child and the question of whether he had lived or died was forever an unsolved mystery.

The Bizarre Tale of the Kidnapped Maiden

On 3 August 1901, a young man ran into the Sheriff's Office in St Joseph, Michigan, to report that his fiancée had been kidnapped. He was barefoot, excitable and out of breath, but managed to tell a story that was both bizarre and frightening.

The man gave his name as Peter Cassiano, and said that he lived in Chicago. He worked for his father – a grocers' wholesaler – and as a result of that, he had become associated with a young Italian woman by the name of Irma Pellas. Pellas worked on her father's market stall and she was greatly impressed with Cassiano's charm and smart appearance. There was only one problem, however. She was apparently promised to another – a young man called William Berni, who worked on a nearby market stall and had known the woman since early childhood.

Cassiano told the Sheriff that in spite of the fact she already had a fiancé, he and Pellas began stepping out. She called off her marriage to Berni and told friends that she would marry Cassiano. This, of course, enraged her former fiancé, and a rivalry developed between the two men. According to Cassiano, he and Irma decided to marry and hastened a trip by boat from Chicago to St Joseph.

As the Sheriff wrote down details of the story, it suddenly became more confusing. According to one version of events, when the couple were on the boat, they noticed jilted lover, William Berni, walking sullenly past their seats. He made no effort to approach or talk to them and then disappeared to the other side of the boat. On their arrival at St Joseph, the couple checked into a local hotel and readied themselves for their forthcoming nuptials.

Later that evening, Irma suggested going for a romantic walk on the lakeside, and during the stroll she somehow managed to drop her handheld fan into the water. As it floated away from the bank, the woman showed great concern, so Cassiano took off his coat, hat and shoes, and waded into the water to retrieve it. By the time he did that, however, he was waist high and quite a way from the shore. Turning around, Cassiano was shocked to see that his fiancée had completely disappeared. On his return to shore, he saw two sets of prints in the sand, and his coat, hat and shoes had gone.

This story was baffling enough, but as police officers grilled him further, the man changed the story almost completely. This time he said that the couple had actually been swimming in the lake, and he had gone further away from the shore in order to show Irma what a strong swimmer he was. When he was a long way from his fiancée, he heard a shout, turned around and saw her being dragged away by former love, William Berni. When Cassiano reached the shore, his clothing was gone, but he found it a few moments later, hidden behind a bench.

After yet more questioning, a third story was added to the mix. This time he and Irma returned to shore safely, but as he was tying his shoes, he was suddenly hit on the head with a sandbag. When Cassiano returned to consciousness, his fiancée and items of clothing had disappeared.

Faced with so many conflicting and baffling stories, the Sheriff's Office came to the conclusion that no kidnapping had actually taken place. They gave word to the newspapers that there was a good chance that Irma Pellas was a con artist who staged the incident so that she could break off the wedding with Cassiano and run off with Berni.

While they were deliberating what had really happened, another bizarre twist occurred. It was discovered that Peter Cassiano was not the man's name after all, and he was really called Will Crew. Not only that, the woman he had been seen with on the banks of the lake was not Irma Pellas but a married woman from Benton Harbor, who went by the name of Mrs

Stephen Crabb. The police declared that almost the entire story put forward by Cassiano/Crew must have been made up.

It was believed that the man had met Mrs Crabb while on his trip, and she was a fraudster, intent on stealing his money. She instigated the walk to the water so that her accomplice could knock the man out and take his belongings. After he had received the bump to the head, Cassiano/Crew became greatly confused and somehow thought that he'd been on a trip with Irma Pellas and William Berni. The woman was not located, however, so this version of events could never be proved.

The matter was wrapped up by the frustrated police, the case closed and Cassiano/Crew sent on his way. However, the question of whether he had ever been involved in a love triangle with Irma Pellas and William Berni – and whether or not they actually existed at all – was never answered. Some believed he had no relation to them, and the entire story and was just a figment of the man's concussed mind.

The Amusing Aberdeen Breach-of-Promise Cases

Many breach-of-promise cases reached the courts in Aberdeen, Scotland, towards the end of the Victorian era. One revolved around the rather dubious story of a thirty-one-year-old woman who was romantically linked to her sixty-four-year-old godfather. The older man had apparently promised to marry the younger woman if she moved in with him, though swiftly changed his mind and denied all knowledge of the agreement the moment the two were intimate. While this particular breach-of-promise case left a rather sour taste in the mouth of journalists, two others won considerable column

inches due to the fact they gave the courts a rare and significant fit of giggles.

The first case happened in October 1895 and concerned two
families within the growing Italian community in Aberdeen.
Ice-cream vendor Agostino Pacitti had been dating Rossina
Rossi for three years, but the couple fell out and the courtship
was called off. Still, Pacitti continued to hold a torch for his
love, so mutual friends and family held a party to try to see
them reconciled. Agostino was positive the two could iron out
their differences, but when Rossina walked into the house, she
refused to have anything to do with him and, after a huge fight,
stormed out.

By this time, Pacitti and other members of the party were
intoxicated and when he saw fellow party-goer Filomena Gizzi,
a 'dark-eyed damsel in her teens', he began flirting with her.
Pacitti's brother was interested in her too and jokingly asked
the woman to marry him. When she declined, Agostino tried
his luck and popped the question too, only this time Filomena
not only said yes, but also pressured the man to name a date.
He did.

The next morning Pacitti bought his new fiancée a hat, and
then they headed to the registrar and local Catholic Church to
publish their intention to marry. While Filomena was deadly
serious about winning Pacitti from Rossina, he just saw the
whole thing as something of a joke; a revenge tactic to make his
former love jealous. 'When a man is a bit angry he does not
know what he is doing,' he later told the court.

If Pacitti was looking for attention from his former lover, it
worked. Rossina was told of the marriage and stormed into his
ice-cream shop to demand he call off the wedding. Not only
that, she decided that instead of marrying Filomena he should

tie the knot with her; and she would personally refund the jilted woman the £5 she had paid towards the ceremony.

Pacitti liked this idea and together they persuaded the registrar to cross out Filomena's name and insert Rossina's. The first wedding was cancelled, much to the chagrin of Filomena, who – with her father's consent – told Pacitti she would sue him to the tune of £50. He thought this was far too much and offered her an out-of-court settlement of £5. The woman laughed and carried on with her plans for £50, though ultimately she was forced to lower it to £12, when the Small Debt Court refused to entertain such a large sum of money.

Rossina set about organising a wedding, and was thrilled that she had won back her love. However, in the midst of all this, Pacitti suddenly got cold feet and decided he wanted to remain single. He told Rossina that he had no intention of marrying either Filomena or her, which sent the angry woman on a mission to reclaim the £5 she had given to his former fiancée.

Meanwhile, the court date arrived and Filomena and Pacitti turned up to thrash out their differences. During a retelling of the farcical union, laughter could be heard echoing around the room and garnered many mentions in newspapers the next day.

'Are you willing to pay anything for damages?' asked the judge, to which Pacitti replied that he would only be prepared to pay £5. When asked who he intended to marry now, the young man first replied, 'Neither of the two,' then showing considerable bravado, added a swift, 'I don't know. I have not made up my mind at all.' The court erupted with laughter, especially when asked if it was true he had promised to marry Filomena while the two were at a party. 'Well, my brother asked first,' Pacitti replied in his defence.

The judge soon got tired of listening to the ridiculous case, especially when lawyer G. M. Aitken declared that no damage could possibly have been suffered by Filomena. 'She might suffer from being laughed at,' the judge retorted. 'I'm afraid her feelings could not otherwise have been hurt, because there was no sweet-hearting before, but I think he should pay for his amusement.'

The man then ordered Pacitti to pay £5, after which Aitken laughed and said that was exactly the amount of money he had offered before Filomena had taken the man to court. 'Still I think that is enough,' said the judge, but once again Aitken pointed out that £5 was originally offered. 'If you say anymore, I will make it £6,' said the weary judge, before declaring the matter well and truly closed.

The next 'Amusing Breach' came exactly six years later, in October 1901. This time the damsel was a nineteen-year-old woman called Wilhelmina Townsley, who attempted to sue her so-called ex-fiancé for £500.

From the very beginning, the case was a confusing one, filled with contradictory anecdotes and information. According to Townsley, thirty-two-year-old widower George Beighton asked her to marry him in 1899. She said yes, but no sooner was a date set than the man's business partner died and he called off the wedding as a mark of respect.

Several years later, Wilhelmina said she tried to get Beighton to the altar again and he agreed. According to her, the would-be groom asked his fiancée's mother for permission, and after she had given her blessing of 'You can please yourself,' a date was set. In August, Wilhelmina persuaded Beighton and several friends to contribute £2 towards the wedding and together they all travelled to the registry office in order to publish the banns. On the way, Beighton apparently bought roast beef for the wedding dinner and a pair of slippers for his fiancée.

It would seem that a great deal of merriment went on before they reached the registrar, as by the time they arrived, two of the wedding party were so drunk they had a fight and were ejected from the office. Beighton and Townsley were considered sober enough, however, and several pieces of paperwork were signed. They were then instructed to come back for the ceremony the next day, before leaving to join the rest of the wedding party, who were still arguing on the road outside the registry office.

Quite bizarrely, on their return to the office on 18 August, Beighton suddenly seemed confused as to who the wedding was actually for. When told he was the bridegroom and the wedding was his own, the rogue promptly ran out of the office, pursued by his fiancée and friends. He then refused to return to the scene, claiming that he must have been so drunk the day before that he hadn't realised what was going on. According to him, the whole episode was a trick, as he had thought he was attending a friend's wedding. No amount of prompting by friend or fiancée would force him to go ahead with the marriage.

Whether or not Wilhelmina had set up the man was not apparent, but after the getaway, her brother insisted Beighton pay £20 to compensate his sister for the pain he had caused. He refused, a fight broke out and the police were called. Several members of the party were arrested, and Beighton was charged with assault and sent to prison.

A month later, Wilhelmina attended court proceedings with her family. There she sat glowering at Beighton, shouting obscenities at him and stabbing her hat pin repeatedly into her chair cushion. This fit of outrage proved to be very amusing for reporters and they devoured each sullen look and inaudible cry.

When put on the stand, George Beighton entertained the court by admitting that he barely knew Wilhelmina and had never pursued her in a romantic way. He was sure he had never agreed or asked to marry the woman. 'Marriage was the last thing on my mind,' he said. 'If I did promise marriage, I was in such a state with liquor I did not know what I was doing.'

Getting onto the weekend in question, the defendant admitted that he did not remember much at all because of his incapacity. He also vehemently denied ever purchasing beef or slippers for his fiancée.

'Did you contribute £2?' asked the judge.

'Yes, but only for a [drinking] spree,' replied Beighton. 'Not for my own marriage!'

In a further twist, the 'groom' claimed that he had no recollection of ever going to the registrar, and that on the day in question, he had been buying a horse and had no contact with Townsley at all. He did remember running away from the wedding, however, but to the best of his recollection, that was several days after it was said to have taken place.

After each statement, laughter erupted throughout the building, and Wilhelmina's expression grew more and more bitter. On the subject of her family, the would-be groom was forthright and described how he had left Fraserburgh in favour of Aberdeen purely to get away from them.

'Did you have a prophetic anticipation of danger?' asked the judge.

'Yes,' replied Beighton. 'The Townsleys had been speaking to other people about marriage, so I thought it wise to gird up my loins and flee.'

'Are you worth £1000?' asked the judge in connection with a rumour he was rich.

'Not even one thousand shillings,' replied Beighton, much to the amusement of the court. His friends then unexpectedly confirmed the groom's insistence that he hadn't proposed, claiming that he never told them of any intentions and when they finally heard the news, they believed it to be nothing but a lark. One of the men greatly infuriated the judge when asked if he had any recollection of marriage plans: 'I don't remember anything,' he said. 'I was in the horrors as I had been drinking for a month before then.'

'You ought to be ashamed of yourself!' shouted the judge. 'And the sooner you get away the better.'

Another witness – William Topp – poured doubt on the idea put forward by Wilhelmina's mother that her daughter was an innocent woman who only had eyes for her fiancé. According to Topp, instead of pursuing Beighton, Wilhelmina had gone after him. When her mother found them making love, she promptly gave the lover 'a hiding' and sent him away.

When Wilhelmina took to the stand, she described how she and Beighton had met several years previously, and recounted the wedding that was meant to take place before Beighton's business partner had died. She then said that the intention to marry the second time was brought about by the groom himself, and that he was perfectly sober on the day of the intended ceremony.

'Since the breach of promise,' she said, 'I have been ridiculed many times. My feelings have been injured.'

Injured or not, the judge soon got tired of the case and finally called things to a halt. After a week of deliberation, he called the party back into his chambers and said that Beighton had not given any real evidence that he was indeed too drunk to know what he was doing. He ruled in favour of Townsley and agreed that on going to the registrar, her fiancé knew that he was supposed to marry her. It was only once there that he changed his mind, causing her loss and emotional injury, as well as humiliation when he claimed to have been coerced into marriage.

While this was good news for Wilhelmina, any celebration was dampened when instead of awarding £500, the judge lowered it substantially to £15 plus expenses. His reason for the smaller amount was simple: if he had set it any higher, Beighton may think his worth as a husband was significantly better than in reality. 'He made a miserable plea in defence,' the judge remarked.

The Kidnapping of Carrie Stevens

SHE IS FOUND! So screamed the headline in the 18 March 1901 edition of *El Paso Daily Herald*. This story was the conclusion of a tale that began some six years earlier, when a small child by the name of Carrie Stevens was reported missing by her mother, Anna.

Anna had been an orphan from the age of eight, and her first marriage to a railway foreman gave her two children – Victoria and Carrie. Unfortunately, her happiness ended when her youngest daughter was just one year old and her husband suddenly passed away. She was later rumoured to have married a cattleman who got caught up in a train robbery scandal, but he died shortly afterwards. This sequence of tragedies left Anna and her two daughters in rather dire circumstances.

The woman decided to turn her life around, and took over the care of a boarding house in El Paso, Texas, where she rented rooms out to respectable townsfolk. During this time, she was introduced to a woman called Mrs Taylor. She had once been an actress, but was now married to an old friend of Anna's first husband. The woman and her husband took a great deal of interest in the two children, and showed a particular bond with Carrie. At that time, both infants had contracted scarlet fever and Mrs Taylor suggested it would be better for the youngest child if she moved into her home to recover. Anna objected wholeheartedly to this offer, and no more was said.

Despite the woman's somewhat obsessive behaviour towards Carrie, the two women remained friends. A short time later, Mrs Taylor was going on a week-long trip to Valentine in Texas, and asked if she could take Carrie with her, the idea being that the change of scene would be good for her recovery. This time Anna said yes, and was pleasantly surprised when her daughter returned a week later, her health greatly improved.

On 8 August 1895, Mrs Taylor asked if she could once again take Carrie on a trip; this time to Albuquerque in order to visit family. Since the child had such a positive time on the last trip, Anna saw no reason to say no, but insisted that the woman keep in constant contact with her. She agreed.

'It was the last time I saw my baby,' Anna explained. 'Mrs Taylor had promised to write me from day to day about my little one, but as no letter came after some days had gone by, I became anxious and wrote to her addressing my letter to Albuquerque. I received no reply and then I telegraphed her, but in vain. Then I became perfectly frantic. I went to Sheriff Simmons and Captain Hughes and told them all about the matter.'

The disappearance of little Carrie Stevens garnered considerable whispers around El Paso and neighbours wondered if the child really had been kidnapped. Even newspapers unfairly questioned the sincerity of Anna's grief, though they never gave any reason for their suspicions. For her part, the woman travelled far and wide looking for her daughter, and made several long journeys to different states. One of these visits was to Denver, where a supposed sighting had been made of the little girl. When Anna arrived, however, she was met by the bad news that her daughter had not been found, and the long and painful search began again. Frank Simmons, from the Sheriff's Office, told reporters what happened next:

'I am positive that Mrs Stevens made every possible effort to locate the abductors. She was almost frantic for a time and urged the officers to assist. I wrote hundreds of letters trying to trace the missing kidnappers, but to no avail. They had disappeared as completely as if the earth had swallowed them up and left no clue behind by which they could be traced. We have never to this day learned what happened to the child. Mrs Stevens had but little money and was unable to prosecute a widespread investigation.'

This was not altogether true. While there really was no trace of Mrs Taylor or the missing child in the beginning, another detective eventually traced them both to Las Vegas. This discovery was enough to send Anna off to the lawyer who had handled her husband's business affairs. There she begged him to give her some money from the estate in order to make the long trip to Nevada and confront the woman herself. He refused to release the money, but promised to telegraph Mrs Taylor and insist she send the child back. 'If she does not,' he added, 'I shall make things hot for her.'

Why anyone thought this light approach to such a serious matter would resolve things is a mystery. Needless to say, as soon as Mrs Taylor received word that Anna had discovered where she and Carrie were living, they boarded the nearest train and totally disappeared for the next six years.

'I spent all the money I could get my hands on trying to find my little one but without avail,' Anna said. 'Sheriff Simmons also spent a good deal of money. For a long time I was prostate with grief but as year after year went by and I could get no tidings of my lost one I had to give up the search.'

People stopped talking about the event, and Anna was forced to go on with her life. However, her memories of her daughter did not fade. 'Her dear little baby face has always been in my mind throughout these long years,' she said, 'and her voice as she used to jump up into my lap and say, "Mammy, rock me to sleep," has echoed in my ears through many a long and weary day.'

In order to make a new life for herself, Anna moved to Mexico, while her eldest daughter, Victoria, grew up and had a custody battle of her own. She had been married for a year and had recently had a baby. The child was placed in the care of a hired nurse from the day of its birth, but when the marriage broke up just a year later, the nurse refused to hand the baby back. Victoria had to take the case to court, where she was eventually awarded full custody of her child.

In early 1901, a strange report came from Danville, Indiana, which stated that Carrie Stevens had been found. It had been six years since the girl had disappeared, and she was now eleven years old. Reporters rushed to try to find out as much about the story as they could, but by this time the tale of her disappearance was long forgotten. One journalist complained that, 'It was with difficulty late last night that anyone could be found who remembered the details of the disappearance with sufficient distinctness to relate them accurately.'

While reporters scrambled to find a story, word reached Anna that Carrie was alive and well. The shocked woman was beside herself and left Mexico straightaway in order to travel back to El Paso. Her eldest daughter also arrived in town and a member of the Sheriff's Office was sent to collect the child. When Carrie arrived in the city by train wearing a smart woollen jacket and large red hat, Anna and Victoria were there to meet her. The three rushed into each other's arms, and had a reunion worthy of any romantic novel. 'To those present, the scene of this reunion was a most affecting one,' wrote one reporter from *El Paso Daily Herald*, before sitting down to an interview with the family.

After talking at length with Anna, the journalist turned his attention to Carrie. She gave a story that was sadder than anyone could have imagined. According to the child, she had no real memories of her mother, except for the colour of her hair and eyes. Mrs Taylor had shown moments of kindness to her, but frequently emotionally abused the child. 'When I got mad about anything she would tell me that my mother was still alive, and then when I was good again she would say that she died a long time ago.'

For the first six months with Mrs Taylor, Carrie travelled extensively under the name of Lottie; first to Las Vegas, and then Nashville and Louisville. It was at the final city that the two encountered a travelling circus. Mrs Taylor suddenly had a yearning to revisit her acting days and so she signed up herself and Carrie as part of the entertainment troupe. In the months ahead, the young child was trained as a trapeze artist and worked every night. However, when the circus reached the town of Lafayette in Louisiana the pair hit a problem.

A woman by the name of Victoria Brazier saw the way Mrs Taylor treated the child and took pity on her, taking Carrie out of her care as soon as she could. This should have been the end of the kidnapping story, had Miss Brazier investigated why Carrie was with the woman in the first place. Instead, she merely placed the girl into the care of a children's home. The child was at the establishment for four years before it was reported that her 'mother', Mrs Taylor, had passed away. It was only when the child told staff that the woman was not related to her at all that Carrie's true identity was revealed.

'They were very good to me in the home,' Carrie told the reporter during the interview. 'I was happy there, but I am glad to have a home of my own, and my own mother.'

'She says it's all so strange to her,' added Anna, 'and the strangest part of it is to call anyone mother.' The woman then announced her intention to set up home in El Paso, concerned that if she moved her child to Mexico, the heat would be bad for her health.

'The mother's voice was full of indescribable pathos and tenderness,' wrote the reporter, 'as with tears rolling down her cheeks she drew the girl to her side . . . It is safe to say that a happier trio could not be found in all El Paso than Mrs Stevens, Victoria and little Carrie.'

Mrs Lewsey's Child Disappears in London

On 26 August 1896, Captain Lewsey from the Royal Dublin Fusiliers waved his wife and child goodbye from Newport station in South Wales. Mrs Lewsey and four-year-old Harold were on their way to London, but as his wife and child set off on their adventure, little did they know that the story of their trip would soon be hitting the newspapers.

On their arrival in the capital at 11.40 p.m., the pair were taken to what she thought was a Paddington hotel and checked in. The next morning Mrs Lewsey decided to go shopping, so told her child she would be back soon and left him in the room. Unfortunately, she did not return that day, or the day after that, or the day after that.

While it may have looked like a case of abandonment, the unfortunate situation came to be because as Mrs Lewsey left the premises, she promptly forgot which hotel she was staying in. Because it was dark when she had checked in, the woman had not taken any mental note of what the building looked like, and on her return from her errand could no longer remember where it was or how to get back.

Panicked, the woman enrolled the help of Scotland Yard but in the days ahead, no trace could be found of the hotel and – more importantly – her son. Word was sent to Captain Lewsey that the child had gone missing, and he broke down and had to be supported by colleagues. In a last-ditch attempt to find his son, the man wrote to Bow Street magistrate, Mr Lushington, to ask that the matter be told in the newspapers.

The case was so strange that journalists did indeed pick it up, and over the course of the next week, the story was reported up and down the country. The tale was always the same, but the headlines varied from the mundane 'A Remarkable Story' and 'An Extraordinary Case' to the intriguing 'Lost in London' and 'Phantom Hotel'. The *Sheffield Daily Telegraph*, however, went with something more hard-hitting: 'A Mother's Carelessness' was its headline, placing the blame for lost Harold on Mrs Lewsey.

Adding fuel to the fire of the bizarre tale was the matter of when and why the woman had left the hotel in the first place. Most reporters told readers that she had left 'to make a small purchase' on the night they had arrived in London, i.e. at almost midnight. But the need to go out so late was bewildering and when police told reporters that she had actually left in the morning, they were sceptical. 'No mention of that was made in the husband's letter,' said one unbelieving journalist.

While newspapers revelled in the terrible story, the coverage paid off when Harold was found alive and well. It had taken almost a week, but on 1 September 1896, he was located in a hotel miles away in Bishopsgate, not Paddington as first thought. The boy was in the care of the manager, who had discovered him on his own in the room. Quite bizarrely, instead of reporting the matter to the police straightaway, the man did not come forward until he saw the stories in the newspapers and realised Harold was missing, not abandoned.

'This incident is a curious example of the sudden and temporary lapse of memory familiar to medical practitioners,' wrote one newspaper, while another described it as, 'Surely one of the strangest ever related in a police court.'

Where Did You Go, Sarah Ann Main?

Benjamin and Ellen Main lived a fairly quiet life in Cardiff, Wales. Benjamin worked as a dock labourer and by 1873 there were seven children living in their humble family home. However, in June of that year, their lives were rocked by a mysterious and baffling disappearance, all because of a teenage quarrel.

Sarah Ann Main was an apprentice milliner and fifteen-year-old daughter of Benjamin and Ellen. On 19 June she argued with her parents over something undoubtedly trivial, and stormed out of the house. But while most children would have returned when they had calmed down or when their stomachs began to churn, Sarah Ann was determined that she would not go home at all that night.

The girl walked around the streets until she reached the workshop of a Mr Reece. The man asked what she was doing there. 'She stated she was in trouble,' he wrote. 'She had quarrelled with her parents and said she would not return home again. Fearing the girl might have come to harm, I told her to go and see my wife and ask if she could stay there. She went and my wife took her in . . .'

This teenage act of rebellion led to her anxious parents asking neighbours, friends and relatives if they had seen Sarah Ann. Nobody could provide any information at all, and they grew increasingly worried. Then just over a week after the disappearance, there came something of a breakthrough. A woman by the name of Augusta Paget Brown came forward to say that she had not only seen Sarah Ann, but also knew that she was perfectly safe and well. 'I know where the girl is,' she told Mrs Main. 'She should be brought home soon.'

The family were confused but Paget Brown offered no further explanation until three days later when she delivered a letter, apparently written by their daughter. The address given was Tooley Terrace, but when the family tried to find the street, they discovered there was no such address. The next day Paget Brown returned to the house and promised to help Mrs Main find her daughter. Together they travelled to Penarth but once again the trip was fruitless and the mother returned empty-handed. When yet another letter was delivered, hope was somewhat renewed, but once again the location was discovered to be false.

After so many dead ends, the family grew understandably suspicious of Paget Brown, and that was cemented when the woman turned up at their door on 25 June.

'Your daughter is married to a barrister,' she told Sarah Ann's confused father. 'They are at the Windsor Hotel and he will come to visit you soon.' Then to 'prove' it, she produced another letter supposedly from Sarah Ann. In the note, the girl told her father that she had been married by Reverend George Tong at St Paul's church, Swansea. However, after sending one of Sarah Ann's brothers to investigate the hotel, he came back with the news that no such person had ever worked there.

By now the family were at their wits' end and decided to call in the police. On hearing the story of the disappearance of their daughter and the visits from Paget Brown, officers decided to take the woman into custody and investigate her claims. She was questioned extensively during this time, but none of her stories added up.

They became further obsolete when on 5 July, Sarah Ann suddenly turned up at her parents' house without any explanation as to where she had been or what she had done. It was soon realised that Paget Brown's claims were utter nonsense and her misguided motive seemed likely to be one of obtaining money under false pretences.

While Sarah Ann refused to go into details about what had happened during her disappearance, the couple who took her in wrote to newspapers to give their side of the story. After explaining that the girl had told them of a quarrel with her parents, they added, 'The statements made to her parents by Mrs Paget Brown were entirely false, as she knew nothing of the girl's whereabouts. I simply send you this as the reports made may have a tendency to stain the girl's character.'

Selected Bibliography

Books

Bondeson, Jan, *Murder Houses of London* (Stroud: Amberley, 2014).

Clay, Jeremy, *The Burglar Caught by a Skeleton and Other Singular Tales from the Victorian Press* (London: Icon, 2014).

Goodman, Ruth, *How to Be a Victorian* (London: Penguin, 2014).

Hyman, Alan, *The Gaiety Years* (London: Cassell & Company, 1975).

MacQueen-Pope, W. *Gaiety: Theatre of Enchantment* (London: W. H. Allen, 1949).

Parker, John, *The Green Room Book, or Who's Who on the Stage* (London: T. Sealey Clark and Co., 1908).

Usher, Shaun, *Letters of Note: Correspondence Deserving of a Wider Audience* (Edinburgh: Canongate, 2016).

Websites

The following provide essential reading for anyone interested in Victorian crime and other stories:

London Old Bailey: www.oldbaileyonline.org
British Newspaper Archive: www.britishnewspaperarchive.co.uk
Newspaper Archive: www.newspaperarchive.com
Also, various newspaper archives available through many libraries via
    ProQuest: proquest.com

Index